A Stern

USEFUL SERVANTS

Johann Wolfgang von Goethe, 1749–1832. *Zur Farbenlehre.*
Tübingen, J. G. Cotta, 1810. The Michaelis Collection. Gift of J.
Philip Gibbs, Jr. Courtesy of the Bryn Mawr College Library.

USEFUL SERVANTS

Psychodynamic Approaches to Clinical Practice

by
Susan S. Levine, M.S.S.

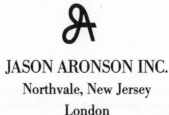

JASON ARONSON INC.
Northvale, New Jersey
London

This book was set in 11 pt. Bodoni Antiqua Regular by Alabama Book Composition of Deatsville, Alabama and printed and bound by Book-mart Press of North Bergen, New Jersey.

Library of Congress Cataloging-in-Publication Data

Levine, Susan S., 1957–
    Useful servants : psychodynamic approaches to clinical
practice / by Susan S. Levine.
        p. cm.
    Includes bibliographical references and index.
    ISBN 1-56821-844-3 (h/c : alk. paper)
    1. Psychoanalysis—Philosophy. 2. Psychodynamic psychotherapy—
Philosophy. I. Title.
    [DNLM: 1. Psychoanalytic Theory. 2. Psychoanalytic Therapy.   WM
460 L6655u   1996]
RC506.L485   1996
616.89'17—dc20
DNLM/DLC
for Library of Congress   96-12695

Manufactured in the United States of America. Jason Aronson Inc. offers books and cassettes. For information and catalog write to Jason Aronson Inc., 230 Livingston Street, Northvale, New Jersey 07647.

For Madeleine and Steven

Contents

ACKNOWLEDGMENTS

This book could not have been written without the assistance of the following colleagues who understand, I hope, how deeply I appreciate their generous sharing of expertise: Salman Akhtar, M.D., Jeffrey Applegate, D.S.W., Charles Ashbach, Ph.D., Margaret Baker, Ph.D., Barbara Breitman, M.S.W., Sydney Pulver, M.D., Steven Rolfe, M.D., Carol Tosone, Ph.D., and Thomas Wolman, M.D. I would also like to express my gratitude to J. Alexis Burland, M.D., Henri Parens, M.D., Newell Fischer, M.D., Philip Lichtenberg, Ph.D., Ira Brenner, M.D., Elisabeth Young-Bruehl, Ph.D., David Sachs, M.D., Philip Escoll, M.D., Doris Mirowski, M.D., Ann Salyard, Ed.D., James Youakim, M.D., Anne Sclufer, Ph.D., Leon Hoffman, M.D., Owen Renik, M.D., Sue Benston, M.D., Kim Benston, Ph.D., and Deborah Rolfe, M.A. for the various ways in which they have taught, supported, constructively criticized, and encouraged me or otherwise facilitated my work. Although it would be impossible to acknowledge individually all those who have contributed to my training, I am indebted to the candidates and faculty members of the Philadelphia Psychoanalytic Institute and of the Philadelphia Psychotherapy Training Program where rigorous clinical inquiry flourishes. And perhaps most important, I thank my patients, supervisees, and students for their trust and for the privilege of learning from them.

Jason and Joyce Aronson provided immeasurable encouragement and wonderful advice over many years. I thank Steven Levine for invaluable criticism of the draft, years of library legwork, and more than I could possibly put into words. As Orson

Welles might have put it, my husband would read no text before its time. I am grateful to Madeleine Levine for being simultaneously my adoring (and adored) fan and my primary source of hubris prevention; she graciously volunteered companionship and nimble fingers in the task of using Spellcheck. My gratitude to Herbert Schmelzer, Reevan Levine, and Natalie Levine for their high standards; to them as well as to Anne Schmelzer, Herbert Levine, and Ellen Frankel for never having asked why I took ss-o-o-o long to write this book. My editors, Catherine Monk and Judy Cohen, were efficient, enthusiastic, and a pleasure to work with, as was the entire staff at Jason Aronson Inc. Helen Horton Peterson, Associate Director of Academic Computing at Bryn Mawr College, supplied crucial solutions for word processing problems. My thanks, too, to the Camargo Foundation in Cassis, France for the use of their library in 1989.

To Mary Leahy, Seymour Adelman Rare Books Librarian, and James Tanis, Constance A. Jones Director of Libraries of Bryn Mawr College, who helped me select the frontispiece, my gratitude for their time and excellent taste. John and Joanne Payson were generous and helpful in giving and securing permission to use the stunning image on the dustjacket. And to the artist, Yvonne Jacquette, my warmest thanks: as anyone who has ever been in a traffic jam knows, bridges and cars can be useful servants, but we must not allow the tools we create, whether machines or psychoanalytic theories, to be our masters. Theories, like candles and headlights, can guide and illuminate in the neverending task of knowing ourselves and our patients.

INTRODUCTION

Theory . . . is a useful servant but a bad master, liable to
produce orthodox defenders of every variety of the faith. We
ought always to sit light to theory and be on the look-out for
ways of improving it in the light of therapeutic practice. It is
therapeutic practice that is the real heart of the matter.
                                                    —Harry Guntrip

This book outlines the major elaborations and revisions of the
psychoanalytic theory Freud pioneered in the waning years of the
last century, offering a clinician's perspective on psychodynamic
thinking. Clinicians new to psychodynamic thought (as well as
laymen who have some basic familiarity with psychoanalytic
ideas) will find this a useful introduction to the variety of clinical
approaches to psychotherapy that have resulted from Freud's
influence. Each theory offers the clinician a different listening
strategy, alternative structures with which to make sense of a
patient's narrative. I have tried to write the book I needed to read
when I was a new clinician, confused and fascinated by the range
of psychoanalytic theories. Why did these clinicians fall into
different "schools" when they all seemed to be saying useful
things? What were the inconsistencies within each theory as well
as between theories? With which sorts of patients might a particular theory be useful? Can one mix and match theories as
needed?

The question is not which theory is "right" in a scientific way,
for in a sense they are all equally right (or equally wrong!). Each

clinican must select what is useful both as a general outlook and in specific circumstances as clinician and patient explore the phenomena of the human mind. Which view of development and psychopathology leads the clinician to interventions that make sense to the patient? Which perspective on the human condition best matches the clinician's own beliefs? Which set of ideas seems to explain or fit best a specific symptom or transference phenomenon? Which theory suggests the most interesting or productive questions to ask in a given situation? Clinical outcome research suggests that no single theoretical perspective is superior to any other, but that it is crucial for the therapist to possess some unifying perspective that orients the work with a patient; in other words, what matters is the fact that one has an orientation rather than what the specific orientation is. This book offers some of the best theories available, and the case illustration in each chapter demonstrates how one talented clinician has applied these ideas. One could choose to think of this as a *prix fixe* menu that places no limit on the order of courses or on how much one may eat—it is up to the diner to craft a harmonious meal. I find delicious elements in each theory.

Many theorists seem to claim to be the true inheritors of Freud's legacy. Generally, however, each one has taken up a particular philosophical trend in Freud's thinking from the standpoint of clinical work, greater diagnostic precision (particularly in regard to personality disorders), or the direct observation and treatment of children. By "philosophical trend" I refer primarily to metapsychology, theoretical constructs used to help organize observed data. No dissection of a brain, however, has ever revealed egos, ids, or superegos, much less ego nuclei, narcissistic lesions, or internalized objects. As Greenberg and Mitchell (1983) put it, "Nobody has ever seen an instinctual drive and nobody ever will" (p. 339). Although these structures may seem to be the most parsimonious in explaining clinical data, they do not exist. Even further from our observing senses are notions such as libido and the death instinct. These concepts are important because they are shaped by the clinical and life experiences of clinicians, who, in turn, shape what each of them and each of us has the capacity to see. Freud was bound by the time in which he lived, and his outlook derived from not only his clinical observations but also his classical education, which included the serious study of literature and philosophy. Freud's immersion in a set of intellectual traditions shaped his approach to medicine and psychoanalysis and is in part responsible for the immense influence his work has had in our culture. Although we do in fact align ourselves with centuries-old philosophical traditions when we select our clinical perspectives, these intellectual issues are, in great part, only minimally relevant to the day-to-day judgments and decisions made in psychoanalysis and psychotherapy.

This précis of the major schools of psychodynamic thought outlines the metapsychological debates while maintaining a focus on the less abstract clinical contributions of each school. The book presents nine psychodynamic perspectives, in approximately chronological order, and demonstrates how these perspectives translate into listening strategies or attitudes in the clinical setting. Those who find it easier to engage with clinical material than with theory are invited to begin each chapter by reading the case material. I have chosen to include lengthy quotations from each writer in the hope that the reader will feel encouraged to read the original material. Beginning clinicians might choose to think of this book as a kind of Rosetta stone that will help them scan the literature and decipher the metapsychological affiliations of the various writers. For concise definitions of all terms used in this book (with the exception of Lacan's for which, as far as I am aware, no concise source exists) the reader should consult Moore and Fine's *Psychoanalytic Terms and Concepts* (1990) or Laplanche and Pontalis's *The Language of Psycho-Analysis* (1973).

For the sake of clarity each theory has been presented as a distinct and discrete clinical style, but it should be recognized that any classification of theorists into schools oversimplifies the interdependence of thought in the field. Clinical situations are rarely so straightforward that one explanatory model is sufficient. Patients seldom benefit from only one theoretical listening stance over the entire course of psychotherapy, although some clinicians impose a single theory on the patient's material. In practice, however, even the most disturbed patients seen in outpatient psychotherapy possess areas of healthy functioning or higher neurotic conflict associated with the effort to resolve the Oedipus complex. Conversely, the most apparently neurotic and high-functioning patients display vulnerabilities from the preoedipal years prior to the establishment of the structure of the mind. Thus, rigid adherence to one theoretical or developmental perspective is likely to be detrimental to the patient.

For the most part, the history of psychoanalysis after Freud is that of the changing focus from the oedipal to the preoedipal period. The Freud case I have chosen to summarize in Chapter 1, Dora, demonstrates Freud's courage and brilliance — but also the way in which his theory could not account for certain clinical phenomena. The ego psychologists discussed in Chapter 2, most notably Anna Freud and Heinz Hartmann, continued the focus on the ego that characterized Freud's later years. They preserve the metapsychological primacy that Freud assigned to the drives. Other well known writers in this tradition include Otto Fenichel, Ernst Kris, Rudolf Loewenstein, David Rapaport, Erik Erikson, Robert Waelder, Charles Brenner, Roy Schafer, Paul Gray, Jacob Arlow, Gertrude and Ruben Blanck, and Edith Jacobson (whose work provides a transition to that of Otto Kernberg).

Melanie Klein, the subject of Chapter 3, remained a loyal believer in the more pessimistic Freud who articulated, albeit tentatively, a theory of a death instinct. She thus took a divergent path from Anna Freud. The close followers of Klein include Joan Riviere, Susan Isaacs, Paula Heimann, Hanna Segal, and Betty Joseph. Otto Kernberg was also heavily influenced by Klein. Klein's heirs, the object relations theorists, put aside Klein's emphasis on death and aggression but retained and elaborated her study of preoedipal intrapsychic life. More important, the object relations theorists repudiated the primacy of the drives, saying instead that infants derived pleasure from the relationships themselves and not solely from the satisfaction of physical need that the other could provide. This book offers a summary in Chapter 4 of the contributions to object relations theory of D. W. Winnicott. Other important writers and clinicians in this tradition include W. R. D. Fairbairn, Ian Suttie, Harry Guntrip, Michael Balint, Patrick Casement, and Christopher Bollas (whose work is also influenced by Lacan).

Margaret Mahler, while remaining in some ways philosophically loyal to ego psychology and drive theory, did detailed studies of the object relationships and intrapsychic states of infants and toddlers. Her separation/individuation theory, the focus of Chapter 5, has gained wide acceptance in the field. Others who have collaborated with Mahler or continued to explore the implications of her theory include Manuel Furer, Anni Bergman, Fred Pine, John McDevitt, Henri Parens, and Selma Kramer. René Spitz also did important infant observational work. Although some ego psychologists interpret Mahler's conclusion as supporting their faith in the autonomous ego functions and the resulting stance that the "lion's share" of the responsibility for development rests with the infant,[1] a more usual reading of Mahler reveals multiple potential (and likely) points at which maternal difficulty places a child's development at risk.

Chapter 6 focuses on Otto Kernberg's attempts to integrate an object relations perspective with classical drive theory. Although he may be less than successful, philosophically speaking, in achieving this impossible goal, he nonetheless produces an impressive theory of the central role that affects play in the development of self and object for the infant. Many prominent clinicians,

---

1. Gertrude Blanck, in comments made on October 26, 1995 at the clinical conference of the National Membership Committee on Psychoanalysis in Clinical Social Work, said that although it was a slight exaggeration to say this, she did not believe in maternal failure.

for example Vamık Volkan, rely on Kernberg's concept of internalized object relations as a listening device. Kernberg is less well known for his metapsychology, persuasive though it is, than for his insights into the treatment of borderline conditions.

An enthusiastic group of self psychologists has followed in the footsteps of Heinz Kohut, the subject of Chapter 7, whose work with narcissistic patients resulted in a metapsychological position rather closer to the object relations school than he acknowledged. Kohut thoroughly repudiated drive theory as explanatory of preoedipal pathology, instead seeing the infant's development as dependent on appropriate empathic responses from the parents. Major contributors in this tradition include Arnold Goldberg, Paul and Anna Ornstein, Ernest Wolf, and James Fosshage. The intersubjective perspective can perhaps be thought of as Kohut's grandchild.

Chapter 8, which takes up two related theoretical threads, introduces the intersubjective school, represented most prominently by Robert Stolorow, as well as others such as Frank Lachmann, Joseph Lichtenberg, Robert Emde, and Stephen Mitchell. While the inspirational spark comes from Kohut's work, important information about intersubjective aspects of mother–infant relationships has emerged from the work of infant researchers. Daniel Stern's work in this area is discussed in this book. Beatrice Beebe is another prominent infant researcher. John Bowlby's work on attachment theory is also relevant to this area. The most fundamental shift that intersubjectivity represents is perhaps characteristic of our post-relativity Zeitgeist; clinical "truth" is no longer seen as an absolute but rather as something that is interpersonally determined and discovered, and socially constructed. As the case presentation in this chapter shows, this can result in a heightened appreciation of the "real" effect of the therapist on the patient.

Finally, in Chapter 9, I offer an introduction to the enigmatic but important contributions of Jacques Lacan. My chapter on Lacan attempts only to distill from his work that which may be of interest to clinicians. I thus stress his view of development, even though he did not consider that this perspective was central to his thinking after he wrote "The Mirror Stage as Formative of the Function of the I as Revealed in the Psychoanalytic Experience" (1936). In an effort to make Lacan less alien and alienating, I compare, contrast, and link his views with those of the other theorists in this book. Most French psychoanalysts have been influenced by Lacan, whether positively or negatively. Thus, echoes of or reactions to his holdings can be discerned even in work not overtly Lacanian, such as that of André Green or Joyce McDougall. Americans writing and practicing in a Lacanian style include Stuart Schneiderman and John Muller. In the United States, however, Lacan's influence has been felt more powerfully in such academic fields as philosophy, literary criticism, and art history; the best introductions to Lacan I encountered were written not by clinicians but by philosophers or sociologists. Possibly in homage to their mentor, Lacanian clinicians tend to write in dense and impenetrable ways—at least it seems so to the non-Lacanian outsider. However, there does seem to be something about Lacan's ideas that provokes the desire to play with words!

The clinical material used in this book has been selectively disguised to the point where it *cannot* be used for scientific study of any kind. Although the core dynamics and therapeutic process have been preserved, each case must be considered as an illustration or parable rather than a report of any particular population, syndrome, or pathology. Regarding treatment modality, I believe that psychotherapy and psychoanalysis are on a continuum, so that clinical wisdom from the one may be applied to the other. I am not unaware, though, that many would argue that there exist significant differences in both technique and substance. The developmental dynamics outlined in this book occur in all patients, although they are easier to observe at greater frequencies of sessions. For that reason, the treatments illustrated here are of relatively long duration and intensity.

Two notes on terminology. I am uncomfortable with, but see

no alternative to, the use of the universal "he"; to use "he or she," "to him or to her," and "himself or herself" would feel more accurate and respectful, but it is terribly cumbersome to both writer and reader. I have chosen, too, for the sake of consistency in the text, to refer to the individuals being treated as "patients" rather than "clients." This may represent a mild repudiation of my own training as a clinical social worker. Yet I found over my years of practice that many clients regard themselves as patients insofar as they seek relief from suffering; in this sense, the medical model provides a powerful and appropriate metaphor for the psychotherapeutic situation. I think it crucial, though, that clinicians from all the mental-health disciplines regard "patients" as "clients" who have the right to be treated without condescension or paternalism. As our theories are for us, we clinicians must for our patients be useful servants.

1 THE INCREASINGLY COMPLEX POSITIONS OF SIGMUND FREUD

There are many comprehensive chronological and clinical descriptions of Freud's work and this outline is intended to serve only as a review of the metapsychological and clinical areas about which there would later be so much disagreement. It is confusing for the student of psychodynamic theory and practice that theoreticians who disagree with each other nonetheless find specific support for their positions in the writings of Sigmund Freud. But Freudian theory is not a clear and unified statement; rather, it is several sets of increasingly complex positions, each of which is dependent for its existence on the unanswered questions posed by the previous theoretical construct. Hence, many different readings of Freud are indeed possible. Freud kept offering new and improved versions of his theories as psychoanalysis developed; however, he did not clarify the situation by retracting outdated positions. This chapter offers not an exhaustive account of these complicated paths but rather an orientation to the issues later thinkers have addressed. In this chapter, as throughout the book, I will focus on those theoretical concerns that relate directly to clinical practice.

Sigmund Freud (1856–1939) was trained in Vienna as a

physician. He did highly respected work in biology and neurology before turning to the study and practice of psychiatry. Retained from his early training, though, was a belief that mental functioning operated according to the logical principles of the natural sciences; it would have been impossible for Freud to escape totally the weltanschauung of the nineteenth century. Like a biologist, Freud attempted to discern in the mind various structures and functions. This faith in the power of empirical, observable, scientific data (known as positivism) represented a true revolution in the predominant view of psychopathology. Although some, including Janet and Charcot (French physicians) and some Americans, were beginning to question the generally accepted view that psychopathology was hereditary and therefore largely immune to psychological influence, Freud's work for the first time made it possible to understand that there existed meaning in such symptoms as hysterical paralysis, obsessions, and hallucinations. Although psychoanalysis as a treatment method is now considered time-consuming and expensive, in Freud's time it was vastly less restrictive (and more effective) than electrical treatments, confinement in sanitoria or spas, or other rest cures.

EARLY THEORY – THE UNCONSCIOUS AND THE STRUCTURE OF THE MIND

Out of Freud's work with hysterics emerged perhaps the most significant contribution of his career: the postulation of the existence and significance of the unconscious. In truth, Freud did not discover the unconscious; philosophers, poets, and novelists had written of it for years and other psychologists suspected its existence. More than a few psychiatrists, neurologists, and hypnotists both in America and in Europe utilized some conception of unconscious mental functioning in their theories and treatments. Freud's unique contribution was a description of the manifestations of the unconscious, an outline of its methods of functioning, and a theory of its contribution to psychopathology. The conscious mind became the proverbial tip of the iceberg, with the content and direction of mental life being under the control of the unconscious. Freud came to believe that the hysterical symptoms he and Josef Breuer, his collaborator, studied were created through conversion and that they symbolically expressed ideas through the medium of the body (Laplanche and Pontalis 1973). Clinical material gained through the use of hypnosis with these patients seemed to give ample evidence of a mind that functioned outside of conscious awareness. One of the metapsychological assumptions underlying this theory came to be called the *economic point of view,* and it held that mental processes involve the action of physical or instinctual energy. And the laws of physics tell us that energy is neither created nor destroyed. Thus, when Freud observed an idea, such as an obsessional behavior, without associated affect or, as with hysterics, affect and behavior in the absence of the original cognition, he assumed that the thought or feeling was present in the unconscious. The cause of mental illness was the patient's inability to experience, and thus discharge, the excitation of the initial event. Another principle borrowed from the natural sciences was *homeostasis*—the organism's tendency to discharge excess excitation and to maintain a kind of steady state. Paradoxically, all living organisms do require a certain amount of constant excitation in order to support life.

The notion that all psychical energy requires discharge derives from neurological theories of nerve function that Freud addressed extensively in his work of 1895, the *Project for a Scientific Psychology.* He used the term *cathexis* to refer to the attaching of psychical energy, either positive or negative, love or hostility, to an idea or object such as a person, a part of one's body, an event, or an inanimate object. Cathexis, a cumbersome translation from the German, is sometimes replaced by "investment" (Laplanche and Pontalis 1973); it can be understood according to the metaphor of an electric wire that is charged with electric current when a switch is turned on. The concept of defense mechanisms rests on the concept of cathexis – that psychical energy, if excited but not discharged, does not simply disappear but must obey the Newtonian law of conservation. Positing the existence of *repression* (other defense mechanisms were identified later) and this process of mental hydraulics allowed Freud to trace the path in the mind of his hysterical patients of the missing idea or affect (the undischarged psychical energy).

Freud and Breuer (1893) wrote that hysterical patients "suffer mainly from reminiscences" (p. 7). The two investigators came to disagree, though, on the efficacy of the treatment they were then using with these patients – hypnosis, a method ideally suited to the uncovering of forgotten memories. Freud was learning that the simple catharsis that successful hypnosis offered provided no more than a temporary cure; he believed that this was explained by the strength of the mental force, repression, that had led originally to the banishment of the thought or memory from consciousness. *Resistance* to getting well through hypnosis or psychotherapy is another manifestation of the repressive force; resistance can be thought of as a tendency that prevents gaining conscious access to unconcious, repressed material and, more specifically, that abhors relinquishing symptoms in therapy. Hypnosis resulted not in permanent cures but rather in temporary ones or in the substitution of one symptom for another; in addition, not all patients were capable of achieving a hypnotic state. Freud thus broke with Breuer and instead attempted to uncover the same unconscious material through requesting his patients to engage in the "uncensored talking" (Gay 1988, p. 71) that would come to be known as *free association*. Simply put, patients were asked to say whatever thoughts came into their minds during the treatment sessions. Freud found that by following the threads that seemed to connect the patient's topics, he could discern the unconscious material. During his first experiments with free association, Freud would place his hand on the patient's forehead and apply pressure in order to help the patient concentrate and overcome resistance to speaking freely. Later he found that this technique was not necessary.

Freud later extended his metapsychology far beyond the theory of psychical energy—the so-called economic point of view—to a conception of the *topographic point of view,* dividing the mind into three systems: the conscious, the preconscious, and the unconscious. (The second and final topography of the mind was the *structural point of view,* that is, the structures id, ego, and superego.) This topographic point of view, this first structuring of the mind into systems, should not be confused with the way in which Freud conceived of hysteria, for "unconscious" referred here to a quality of a thought, as an adjective rather than a noun. Although these concepts remained descriptive and not elaborated into a structure, they were nonetheless central to the theory of hysteria.

Preconscious material is that which, although not in one's awareness, may readily become conscious; a psychoanalytic interpretation would promote access to preconscious thoughts, as would the examined content of a dream. When affects and ideas are for some reason intolerable to the censoring agency of the mind, they are rendered unconscious via the mental operation of repression, the prototypical defense mechanism that occurs both in normal and in pathological functioning. Since all the defense mechanisms occur as unconscious processes, they all include repression as one of their constituents. And why would there come to exist a censoring agency in the first place? Why would the mind need not know certain things? The answer leads to one of the central topics in psychoanalytic theory—the concept of anxiety.

At this early point in Freud's psychoanalytic career, anxiety was thought to result from sexual frustration, from libido that had not been discharged. In the etiology of each hysterical patient could be found some sexual element, such as a forbidden desire (e.g., a governess falling in love with her employer), wishing to marry one's dead sister's husband, or a traumatic event (sexual advances made to a 14-year-old by her father [Freud and Breuer

1893]). This view that there was a sexual event at the root of each case of hysteria is sometimes referred to as the *seduction theory*. But sometimes, as noted above, the problem seemed to be one of the patient's desire. As Freud continued his self analysis, he, too, found "memories" of having been seduced as a child, and, believing these must be false, he concluded that many seemingly real memories reported by patients were in fact fantasies or memories of childhood fantasies. Ann Salyard (1994) emphasizes how central to the development of early theory was Freud's self-analysis; her close analysis of Freud's early writings and letters leads her to believe that Freud did in fact have early sexual experiences. Thus, Freud's espousal and later rejection of the seduction theory remain controversial and historically unsettled areas.

Some mental health professionals and many laymen are dubious about the existence of so-called false memories; but the great difficulty of distinguishing memory from fantasy has been part of the psychoanalytic discourse since the early twentieth century.

CURES, DREAMS, AND MENTAL PROCESSES

If it is anxiety-provoking unconscious affects and ideas that lead to symptom formation or psychologically determined distress, then a cure would require making these anxiety-provoking elements conscious and helping the patient to tolerate them. Freud believed that discharging the excitation could occur through remembering and through speech, not only through action (he was still dealing with his hydraulic neurology here). It is through interpretation to the patient of the latent meaning of his or her communications that the unconscious (more accurately, the preconscious) can become conscious. The patterns and content of speech and behavior in the consulting room readily permit the discovery of latent meaning if the patient indeed follows what

Freud termed the *fundamental rule*, which he advised the analyst to impart at the beginning of treatment in the following fashion:

> "What you tell me must differ in one respect from an ordinary conversation. Ordinarily you rightly try to keep a connecting thread running through your remarks and you exclude any intrusive ideas that may occur to you. . . . But in this case you must proceed differently. You will notice that as you relate things various thoughts will occur to you which you would like to put aside on the grounds of certain criticisms and objections. You will be tempted to say to yourself that this or that is irrelevant or nonsensical, so that there is no need to say it. You must never give in to these criticisms, but must say it precisely *because* you feel an aversion to doing so." [Freud 1913, p. 135]

Patients who applied this fundamental rule very often found themselves reporting their dreams, and Freud (1900) came to regard dreams as "the royal road to a knowledge of the unconscious activities of the mind" (p. 608). Mental functioning displayed in dreams exemplifies what Freud called *primary process* thinking, in which the laws of logical connections, the ability to delay gratification, the need to avoid gratification of unacceptable wishes, and the avoidance of contradictory attitudes — all of which characterize *secondary process* mental functioning — do not apply. Dreams, Freud argued, represent wish-fulfillments, often couched in metaphors that remain unrecognizable to the conscious mind; at the root of dreams and of psychopathological symptoms lies a desire (wish), primitive or infantile in nature, which if expressed consciously would cause overwhelming anxiety. This infantile wish attaches itself to the dreamer's more contemporary desires and the dream as recalled is a product of displacements, condensations, reversals, and layers of revisions that permit the discharge of the wish, its satisfaction in fantasy, while still protecting the conscious mind from anxiety. The so-called day residue, the contemporary subject material of the dream, functions as a carrier for the infantile wish. The vocabulary of the dream is symbolic images and the dream's grammar is expressed in the narrative sequences. In short, the dream reveals the processes of the mind itself. Freud's dream theory was particularly controversial because he identified in the minds of normal people and in children the very same mechanisms at work in the minds of those who suffered from mental illnesses, disease entities many considered hereditary.

THE ROLE OF SATISFACTION

How does the infant, primitive and demanding, whose mind functions according to primary process, come to be "civilized," to accept the nongratification or delayed gratification of needs and desires? At the beginning of life we operate according to the *pleasure principle*, procuring as much pleasure as possible while avoiding unpleasure. To a great extent the infant's unpleasure involves uncomfortable levels of excitation or stimulation that can be internal (e.g., being hungry) or external (e.g., being in a noisy room) in origin. Thus, the *experience of satisfaction* results from a reduction of tension and a return to homeostasis (Laplanche and Pontalis 1973). An infant who experiences a great deal of satisfaction and very little pain develops what Therese Benedek (1938) later called "confident expectation" and Erik Erikson (1950) thought of as "basic trust." Both of these concepts refer to the infant's belief that his needs will be met, which is the foundation of the ability to tolerate delays in gratification. In other words, the discomfort involved in the wait for satisfaction comes to be encoded in the mind as part of the experience of satisfaction. The pleasure of eating is a counterpoint to the hunger that the baby has been allowed to develop. It is only repetitive and excessive delays of satisfaction that lead to an encoding and remembering of an experience of pain (Stern

1985). The baby who has received adequate and timely gratification learns to tolerate reasonable levels of hunger and other potentially uncomfortable sensations.

The *reality principle*, which shapes the functioning of most older children and adults, permits "the search for satisfaction [not to] take the most direct routes but instead [to] make detours and [to postpone] the attainment of its goal according to the conditions imposed by the outside world" (Laplanche and Pontalis 1973, p. 379). The defense often facilitating this process is *sublimation*, which involves the satisfaction of a wish through an altered aim or object. Generally considered to be a healthy or high-level defense, sublimation derives its psychic energy (again in the hydraulic-economic model) from desexualization of libido. (Hartmann addressed this issue with his concept of neutralization.) Although it is a defense insofar as it averts the consequences of the direct expression of an instinctual wish, sublimation is not defensive in that the wish is gratified and not left entirely unsatisfied or repressed.

The important concepts of *regression* and *fixation* are tied to the question of satisfaction. To understand the difference between the two, one need only remember the distinction between being broke and being poor.[1] If a child experiences too much pleasure or too much pain at any stage of development it is possible to develop a fixation, and psychological development becomes arrested. A lesser degree of excessiveness renders the child prone to a regression, a potential return under conditions of stress to the level of experiencing at which satisfaction was last achieved comfortably. The stages of development refer to the oral, anal, and phallic—the maturational progression of primary zones of satisfaction; Freud (1905b) outlined his theory of development and of infant sexuality in his "Three Essays on the Theory of Sexuality."

---

1. I thank Raymond Catton, M.D., for this analogy.

ID, EGO, AND SUPEREGO

Freud's clinical experience suggested that the unconscious/ preconscious/conscious system was insufficient to explain the functions of the mind. For instance, this topographic point of view could not explain why the defensive process itself was an unconscious one; within this model, the conscious mind was thought to contain what would later be called ego functions as well as the moral force of the superego. Also, the topographic could not account for the existence of the unconscious sense of guilt (Moore and Fine 1990). Freud in the 1920s formulated a second topography of the mind—the agencies of id, ego, and superego. This is known as the *structural point of view*. Although the ego is the most representative of the reality principle and the id of the pleasure principle, no simple correspondence exists between these agencies and the systems of consciousness or the economics of pleasure and unpleasure; for instance, the id remains entirely in the unconscious, while the ego and superego have in addition conscious and preconscious elements. The id represents "the instinctual part of the personality"; the ego "puts itself forward as the representative of the whole person"; and the superego "provides judgment and criticism, constituted by the internalization of parental demands and prohibitions" (Laplanche and Pontalis 1973, p. 452). The superego, however, consists not only of the judging and prohibiting functions but also of a positive sense of how one would like to be; in fact the original term for the superego was *ego ideal*.

These agencies of the mind are often in conflict over which strivings or desires will be permitted expression; thus in addition to the external conflicts involved in securing satisfaction in the environment, there are also internal psychological conflicts— *intrapsychic conflict*. Although he did not include the superego in this image, Freud (1933) used the following analogy to capture the complicated relationship of ego to id, of reality to pleasure:

The ego must on the whole carry out the id's intentions, it fulfils its task by finding out the circumstances in which those intentions can best be achieved. The ego's relation to the id might be compared with that of a rider to his horse. The horse supplies the locomotive energy, while the rider has the privilege of deciding on the goal and of guiding the powerful animal's movement. But only too often there arises between the ego and the id the not precisely ideal situation of the rider being obliged to guide the horse along the path by which it itself wants to go. [p. 77]

The ego, then, is in constant battle to satisfy the demands of id and external reality. Its own internal taskmaster, the superego, is the representative of parental and societal prohibitions; the often punitive quality of the superego results from the fact that the child tends to internalize not a well-rounded parental voice but rather the parents' superegos, their harshness unrelieved by the efforts parents may make to temper their judgmental acts. The child's fantasy of what the parents would condemn also plays a role in superego formation.

ANXIETY, CONFLICT, AND THE DRIVES

It is anxiety that fuels *conflict* and motivates compromise on the part of the ego, anxiety that is the response to the perceived danger in not obeying the demands of external reality, id, and superego. Freud also at this time radically revised his theory of anxiety. Instead of holding that anxiety resulted from repression, he did an about-face; now anxiety caused repression. Moreover, *signal anxiety* was the way in which the ego communicated the need for defense. This anxiety could result from anticipation of danger in the event that id impulses were satisfied. *Traumatic anxiety*, on the other hand, resulted from the overwhelming of the stimulus barrier and the ensuing helplessness of the ego; to this day, controversy exists over whether trauma (in an adult) ever occurs independently of the preexisting personality. A series of prototypic dangers followed the child's development: loss of the object (the loved and needed caregiver), loss of the object's love, loss of bodily integrity (castration), and loss of the superego's love (guilt). The maturing organism's changing biological and instinctual needs fuel this process, or, to follow Freud's analogy, set the horse off down the path in the first place. Thus, the producers of conflict are the instincts, or *drives*, which Freud (1915) saw as a quasi-biological, or somatopsychic, pressure on the organism:

> By the pressure of an instinct we understand its motor factor, the amount of force or the measure of the demand for work it represents. . . . The aim of an instinct is in every instance satisfaction which can only be obtained by removing the state of stimulation at the source of the instinct. . . . The object of an instinct is the thing in regard to which or through which the instinct is able to achieve its aim. It is what is most variable about an instinct and is not originally connected with it, but becomes assigned to it only in consequence of being peculiarly fitted to make satisfaction possible. . . . By the source of an instinct is meant the somatic process which occurs in an organ or part of the body and whose stimulus is represented in mental life by an instinct. . . . Although instincts are wholly determined by their origin in a somatic source, in mental life we know them only by their aims. [pp. 122–123]

Conflict is produced when instinctual wishes encounter prohibitions. Actual conflict later becomes internalized, intrapsychic conflict as the superego stands in for the actual parents. Conflict cannot exist, therefore, before the age when prohibitions can be perceived; prototypic conflictual processes include toilet training and the working through of oedipal strivings. Before turning to Oedipus, though, it is important to understand further the place of the instincts in very early childhood, a topic that has generated much dispute in the field of psychoanalysis.

NARCISSISM, DEATH, AND INFANTILE SEXUALITY

Freud saw the drives as being the sole motivating factor in infancy, holding that infants seek human relationships in order to meet these psychobiological needs, a position that the object relations school later rejected. Drive theory sees the infant turning toward people (objects) as the method by which unpleasures may be eliminated, as a measure through which homeostasis may be restored. The object is important as a facilitator of tension reduction. The helping objects are experienced as extensions of the self as the infant is postulated to exist at this early stage in an undifferentiated state in which no distinction between self and environment is perceived. Freud also referred to this period as that of *autoerotism*. Until recent years little knowledge was available about the psychology of early infancy, but sophisticated research strategies (see Chapter 8) and reexamination of existing thought (see Chapter 5) have led to strong challenges to this concept of *primary narcissism*. In this state, the infant relates to the environment, but he does so without true object relations; the object is not cathected and there does not exist an intrapsychic mental representation of it. It is only the ego, used in the sense of "self," that is cathected (Moore and Fine 1990).

Although the term *narcissism*, thanks in great part to Kohut, is commonly used today to refer to the broad issue of self-esteem, its history as a psychoanalytic theory is complex (Pulver 1970). Freud selected, but did not invent, the word in order to echo the Greek myth in which Narcissus looked in a pond and fell in love with his own image. In early psychoanalytic usage it thus refers to the infant's cathexis of the self. It later was used to characterize a sexual perversion, as well as a particular style of object relations — seeking others like the self — in distinction to *anaclitic* (leaning on something) object relations in which the model was the dependence on the mother. Narcissistic object relations, although they appear to be relationships, in fact are not truly social because the fantasy and wish is for a love relationship with the self; primary narcissism is, by definition, centered on the self. Freud dated the developmental occurrence of primary narcissism at various times, but his last position was that it was coexistent with the autoerotic phase in the earliest weeks of life (Laplanche and Pontalis 1973). This theoretical position concerned what was and is still essentially unknowable – the state of mind of the neonate.

This relatively academic controversy over infants had little to do with Freud's popular reputation as a man of controversy, which was based on his heretical pronouncements about sexuality. Particularly difficult for nineteenth-century folk to stomach were the concepts that sexuality began in infancy and, moreover, that we are all bisexual by nature. Freud used *sexuality* to refer not simply to the adult experience we would normally associate with that term but instead to a larger range of sensual pleasures that could not adequately be explained as motivating factors for self-preservation. These, Freud said in his early psychoanalytic writings, are the two major classes of instincts, the self-preservative and the sexual, and it was the study of sexual pleasure that led him to the now-familiar but then startlingly new outline of the stages of childhood sexual development. (To this day, many find the concept of childhood sexuality shocking, repugnant, and unacceptable.) If this classification of instincts sounds unfamiliar it is because Freud later revised them. Forced to account for such clinical instances of self-directed aggression as sexual masochism, the negative therapeutic reaction (paradoxical worsening of illness in response to treatment), and to the *repetition compulsion*, Freud postulated a *death instinct*. Thus, this death instinct, *Thanatos*, and the sexual or life instinct, *Eros*, shaped the human struggle. The aim of life, Freud said, was death, pointing to the tendency of the organic to return to the inorganic. The death instinct was accepted only by few clinicians and theorists (most prominent among them Melanie Klein and Jacques Lacan), but the aggressive drive became an accepted part of the psychodynamic lexicon. Currently accepted is the notion that some admixture of aggressive and libidinal wishes characterizes most human actions. Indeed, aggression is necessary to thrive and underlies what is has become fashionable to call "assertiveness."

Freud's theory of *psychosexual stages* was completed before the formulation of the death instinct. Libido, as reflected in sensual gratification, is centered successively upon different zones of the infant's body that, in turn, tend to characterize in a more general sense the child's experience of the world. It makes sense that in the first months of life the infant receives most pleasure via the mouth and explores the environment orally as well. Sucking needs, which reflect the pleasure instincts, very often exceed physical hunger, the self-preservative instincts; witness the pleasure that infants derive from the thumb or the pacifier. Much to the horror of their caregivers, babies also put anything and everything in their mouths in what we assume is an effort to become familiar with the nature of their surroundings. The primary zone of pleasure shifts from the *oral* to the *anal* from the ages of about 2 to 4 as the child expels or retains the feces and struggles along these lines with self-control versus lack of organization, activity versus passivity, and generosity versus parsimony. Freud elaborated later sexual development in a masculine paradigm, believing the phallus—the penis and its symbolic meaning—to be central to both girls and boys. Similar to the active-passive polarity of the anal stage is the opposition of "phallic" and "castrated" (Laplanche and Pontalis 1973) in what Freud termed the *phallic* phase. Boys develop anxiety about castration, whereas girls believe they have already suffered this fate; girls become envious of the penis. These tensions brought on by the emphasis on the phallus are resolved by the working through of the Oedipus complex, which allows the attainment of the *genital* phase in which affectionate and sensual strivings are united. Note that sexual development unfolds from infancy to adulthood not in one smooth progression but with two peaks of activity, in early childhood and then again in adolescence. The working through of the *Oedipal crisis* ushers in a period known as *latency*, of relative freedom from instinctual pressure, although in some latency-age children, this reduction may seem minimal. As Elisabeth Young-Bruehl (1992) has noted, "Latency is when your child sits still a little bit longer!"

THE OEDIPUS COMPLEX

Freud became aware in his self-analysis of conflicting feelings of jealousy and affection for his father and of love for and the wish to possess his mother. Utilizing his own experience, he attended to similar tensions in his patients' dreams and memories. He came to call this the *Oedipus complex* after the Greek mythic character who, despite having been left to die by his parents, fulfilled the prophecy that he would kill his father and marry his mother. It is the working through of one's desire for the opposite-sex parent and one's wish to eliminate the obstacle of the same-sex parent that leads to the final stage of sexuality, the so-called genital stage, in which one's wishes to love and to be loved both affectionately and sexually are directed toward the opposite sex. This end is achieved through the realization that the longed-for parent in fact prefers the spouse rather than the child. The child then overcomes the wish to kill the intervening parent through an identification with that parent, by trying to become like the parent of the same sex. The repressed sexual attraction toward the same-sex parent, a reflection of our natural bisexual tendencies, has come to be known as the *negative Oedipus complex*.

The oedipal scenario is experienced differently by boys and girls. For one thing, the boy retains the adored mother of infancy as the desired object, while the girl shifts her interest to the father. According to this view, the negotiation of the oedipal drama is more difficult for girls. Current views dispute this point, although it is generally agreed that the readily identifiable locus of sexual sensation in boys (as compared with the more diffuse and mysterious sensations in girls) does permit a more easily identifiable end to the oedipal wishes. For boys, the father's prohibition against attainment of the mother is perceived as a threat of castration. The notion that castration is a possibility follows the recognition that there are some people, such as mother and sister, who do not have penises. The threat disappears when the boy relinquishes desire for his mother and subsequently identifies with his father. Girls, in this schema, believe thay have already been castrated; the belief that they have already lost something renders girls prone to depression from an early age. Girls resolve the oedipal conflict by replacing the wish to possess a penis with the desire to bear a child. Despite the father's preference for the mother, the wish to give the father a gift of a baby, as the mother did, dissipates slowly in contrast to the more easily defined end of the complex for boys.

The significance of the Oedipus complex lies not only in the development of sexuality but also in the final structuring of the agencies of the mind. It is the internalization of the prohibition against incest and the ensuing identification with the same-sex parent that add the final building blocks of the superego and of gender and sexual identity. Because the Oedipus complex wanes slowly for girls, Freud felt that girls were in a disadvantaged position with regard to superego development and were at much greater risk for developing neuroses. In other words, what is forbidden to the little girl is the wish to marry her father and have his child, a wish that is specific in content but vague as to the physical methods necessary to achieve it. Only in very rare instances even today are little girls made aware of all the elements of their genital anatomy so that they understand the source of their pleasurable sensations and how they will be able to create and give birth to a child. The little boy, on the other hand, is forbidden actions with his easily observable penis, which he prizes and fears losing. Indeed, Freud believed that as a result of the different oedipal experience, women never develop the high level of conscience and morality possible for men. Current views on the comparative psychologies of men and women suggest that the situation is not exactly as Freud described. Carol Gilligan's (1982) work, for instance, describes different but equally strong moral styles in her studies of how boys and girls respond to moral dilemmas. Girls try to weigh relative rights and wrongs in a situation, while boys tend toward a morality more cut-and-dried, so to speak. Also central to Gilligan's understanding is the differing weight played by the conflicting values of affiliation and autonomy in the morality of boys and girls.

One of the most common criticisms of Freud's work is of his view that development is generally finished with the resolution of the oedipal crisis. Latency, the period beginning with the end of the Oedipus complex at age 5 or 6 and extending to the onset of puberty, ushers in an emphasis on affection rather than sexuality in relationships. This is accompanied and promoted by increased use of repression and sublimation. Puberty carries an upsurge in sexual interest, which reflects, in the choice of object, the compromises or conflicts with which the child resolved the oedipal situation. The crises and intense relationships of adolescence reflect the resumed working through of oedipal conflict, which includes attempts to consolidate identity, sexual preferences, and morality. In other words, Oedipus was king in ancient Greece and king of human development to Freud. By contrast, Erik Erikson (1950), a prominent post-Freudian analyst, saw development as continuing throughout adult life, with different crises characterizing each stage of life.

A brief comment on Freud's views about homosexuality is in order, for the psychoanalytic establishment today is considered by many to hold the position that homsexuality is unquestionably an illness. Freud seems to exhibit different attitudes at different points in his work. He did include homosexuality as one of the *perversions*, a perversion being defined as when what would be no more than a component of "normal" heterosexual sexuality instead becomes the central focus of and condition for sexual pleasure. (More accurately, homosexuality is termed an *inversion*, referring to the fact that it is opposite from the normal choice of turning outward, away from the image of oneself.) But he also recognized that the matter of sexual object choice in adults was not subject to easy change or influence. It would be as easy to change a homosexual into a heterosexual as it would be to change a heterosexual into a homosexual. Indeed, one of Freud's most radical suggestions was that heterosexuality, too, needed to be explained, that there was nothing inevitable about it. And equally radical was Freud's (1905b) recognition that the quality of sexual fantasy rather than the physical gender of the partner determined whether the mental attitude was one of hetero- or homosexuality:

> Psycho-analytic research is most decidedly opposed to any attempt at separating off homosexuals from the rest of mankind as a group of a special character. By studying sexual excitations other than those that are manifestly displayed, it has found that all human beings are capable of making a homosexual object-choice and have in fact made one in their unconscious. Indeed, libidinal attachments to persons of the same sex play no less a part as factors in normal mental life, and a greater part as a motive force for illness, than do similar attachments to the opposite sex. . . . Thus from the point of view of psycho-analysis the exclusive sexual interest felt by men for women is also a problem that needs elucidating and is not a self-evident fact based on an attraction that is ultimately of a chemical nature. [pp. 147-148]

IMPORTANCE OF THE PREOEDIPAL PHASE

The Oedipus complex constitutes an important dividing line in development and has become a dividing line of sorts among post-Freudian thinkers as well. Freud and his closest followers held that the goal of clinical psychoanalysis was to make conscious via interpretation the patient's oedipal wishes and the conflicts surrounding the castration complex (in men, the fear of losing the penis; in women, the wish for a penis). After repression and resistance have been overcome, these conflicts are accessible to the patient since they originate at a time in life when the child has a basic command of language. Memories are thus encoded in language, the predominant mode of adult communication. Preoedipal problems tend to be much less easily verbalized, even assuming the patient would be able to reach behind the barrier of forgetting that comes to enshroud early childhood, since the memories are deposited only partially in language. Thus they tend to be displayed as reenactments with the therapist rather than as displacements onto the therapist. Freud (1914) himself postulated and wrote of the importance of these early events that he was unable to reach either in his patients or in his self-analysis (although he had not yet understood that the transference and the countertransference would be a gold mine for preoedipal gems):

> There is one special class of experiences of the utmost importance for which no memory as a rule can be recovered. These are experiences which occurred in very early childhood and were not understood at the time but were *subsequently* understood and interpreted. One gains a knowledge of them through dreams and one is obliged to believe in them on the most compelling evidence provided by the fabric of the neurosis. [p. 149]

Much of the disagreement in the field of psychoanalysis can be traced to the issue of whether there exist any conflicts outside oedipal issues and whether material from this very early period may be interpreted in treatment. *Deficit* is one of the code words referring to this controversy, referring to so-called missing elements in the prestructural, pre–id-ego-superego, mind. Deficit and conflict are often thought to be mutually exclusive explanations for various pathological qualities, but in reality each personality and every symptom has both oedipal and preoedipal components. Another question is whether what clinicians observe is actually the result of deficit, that is to say "lack of mental structure," or is it rather a weak, inefficient, or bad mental structure? This controversy has been most fruitful, much innovation in the field having resulted from efforts to reach patients with problems of predominantly preoedipal origin, that is, those with character (personality) disorders more serious than neurosis.

TRANSFERENCE AND COUNTERTRANSFERENCE

Knowing what we do about the current proportions of neurotic to narcissistic and borderline patients, it is quite clear that psychoanalysis as Freud conceived and practiced it is a treatment for the few and not the many. A prospective analysand must be able to tolerate the absence of gratification of the analytic treatment and must possess strong motivation to gain self-knowledge. (Some Freudians felt that the treatment was only suitable for the educated classes, although early analysts in the United States drew patients from the general population of mental hospitals.) However, many patients, including some of Freud's, either were not capable of this or had problems of a narcissistic or psychotic nature. Problems arose when clinicians wished to expand the type of pathology that could be treated analytically. It seems clear today that several of Freud's celebrated patients, Dora, for instance, presented narcissistic and borderline pathology; indeed, this may account for Freud's less than total therapeutic success. Also, early theories of cure rested on the principles of remembering and abreacting, that is, that recalling the traumatic event or thought and discharging the emotion attached to it would be therapeutic; later views attached equal importance to the analytic exploration of resistances and defenses expressed in the analytic encounter itself.

Like the proverbial chicken and egg, theory and clinical data in psychoanalysis are inextricably intertwined. The subject of developmental pathology, that is, of narcissism and psychosis, leads to the issue of one of the major ways in which this type of problem is diagnosed, via the *transference*. Freud and Breuer discovered early that patients formed very intense relationships to their therapists. Freud with admirable modesty realized that his personal qualities were insufficient to account for the love all his female patients felt for him; he thus discovered transference, that these feelings had been transferred from the true object of affection to him. So important was transference that psychopathology came to be classified by whether a patient could form a transference. It was the patients with the *transference neuroses* — anxiety hysteria (phobias), conversion hysteria, and obsessional neurosis — who had adequately cathected external relationships so as to be capable of developing an analyzable transference. In the narcissistic neuroses, what we today call psychoses and borderline conditions, the libido is withdrawn from external objects and is directed to the ego.

Transference, which constitutes a key element in psychoanalytic diagnosis and treatment, has been called "a process of actualisation of unconscious wishes" (Laplanche and Pontalis 1973, p. 455). Originally conceived as a description of the delimited ways in which the patient experienced the analyst to be similar to figures from the past at specific moments in the treatment, transference grew to embody a wide range of concepts. Transference is often used today in a more general sense, to refer to the entirety of the patient's feelings for the therapist. The analytic patient had to be capable of displacing his or her conflicts onto the analyst while at the same time maintaining a constant sense of a working partnership, now referred to as a therapeutic or working alliance. To address oedipal issues in psychoanalysis, the patient had to be able to develop a neurotic transference, and then, ideally, a "transference neurosis," an organized and consistent re-creation within the analytic chamber of previous difficulties; it is the resolution of the transference neurosis that came to be seen as the primary curative element in psychoanalysis.

The development of a usable transference depends on other conditions in the treatment, namely the *neutrality* of the analyst. Neutrality and the closely related concepts of *anonymity* and *abstinence* characterize the analytic attitude. As Freud (1912) put it, "The doctor should be opaque to his patients and, like a mirror, show them nothing but what is shown to him" (p. 118). In this area, Freud's technical recommendations must be understood along the lines of, "Do as I say, not as I do." Freud would lend money to needy patients, and have patients accompany him on vacation so as not to interrupt the treatment; he committed such no-no's as treating a boy, Little Hans, through advice given to his father, all while the child's mother was in analysis with him; and he analyzed his own daughter, Anna. Freud's departures from his own recommendations notwithstanding, the goal of maintaining a neutral stance was to permit the patient to experience with the analyst as full as possible a range of transferred feelings, which were to include negative reactions. Any knowledge about the actual thoughts or opinions of the analyst would impinge on the patient's freedom to project. Anonymity, however, is always relative, for the analyst may be well known in the community (as Freud certainly was in Vienna) and the analyst always makes himself known in certain unavoidable ways by the decoration and location of the office, manner and attire, and by his professional style. Similarly, abstinence (refusing to gratify the patient's wishes that derive from libidinal sources) forced these wishes into the analytic dialogue. Putting thoughts and feelings into words rather than permitting their discharge in actions is one of the cardinal principles of psychoanalytic treatment.

Although Freud referred only on few occasions to the transference's companion, the concept of *countertransference*, the analyst's unconscious contributions to the relationship with the patient, this idea is nonetheless part of his bequest to later clinicians. Countertransference is often used today in an expanded sense, although some argue that it would be beneficial to restrict the usage to the original meaning. Countertransference used to be thought of as a Bad Thing. Having feelings, unconscious or conscious, about the patient was thought to indicate that the analyst needed more personal analysis. For this reason, clinicians were reluctant for many years to reveal the extent to which this was a practically universal experience. Today, countertransference is seen as a rich source of information about the patient, for one does not have the same reactions to all patients. However, countertransference is valuable if it is used as data, not if it is unconsciously acted out with the patient. It is essential, therefore, that the analyst be well analyzed. The analysts trained and treated by Freud generally had training analyses of a few months' duration; today, a training analysis lasting five years is not considered especially long. Although Freud clearly had no choice in the matter, at least at the beginning, for he was the first psychoanalyst, it is well to remember that he never himself underwent analysis except on his own. In his self-analysis, the study of his own dreams and associations, Freud displayed a remarkable ability to examine deeply personal material in an objective manner, but it would have been impossible for him to appreciate either the power of transference and countertransference or the influence of preoedipal/preverbal states particularly in regard to the early relationship to the mother.

THE CASE OF DORA

DORA'S BACKGROUND

It was Freud's early treatment failures such as with the young woman he called Dora (later identified as Ida Bauer) that clarified the importance of the transference and signposted the way to the later understanding of the centrality of the transference neurosis. Technically, Freud's title of the Dora case, "Fragment of an Analysis of a Case of Hysteria" is correct—he *was* able to analyze Dora's symptoms and interpret to her a highly specific understanding of her unconscious conflicts. A brief examination of this case will demonstrate Freud's intellect, underline the inadequacies of the topographic model that defined the therapeutic task as simply making the unconscious thought or affect conscious, and highlight the importance of transference and countertransference elements.

Hysteria, Dora's malady, refers to somatic symptoms, often shifting from one to another area of the body, that result from psychological conflict. "Conflict" is used here in the technical psychoanalytic sense – a clash of opposing wishes of different agencies of the mind. The conflict in hysteria results from the censorship agency of the ego trying to prevent unacceptable unconscious wishes from being expressed. The repression of these forbidden wishes is not altogether successful, hence resulting in the symptom – a compromise formation. Hysteria, as Freud (1905a) saw it, required three ingredients: a psychic trauma, a conflict of affects, and a disturbance in the sphere of sexuality. Insofar as Freud still believed that cure depended on the breaking of the repression barrier and in attaining knowledge of these repressed elements (wishes and conflicts), early psychoanalytic treatment and the clinical use of dreams had not moved far from its roots in hypnosis. In the case of Dora, Freud describes a therapeutic failure that simultaneously seems to have represented for him an intellectual and, certainly, a literary victory.

Dora was brought to Freud by her father soon after he had discovered a suicide note she had written. Her affectionate, positive attitude had changed, and she was displaying a nervous cough, periodic loss of her voice, and such signs of depression as fatigue, poor concentration, and social isolation. Dora had reported to her father that a certain Herr K., a close family friend, had propositioned her as they walked by a lake. Upon questioning by Dora's father and uncle, Herr K. denied that this had taken place. The father suspected, he told Freud, that Dora had become overexcited reading books about sex and that she had thus imagined the entire incident. But Dora, in addition, was demanding that her father terminate the friendship with Herr K. and especially with Frau K. Herr Bauer requested that Freud "try and bring her to reason" (Freud 1905a, p. 26).

Freud, however, learned from Dora a most complicated and sordid story—that there existed a sexual liaison between Dora's father and Frau K., that both Herr K. and Dora's father "got nothing out of their own wives," and that the father's refusal to acknowledge the truth of Dora's story amounted to a trading of his daughter in exchange for Herr K.'s continued collusion concerning the affair with Frau K. Freud concluded that the shock of Herr K.'s proposition constituted a trauma for Dora, for one thing because it recalled to Dora an earlier incident, more flagrant, when Herr K. pressed his body to Dora's and kissed her. And yet these were insufficient to explain Dora's hysteria at age 18 because symptoms such as a nervous cough and loss of her voice had appeared as early as Dora's eighth year. Trauma requires not only an event of sufficient magnitude to create shock but also a psychological breeding ground made vulnerable by innate constitution or by past experience. What Dora described from the first attempted seduction was the sensation of disgust and of Herr K.'s pressing against the upper portion of her body; this sensation and the disgust returned to her periodically after the actual event. Freud understood this to be a displacement upward and a reversal of affect; Dora repressed her sexual excitement and the memory of feeling Herr K.'s "erect member against her body" (p. 30). From that time forward, Dora made great efforts to avoid seeing all men who might be sexually aroused, whether they might be alone or with another woman. The defense mechanism she used here was a phobia—the fear and thus avoidance of simultaneously exciting and upsetting stimuli that further reinforced and protected the initial repression.

Dora at first protested Freud's interpretations that she must be in love with Herr K., then reluctantly agreed that, although it might once have been true, it was so no longer. She was, however, nearly obsessed with her father's love affair with Frau K. and was relentlessly attuned to all the arrangements the two of them made to be alone. Indeed her own suicide attempt may have been an imitation of a similar threat by her father, although Dora asserted to Freud that she had understood her father's threat to have been only another excuse for him and Frau K. to be alone. Another complaint Dora had about her father, which she might well have been justified in directing toward Frau K., was that he took advantage of his multiple medical problems to gain various ends. Frau K., for her part, became ill whenever she was faced with the prospect of intimate relations with her own husband. If Frau K. did not desire her husband, though, it would seem that Dora did, for her voice would disappear when Herr K. was absent. Dora's hysterical mutism possessed a certain neurotic logic: "When the man she loved was away she gave up speaking; speech had lost its value since she could not speak to *him*" (p. 40). With her exposure to this hotbed of hypochondria it is not surprising to find imitative and identificatory elements in Dora's symptoms. Note that in hysterical symptoms, though, there are always two contributors — the psyche and the soma. The thought alone is insufficient to create a bodily symptom. There must exist both a psychic wish as well as an organic pathway. In the absence of the somatic participation, another form of psychological symptom (e.g., obsession or phobia) will occur.

Dora's life was further complicated by her governess, who was also in love with Dora's father. This governess, for reasons we may imagine, urged upon Dora the knowledge of her father's love affair. Dora's indignation, then, served her governess's need as well as her own. The governess seems, too, to have been the source of much of Dora's forbidden knowledge of sexual matters in general, reading books to her and asking that she not reveal this to her parents. Dora came to realize that she held interest for the governess only as a means to a connection with her father, and she thus cut off contact with the governess. But there was a painful similarity between herself and this governess for she, Dora, had used her affection for Herr K.'s children as an excuse to be near Herr K. just as she had been used by her fickle governess.

Freud accepted that what Dora reported represented the actual state of affairs, as it were: "I could not in general dispute Dora's characterization of her father" (p. 34). However, he took it all a step further than Dora no doubt had intended: "A string of reproaches against other people leads one to suspect the existence of a string of self-reproaches with the same content" (p. 35). Freud realized that she, too, turned a blind eye to her father's sexual intrigues until the offensive (but unconsciously welcomed) scene at the lake and Herr K.'s denial. After understanding her role as payment for Herr K.'s silence she could no longer contain her disapproval of all involved.

One might well ask where Dora's mother was in all of this. As Dora related the situation to Freud, it was clear that her mother no longer was attractive to her husband. Freud describes her as having a housewife's psychosis (perhaps the obsession we might today call "crazy clean"). The family constellation was completed by an adored brother, one and a half years older than Dora. There seem to have been alliances between mother and son and between father and daughter, such that when father's attention turned to Frau K. it constituted an intense loss for Dora. And this was only one of many losses. Although we are told little about Dora's early life, it is not an excessive stretch of logic to conclude that she had lost any positive elements her mother might once have provided. She was to lose her governess, who desired her father, and also the idolized Frau K., who possessed him.

Thus, there is a convoluted web of desires, jealousies, repressions, and imitations that influenced Dora's symptoms and complaints. All of the characters in Dora's life seemed to use sickness to get what they wanted and to avoid what they did not want. Freud, unlike Dora's father, saw no reason to doubt her version of events and seemed to have felt that Dora was quite an acute observer. (Erik Erikson, in his 1961 commentary on this case, pointed out that the penetrating search for truth in which Dora was engaged is a developmental characteristic of adolescence.) But the fact that Freud actually listened to Dora, assumed that symptoms carried meaning, and considered her to be an acute observer of family life represents a revolutionary hermeneutic position in the history of psychotherapy and psychiatry; it is perhaps too easy, from a modern standpoint, to criticize Freud's failures with Dora and to forget his radical and brilliant contributions.

DORA'S ANALYSIS

Dora's motive for her suffering and for her suicide threat was to detach her father's interest from Frau K. Freud, in discussing the undoubted psychological motives for hysterical illness, lays out a therapeutic strategy that, tragically for Dora, proved ineffective in one important respect: "An attempt must first be made by the roundabout methods of analysis to convince the patient herself of the existence in her of an intention to be ill" (p. 45). Moreover, this is more difficult when the symptoms purport to influence others in addition to their intrapsychic effects. The essential contradiction in Freud's battle plan between *convincing* and *analyzing* proved to be his downfall. Although he writes of his efforts not to give Dora more sexual information than she already possessed, at every point Freud tells Dora more about herself than she is prepared to know. Right he might have been, but right she was, too, to leave this analysis that must have felt like just one more instance of being used. And Freud did use Dora, to prove the utility of his theory of dreams and to teach himself and (eventually, for he delayed publication of this case for four years) his readers about the technique of analysis. Noble though his intentions might have been, they must have held little value for this anguished adolescent.

Freud's theory at the time he treated Dora was that knowledge led to cure, and he hence attempted to give Dora the benefit of his perceptions. With the knowledge we now have, it is painfully easy to criticize Freud's technique. No psychoanalytic therapist of even average judgment and skill would attempt to communicate such interpretations so early in a treatment without a solid therapeutic relationship. Even Freud was aware that there had to be adequate positive transference from the patient to permit a treatment to occur. Some of Freud's interpretations were noxious: tying Dora's throat symptoms (cough, tickle) to a fantasy of fellatio, telling her that she was unconsciously in love with her own father (who had in reality preferred that Dora rather than his wife nurse him through his illnesses), suggesting that her flight from her love for Herr K. was a regression to her earlier love for her father. Behind both of these affections, though, Freud discerned a jealousy about and an attraction to Frau K., whose bedroom Dora would share during her visits to the K.s' house (not incidentally, displacing Herr K. to a guest room—again Dora was used). Dora had been Frau K.'s confidante, and so the picture is complete when Frau K. develops a liaison with Dora's father; every adult whom Dora has trusted has betrayed her. And both her father and Frau K. have taken a love object from her, for Freud believes that Dora has a strong undercurrent of homosexual love for Frau K. The childhood history Freud provides is very incomplete and one would have to wonder about the role of the mother in all of this; the attraction to Frau K. would likely be derived from Dora's negative oedipal complex. Whether Freud ever interpreted the homosexual material to Dora is not clear, but it was at this point in the treatment that Dora reported the first of two dreams, which are then exhaustively analyzed:

"A house was on fire. My father was standing beside my bed and woke me up. I dressed quickly. Mother wanted to stop and save her jewel-case; but Father said: 'I refuse to let myself and my two children be burnt for the sake of your jewel-case.' We hurried downstairs, and as soon as I was outside I woke up." [p. 64]

One purpose for which Freud was able to use the case of Dora was to illustrate and substantiate his recently published theory of dream interpretation in which he outlines the temporal layering of wishes, from the day residue to the most deeply repressed childhood desire; indeed the original title of this essay was "Dreams and Hysteria." From his analysis of Dora's first dream, too lengthy and elegant to capture here, Freud uncovers tier upon tier of unavowable wishes and the defenses against them. Dora feared being sexually persecuted by Herr K., but she was also willing to give both Herr K. and her father what their wives would not. This Dora denied. Freud also divines a history of bed-wetting (which Dora confirmed), which he posits was related to childhood masturbation. Through this chain of deductions Freud comes upon the fact that at a very young age Dora had known her father to have had a venereal disease that he passed to his wife. Like her mother, Dora experienced a genital discharge (a catarrh); Freud attributes this to excessive masturbation but his reconstruction is that Dora must have unconsciously believed that her father had given it to her as he had to his wife.

In addition to the anxiety Dora suffered over masturbation, Freud believed she had also been exposed to primal scenes as a young child. Sleeping next door to her parents' bedroom, Dora likely overheard their sexual exertions. More specifically, Freud attributes Dora's periodic shortness of breath both to this and to masturbation. He postulates that her unwell father might well have sounded quite breathless; if so, this symptom would suggest Dora's identification with her father in the sexual act and would support the suggestion above that Dora's attraction to Frau K. might indeed have stemmed from a desire to possess her mother and a failure to identify with her. Having learned to associate sexual exertion with illness (father's breathlessness, the genital discharge and disease) Dora might then have been frightened that her own breathlessness during masturbation would harm her. One can hardly imagine a less wholesome way in which to learn about sex; Dora's bitterness, cynicism, and pessimistic view of relationships between men and women seem to be almost the logical outcome of this family background.

Freud looks further at the dream and sees a transference

element in Dora's association to the bed-wetting segment; she talks about smoke, and Freud, of course, smoked. Unfortunately, he leaves this issue untouched — unfortunately because this was a harbinger of Dora's soon-to-be-announced plan to break off the treatment to avoid the temptation of wanting a smoky kiss from her analyst. There is much more to the rich analysis of the dream; but, in sum, Freud is able to discern Dora's early sexual knowledge, gaps in knowledge, her anxieties, and how these led to identifications and symptoms in her latency years. He linked her disgust over Herr K.'s touch to her childhood assumption that all men have and pass on venereal disease, and he outlined the contradiction between her anger at her father for making her vulnerable to Herr K. and her wish, expressed as gratified in the dream, that her father would protect her from danger.

There was a second dream, a more lengthy one, that Dora brought to the treatment. It was, however, incompletely analyzed due to Dora's abrupt termination of the analysis. This dream portrays via a "symbolic geography of sex" the fantasy of "a man seeking to force an entrance into the female genitals" (pp. 99–100). The dream contains a revenge wish against her parents: if they are dead, then Dora will be able to gain the knowledge she seeks and act as she pleases. This derives from the reference to reading the forbidden encyclopedia. Exploration of the significance of reading led Freud to understand that an attack of what was thought to be appendicitis was in reality a case of hysterical labor pains, timed exactly nine months after Herr K.'s proposition. Thus, Dora enacted her repudiated wish. At this, Freud was able to prove to Dora that her love for Herr K. was continuing: "And Dora disputed the fact no longer" (p. 104). This technique in which Freud attempts to persuade Dora of his "correct" understanding of her is a far cry from standard psychoanalytic strategy today in which one would seldom try to insist that the patient agree with anything and one would rather explore the patient's resistance, if it was resistance.

Perhaps it is no surprise to the modern reader of this case that

Dora came to a session one day with the pronouncement that it would be the last, admitting that she had decided so two weeks ago. Paradoxically, Freud does not try to persuade her to stay in treatment to work this through as one would be inclined to do today with a patient who so clearly continued to need help. He instead acknowledges her remark and indicates that they will use the session in the customary manner nonetheless. He comments that the two weeks reminds him of the notice one might give a domestic servant, and this elicits the story from Dora of a governess of the K. children after Herr K. had propositioned her. This governess had told Dora enough detail about the invitation and the subsequent sexual liaison so that when Herr K. propositioned her, she recognized his words as the very same ones he had used with the governess. Thus, Dora was insulted by the proposition not only because she suspected she was being bartered off by her father, but more immediately because she did not want to think of herself as no more important to Herr K. than a governess (of whom he had grown tired). It had been Dora's secret hope, Freud felt, that Herr K. would divorce Frau K. in order to marry her. But this hope was dashed when Herr K. denied to Dora's father that he had ever made any move toward her.

This new self-knowledge cannot have been pleasant for Dora, and it certainly did nothing to change her mind about leaving the analysis. Freud took this quite personally despite his effort to behave in a scientific way in Dora's presence: "Her breaking off so unexpectedly, just when my hopes of a successful termination of the treatment were at their highest, and her thus bringing those hopes to nothing—this was an unmistakable act of vengeance on her part" (p. 109).

Perhaps Freud was right. We would be unlikely today to feel that Dora was free of narcissistic or borderline pathology, and she may well have discerned, in the uncanny way that children and borderlines do, that Freud, too, was in part using her for his own purposes. By writing her story, though, Freud got the last laugh, if such a word can be used in connection with this pathetic and unhappy young woman.

Freud did consider whether he ought to have tried to keep her in analysis by expressing interest in her or by showing some personal warmth. It is impossible to know if this would have worked, but Dora might have responded positively to any indication that Freud could put her interests first, as her father and Herr K. obviously did not. But this would only have camouflaged the deeper things that were going wrong in the treatment. Freud did not see what he, himself, helped make so clear to us. Self-knowledge that is only intellectual is not therapeutic, and cure is not as simple as making conscious what is unconscious. The structural model responded to this need to understand and respect resistances to insight and change. Also entirely untouched is the issue of countertransference. Freud did write of the critical need for enough positive transference to sustain the treatment, but one has only to examine the language with which he describes this case to discover strong biases and countertransference responses on his part that impeded the development of what would today be termed a working or therapeutic alliance. These criticisms come easily, though, to those who have the benefit of Freud's later work and that of his many followers. His courage in exposing this pioneering work to us must not be underestimated.

CONCLUSION

This chapter, while not an exhaustive account of Freud's clinical and theoretical contributions, has outlined some of the major theoretical and clinical areas in which there would later be controversy and innovation. These areas primarily concern the domain of preoedipal development. Although Freud's scheme of psychosexual stages does include these early years it proved to be an insufficient explanatory model in that it did not adaquately address the establishment and vicissitudes of the relationship between infant and caregivers. Insofar as the developmental functions as a metaphor for the clinical situation, Freud's model therefore stopped short of being able to teach clinicians how to understand and work with the so-called narcissistic transferences. In a sense it is unfair to present only the case of Dora as representative of Freud's clinical contribution, for his countertransference, I believe, prevented him from doing the work that he was capable of doing at this stage in his career. But this case demonstrates what is best about Freud's theory, what his ideas could explain in brilliant and innovative ways, as well as what was still lacking. Although it can be no more than interesting speculation, one wonders how each of the clinicians discussed in the following chapters might have approached Dora.

2 THE BEGINNINGS OF EGO PSYCHOLOGY: ANNA FREUD AND HEINZ HARTMANN

Freud's psychoanalytic theory centered largely on the discovery of the unconscious and the exploration of the manifestations of the id; as such, it came to be called a "depth" psychology. Toward the end of his career, he began to reconceptualize the role of the ego, and the ego psychologists carried on this strand of his thought. Ego psychology was for some time the dominant force in psychoanalysis as it was practiced and taught in the United States. It was the politically correct barometer of orthodoxy, the true heir to Freudianism, against which all theoretical and clinical innovations were judged. This chapter outlines some of the contributions of Heinz Hartmann (1894–1970), an Austrian physician and psychoanalyst, who, as perhaps the major articulator of the principles of ego psychology, attempted to preserve, protect, and expand the utility of Freud's structural point of view and theory of drives. The psychoanalytic pedigree, though, leads not only to Sigmund but also to Anna Freud (1895–1982), his daughter and analysand, whose study of the domain of the ego opened the door to Hartmann and others.

To review the metapsychological background, Freud described at various stages in his life three points of view, or perspectives, for understanding mental functioning. The *economic* refers to the postulate that there is an instinctual energy that powers psychological functioning; following the laws of Newton, this energy possesses a quantity that can be increased, decreased, or equaled from one psychical event to another. The *topographic* point of view represents the first subdivision of the mind into different components; the distinction Freud made was between unconscious, preconscious, and conscious systems of the mind. The *structural* or *dynamic* point of view (sometimes called the second topography) takes as its departure the now-familiar mental structures of id, ego, and superego; psychical phenomena are seen as "the outcome of the conflict and of a combination of forces ultimately instinctual in origin–which exert a certain pressure" (Laplanche and Pontalis 1973, p. 126). Freud developed the second topography to deal with the increasingly complex defensive structure that seemed inadequately explained by the unconscious-preconscious-conscious systems; his early work addressed almost exclusively the unconscious processes, which he at first attributed entirely to the id. To add to the confusion, the terms *unconscious, preconscious,* and *conscious* continue to be used as to describe qualities a thought or affect possessed. Anna Freud and later Hartmann and his followers, though, concentrated their attentions on ego processes, picking up on Freud's later ideas. Attention to these processes of the ego, particularly in the area of the defenses, is of great importance in the clinical setting.

THE PROBLEM OF REALITY IN PSYCHOANALYTIC THEORY

The problem faced by Freud's followers was to account for the fact that people respond to reality and not just to internal, instinctual drives. Indeed, Freud had faced this problem as well in his early years as a psychoanalyst as he attempted to account for the stories his patients told of their sexual abuse by their fathers.

When he discovered similar memories in himself in the course of his self-analysis, he realized that perhaps these "memories" were actually fantasies; he thus gave up the seduction theory that actual abuse lay at the root of all neurosis. But the problem of how the mind deals with external reality remained even though the thrust of psychoanalysis became the exploration of the instincts and their fantasy representations, for example, the id. One pressure, then, that ego psychologists felt was the need to defend their very interest in the ego—that is, to defend themselves from criticism by depth (id) psychologists. Thus Anna Freud (1966) begins *The Ego and the Mechanisms of Defense*, a landmark book first published in 1936 that outlined a view of the ego within the tripartite mind of the structural model, as follows:

> There have been periods in the development of psycho-analytical science when the theoretical study of the individual ego was distinctly unpopular. Somehow or other many analysts had conceived the idea that, in analysis, the value of the scientific and therapeutic work was in direct proportion to the depth of the psychic strata upon which attention was focused. Whenever interest was shifted from the deeper to the mere superficial psychic strata—whenever, that is to say, research was deflected from the id to the ego—it was felt that here was a beginning of apostasy from psychoanalysis as a whole. [p. 3]

In other words, deeper isn't necessarily sexier (intellectually speaking, that is). And in line with her father's revision of his original equation of ego with the quality of consciousness, Anna Freud (1966) asserts that it is "the task of the analyst to bring into consciousness that which is unconscious, no matter to which psychic institution it belongs" (p. 28). (Recall, too, that Freud's therapeutic strategy of bringing into consciousness that which is unconscious derived from early work in hypnosis but persisted throughout his career.) Anna Freud reminds us that it is psychic conflict of one kind or another that leads to the structuring of the mind. Thus, under nonconflictual circumstances, the structured nature of the mind is not readily apparent. That is, when the ego has no objection to wishes or prohibitions it offers no obstruction, it does not make its presence known, and is a "medium through which we try to get a picture of the other two institutions" (p. 6). But when a conflict does exist, then the ego becomes active and the defensive process occurs. In reality, this occurs often, since much of what people do in civilized society requires the delay of gratification and represents a compromise formation.

Anna Freud points out that while the ego is the major source of resistance in treatment, and does not wish to become known, the id's desires press constantly for satisfaction and exposure. Treatment, she says, is therefore the ally of the id in the sense that ego and superego restrictions on instinctual gratifications may be lessened. Note that this view of analysis, that the main task is to permit the expression of repressed id impulses, represents the treatment strategy for a neurotic patient; it does not address the problems associated with those psychopathological syndromes such as the borderline in which there is too little, or impaired, ego and superego functioning—and too little control of impulses. Nonetheless, the ego Anna Freud studies and bequeaths to Hartmann is not the relatively unempowered ego of her father's horse and rider analogy—"Thus in its relation to this id it is like a man on horseback, who has to hold in check the superior strength of the horse; with this difference, that the rider tries to do so with his own strength while the ego uses borrowed forces. . . . Often a rider, if he is not to be parted from his horse, is obliged to guide it where it wants to go" (Freud 1923, p. 25). Anna Freud described the rich variety of powerful ego defenses; Hartmann later proposed that the ego has some functions and potentials—under ordinary circumstances independent of mental conflict—that are either present from birth or unfold in the maturation process.

Anna Freud stressed that there are therapeutic gains to be made by expanding the focus from exclusively the instincts and their *derivatives* to include a study of the defensive process;

derivative refers to the fact that we never observe an instinct directly but "see" instead how it is translated into particular strivings. By exploring the patient's uses of the mechanisms of defense, she points out, analyst and patient learn about the route of the instinctual wish, that is to say, why its pressure for satisfaction led to unpleasure and thus set the ego's defensive process into motion. This also reveals, she suggests, the history of the development of the ego in the sense that the particular defense very likely began at a specific moment in the patient's past under pressure from the very same wish. This examination of unconscious activities of the ego and its history generally evokes further resistances, which, in turn, need interpretation; Anna Freud (1966) identifies this process as *character analysis*. After all, "insofar as the ego institutions have endeavored to restrain the id impulses by methods of their own, the analyst comes on the scene as a disturber of the peace. . . . In analysis all the material which assists us to analyze the ego makes its appearance in the form of resistance to the analysis of the id" (pp. 29–30). Thus his daughter has made sweet (albeit tart!) lemonade out of the sour lemons of resistance Freud unsuccessfully struggled to squeeze by and avoid during his early years as an analyst. To a neurotic patient, treatment may represent more of a threat to the ego than to the id and the resistances will align themselves accordingly.

INFANT DEVELOPMENT:
ANNA FREUD VS. MELANIE KLEIN

Another challenge the ego psychologists faced was to distinguish their own interest in the way in which the individual relates to reality from the theories of the developing school of object relations (represented by Melanie Klein and her followers), which ascribed object relatedness to the very young infant as a goal in and of itself. The metapsychological obstacle here was to acknowledge the importance of object relations and of the environment to the infant and growing child without violating the principle of primary narcissism (that is, the theory that the infant relates to the environment but does not have true object relations). As Hartmann (1958) puts it, "We should not assume, from the fact that the child and the environment interact from the outset, that the child is from the beginning psychologically directed toward the object as an object" (p. 52). David Rapaport (1958), a collaborator of Hartmann and his translator, exemplified the rivalry between the two schools when he wrote, "The 'theory' of object relations evolved by Melanie Klein and her followers is not an ego psychology but an id mythology" (p. 750). Anna Freud (1966) draws a very specific distinction between herself and Melanie Klein as she tries to describe the earliest conditions under which defenses occur. She points out that it makes little sense to postulate the use of repression until there is enough differentiation of ego from id to imagine that banishing a desire or a feeling from the ego would lead to relief; thus, repression, though perhaps the most central mechanism in neurosis, is not among the earliest defenses.

> Repression consists in the withholding or expulsion of an idea or affect from the conscious ego. It is meaningless to speak of repression where the ego is still merged with the id. Similarly we might suppose that projection and introjection were methods which depended on the differentiation of the ego from the outside world. The expulsion of ideas or affects from the ego and their relegation to the outside world would be a relief to the ego only when it had learned to distinguish itself from the outside world. . . .
>
> According to the theory of the English school of analysis, introjection and projection . . . are the very processes by which the structure of the ego is developed and but for which differentiation would never have taken place. [pp. 51–53]

The key phrase here is "the ego is still merged with the id," with its reliance on the concept of primary narcissism. Note that this predates Hartmann's revised theory of the origins of the ego.

One of the primary ways in which Klein and her followers opposed Anna Freud was in the belief that the infant was affected by external reality from the beginning of life; hence theories such as the early use of projection and introjection. In general, too, the English school after Klein gave great weight to the role of reality and minimized or denied the importance of instincts, or drives. But it should not be forgotten that when Freud asserted that the characteristics of an instinct were its source, aim, impetus, and *object*, this is in fact a theory of object relations. Anna Freud (1966) carries this theme forward when she writes, "The infantile ego fears the instincts because it fears the outside world. Its defense against them is motivated by dread of the outside world, i.e., by objective anxiety" (p. 57).

In line with this belief Anna Freud adds a new element to the therapeutic arsenal of the child analyst—active intervention in the child's environment. The analyst could work to educate parents and teachers about the child's needs and thus to exert benign influence on the actual world in which the child functioned; the goal in this was to ensure that the sources of objective anxiety be reduced. Anna Freud, unlike her father, worked directly and extensively with children. Her knowledge of development came not exclusively from reconstructions made in adult psychoanalyses but from child analyses and the observation of normal children.

HARTMANN'S INTRODUCTION OF THE ADAPTIVE POINT OF VIEW

The stage has been set for the core contribution of Heinz Hartmann—the importance of the adaptive capacities of the human infant and, in a broader sense, of adding the adaptive view to our metapsychological perspectives—the economic, topographic, structural, and genetic (e.g., what caused a particular solution to be adopted at a particular time) points of view. Hartmann's larger purpose was to broaden psychoanalysis from a theory of pathology to a general psychology. This carries on an important strand of thought in Freud's writings expressed, for instance in works such as "The Interpretation of Dreams" (1900), "Jokes and Their Relation to the Unconscious" (1905c), and "The Psychopathology of Everyday Life" (1901). These works, though, all date from 1905 or earlier and it is true that Freud's later focus could be seen to be more on psychopathology, on the exploration of the material produced by his analytic patients. His major contribution to a theory of general psychology in his later years would be the ambivalently proposed and defended notion of the death instinct. Nonetheless, Anna Freud (1966) returns us to the tradition of regarding psychoanalytic theory as being applicable to all when she writes, in relation to the defensive process, "The efforts of the infantile ego to avoid unpleasure by directly resisting external impressions belong to the sphere of normal psychology" (pp. 70–71). So much is this now a part of society's understanding of normality that it is perhaps difficult to appreciate that this was originally a radical and unsavory position when Freud saw no theoretical difference between the dreams of neurotics and normals in *The Interpretation of Dreams* in 1900.

The ego psychologists had also to defend their theory (and their view of Freud) from those object relations theorists who seemed to attack one of the most most basic tenets of psychoanalysis, the centrality of the drives. The traditional view held that object and environment were important only in their role of enabling the drive to be satisfied; the interaction was not a goal in and of itself as writers such as Winnicott proposed. Hartmann (1959) writes: "According to Freud, sexuality and aggression are, among all the drives one could describe, those that come closest to fulfilling the demands psychoanalysis makes on a concept of drives" (p. 327). Earlier in his career, however, Hartmann (1948) had put aside Freud's expanded definition of the drives as the life and death instincts, indicating that he used "the concept of drives which we actually encounter in clinical psychoanalytic psychology, omitting Freud's other, mainly biologically oriented set of hypotheses of the 'life' and 'death' instincts whose interplay is meant to explain 'the phenomena of life'" (Freud 1930, pp. 71–72). This turning away from the death instinct and the resultant tendency toward aggression, admittedly a controversial and unprovable proposition, set the stage both for the orthodoxies of American ego psychological thinking with its focus on the potential for integration and healthy adaptation and also for the violent rejection of these ideas by Lacan and his followers in France. Hartmann (1950), though, proclaimed that he desired to do no more than annotate and flesh out Freud's "findings" on the ego and cites Freud's formula for proper psychoanalytic research:

> Taking as my main points of departure some of Freud's later and not yet fully integrated findings, I have presented a number of synchronizations and reformulations of and additions to some generally accepted tenets of psychoanalytic theory. May I end by quoting a passage from Freud's writings (1926, p. 160): "There is no need to be discouraged by these emendations. They are to be welcomed if they add something to our knowledge, and they are no disgrace to us so long as they enrich rather than invalidate our earlier views by limiting some statement, perhaps, that was too general or by enlarging some idea that was too narrowly formulated." [p. 141]

DEVELOPING A GENERAL PSYCHOLOGY: THE "CONFLICT FREE" EGO

In Hartmann's (1951) words,

> First of all, ego psychology meant and means a broadening of our field of view. "Good" theory helps us to discover the facts (for instance, to recognize a resistance as such) and it helps us to see the connections among facts. This part of our psychology also gives a deeper understanding of the forms and mechanisms of defense, and

a more exact consideration of the details of a patient's inner experience and behavior; corresponding to this on the side of technique, is a tendency toward more concrete, more specific interpretation. [p. 149]

Hartmann's work did permit a fuller consideration of and emphasis on the individual's relationship to the environment. Attention was paid to the ways in which reality affected the child's development. For instance, Anna Freud's work on identification with the aggressor showed the way in which an oppressing person could mold the child's behavior, conscious thought, and defensive structure. Hartmann's aim was to develop a general psychology of mental life, though, rather than a new theory of psychopathology. Freud's extensive exploration of id psychology, instinctual drives, and of neurotic conflict had left unexamined the range of healthy functioning. Hartmann (1958) proposed the concept of the "conflict free ego sphere" to describe

that ensemble of functions which *at any given time* exert their effects outside the region of mental conflicts. Included in these ego functions are perception of the outer world, intention, object comprehension, thinking, language, recall-phenomena, productivity, various phases of motor development, perception of the self, reality testing, time perception, the defenses, "a person's character," and finally "the coordinating or integrating tendencies known as the synthetic function." [pp. 8–9, emphasis added]

Many of these *primary autonomous ego functions* and the potential for them existed from birth, he thought. Hartmann (1950) goes on to define the ego as the sum of its functions:

To define it negatively, in three respects, as against other ego concepts: "ego," in analysis, is not synonymous with "personality" or "individual"; it does not coincide with the "subject" as opposed to the "object" of experience; and it is by no means only the "awareness" or the "feeling" of one's own self. In analysis, the ego is a concept of

> quite a different order. It is a sub-structure of personality and is
> defined by its functions. [pp. 114–115]

Note that these functions are not entirely immune to the vicissitudes of life. Their development depends on the unfolding of the maturational process within an "average expectable environment," and their continued healthy operation can be compromised in situations of mental conflict, for instance, in depression or in response to trauma. Nonetheless, this constitutes a celebration of the capacities of the ego. It is important to understand that when Hartmann writes about environment he has a particular meaning in mind, and that is a biological one. He conceives of environment as a sort of biological backdrop, crucial yet essentially passive, against which the baby's physiological-instinctual needs unfold. This deliberate emphasis on biology stands in sharp distinction to Winnicott, Kohut, and even Mahler who see the infant as deeply embedded in a primary psychological relationship with the mother (Greenberg and Mitchell 1983).

But seeing the biological as the determining force is consistent with the primacy Hartmann ascribes to adaptation. Accordingly, Hartmann sees the ego not exclusively as a psychological precipitate of intrapsychic conflict and social experience but as a product of biological inheritance. As Greenberg and Mitchell (1983) phrase it, "The ego is viewed as the organ of adaptation, of synthesis, of integration, and of organization" (p. 242). In Freud's understanding, the ego developed out of the matrix of the id and derived the psychic energy for its activities from de-sexualized libido, that is, from id energy. Hartmann introduces the concept of *neutralization*, which encompasses the energy that is to be derived from aggression in addition to libido. But the energy for what Hartmann would call the primary autonomous functions of the ego did not come from neutralization, he proposed, but rather from a "primary ego energy" (p. 227). *Secondary autonomous ego functions,* that is to say, capacities that originated in conflict but underwent a change of function, derive their energy from dein-stinctualized sources. (An example of this would be bowel control, which is not an inborn ego skill; however, virtually all children transform this often conflictually learned task into a conflict-free habit.)

FITTING INTO THE ENVIRONMENT: EGO AND DRIVES

Hartmann sees the ego as not only limited to the functions just discussed, but also as the agent by which the drives—the id instincts—may be gratified. These *ego interests* (Hartmann's term for what Freud had initially called *ego instincts*) thus serve the self-preservative instincts as well as the sexual and aggressive drives. The reality principle, through which satisfactions are gained by necessary detours, postponements, and alterations according to environmental conditions, is a function of ego strength. The ego is capable of organizing and tolerating the delays in achieving gratification that the id, operating by the pleasure principle, could not. In the end, the ego and the reality principle, which address actual conditions in the world, realize greater gratification than would the id acting alone. In the sense that the infant must inescapably deal with reality long before the ego can tolerate frustration, it is reality as much as the pleasure principle that shapes the developing psyche. And the ways of addressing real situations are often indirect, as Hartmann (1958) describes:

> It is possible, and even probable, that the relationship to reality is learned by way of *detours*. There are avenues of reality-adaptation which, at first, certainly lead away from the real situation. The function of play is a good example, that is, its actual role in human development rather than any teleological theories about it. Another example is the auxiliary function of fantasy in the learning process: though fantasy always implies an initial turning away from a real

situation, it can also be a preparation for reality and may lead to a better mastering of it. Fantasy may fulfill a synthetic function by provisionally connecting our needs and goals with possible ways of realizing them. [p. 18]

In mental functioning, then, the shortest distance between two points sometimes is not a straight line; or, rather, what looks like a roundabout route may in fact represent the most efficient itinerary.

Hartmann (1958) distinguishes progressive from regressive adaptations; in other words, some adaptations serve healthy development while others may lead to unsuccessful adjustments and thus to neurotic or characterological conflicts or symptoms: "Adaptation achievements may turn into adaptation disturbances. . . . We also know that the neurotic symptom, too, is an attempt at adaptation, though an abortive one" (p. 54). Ernst Kris (1934) coined the term *regression in the service of the ego* to describe the way artistic activity can further development through a seeming step away from reality.

For Hartmann (1958) as well as Darwin the organism's ability to adapt to the environment is crucial. The concept of adaptation is central to his definition of mental health, and "fitting in" and "equilibrium" are important components of mental health:

Generally speaking, we call a man well adapted if his productivity, his ability to enjoy life, and his mental equilibrium are undisturbed. . . . The degree of adaptiveness can only be determined with reference to environmental situations (average expectable— i.e., typical—situations, or on the average not expectable—i.e., atypical—situations). . . .

The observation underlying the concept "adaptation" is that living things patently "fit" into their environment. Thus, adaptation is primarily a reciprocal relationship between the organism and its environment. [pp. 23–24]

Hartmann (1958) sees the newborn as being already equipped with the ability to adapt to the world, in other words, "hardwired" for adaptation:

> The newborn infant is not wholly a creature *of* drives, he has inborn apparatuses (perceptual and protective mechanisms) which appropriately perform a part of those functions which, after the differentiation of ego and id, we attribute to the ego. A state of adaptiveness exists before the intentional processes of Adaptation begin. [p. 49]

Again it must be stressed that this fitting in with the environment that the infant performs is not a striving toward attachment to objects. The infant may be born with certain capacities, but they are used, according to Hartmann, only in the process of seeking satisfaction of id instincts, of reducing pain, and of maintaining homeostasis. The infant seeks objects only insofar as an object will assist in the achievement of these aims. As the child begins to change from pleasure-principle–oriented functioning to reality-principle functioning, "mere motor discharge" (p. 86) wanes and intentional actions occur. These actions, though, are rooted however remotely in the id: "It goes without saying that the apparatuses, both congenital and acquired, need a driving force in order to function; and that the psychology of action is inconceivable without the psychology of instinctual drives" (p. 108).

CLINICAL IMPLICATIONS

Psychotherapy conducted according to Hartmann's principles focuses on the individual's relationship to reality. The clinician must assess the areas of conflict and difficulty identified by Freud within the overall context of adaptation. Hartmann has not written extensively about clinical treatment, but this passage from one of his major works gives a good sense of the goals of treatment:

> We consider an action realistic, first of all, when it is realistic in its intention, that is, when its means are chosen according to its goals in the light of correctly appraised external (and internal) conditions. . . . We also consider realistic those actions which fit into the conditions of the external world so that they actually further the reality relations of the individual. [Hartmann 1958, p. 87]

Treatment is aimed at improving the individual's ability to act effectively in the world while respecting his or her internal demands. Intrapsychic conflicts must be explored in order to produce adequate knowledge of one's own needs and of transferences based on early experience. Transference, though, is not used as a means to rework past problems; Hartmann encourages transference and regression in treatment only insofar as they serve to increase subsequent insight into how better to cope with actual conditions in the world. The major goal of treatment guided by the principles of ego psychology, then, is to foster a strengthened ego better capable of appraising reality and of organizing effective action—in sum, capable of improved adaptation.

In his view of psychoanalysis, Hartmann (1958, p. 64) sees the integrating, or synthetic, role of the ego as crucial. He disagrees with the "often-voiced idea that the unconscious basically 'knows it all' and that the task [of psychoanalysis] is merely to make this knowledge conscious by lifting the defense." He points out that even well functioning people are likely to "conceal their mental life from themselves":

> Every instance of self-deception is accompanied by a misjudgment of the external world also. Psychoanalysis has systematized and can remedy these self-deceptions. Indeed, a great part of psychoanalysis can be described as a theory of self-deceptions and of misjudgments of the external world. In the course of the psychoanalytic process one learns to face one's own mental contents as objects of experience and thought and to see them as part of a causal network. Thus, psychoanalysis is the highest development of thinking directed toward the

inner life, in that it revises and regulates adaptation and fitting together (with all the biologically significant consequences for the individual that this implies). [pp. 64–65]

CONCLUSION

Anna Freud's and Heinz Hartmann's work on the ego has been so thoroughly integrated into psychotherapeutic thinking that it is difficult to appreciate that at one time we did not know all this. Today, these ideas have the quality of being clinical "common sense." Yet what came along with the exploration of the ego's functions and role was the belief in the strength of the ego, and the goodness of the ego as a mental structure. While the object relations theorists do not address this topic directly, there is in their work the assumption that such strength develops from adequate relationships in infancy and childhood; they do not attack the ego or its presumed beneficial nature. Though Kohut's self psychology would appear to be quite far theoretically from ego psychology, in fact it was Hartmann who brought a concept of the self as distinct from the ego into classical theory and refined Freud's definition of narcissism (from "the cathexis of the ego" to "the cathexis of the self") (Greenberg and Mitchell 1983). It would be Jacques Lacan, however, who, as early as 1936, attempted to question the underlying assumption that the ego was a Good Thing.

CASE ILLUSTRATION–
ADAPTATION AS PATHOLOGY

In the following case, adaptation became the concept that organized the therapist's understanding of the patient. The patient's seemingly admirable ability to adapt to the demands of her environment represented a character style that left her frustrated and unhappy, but with almost no understanding of why this was so. The therapist works with this patient along the lines of Hartmann's recommendation, addressing transference not as a primary goal but insofar as the transference intruded into the therapeutic work. As will become clear, the extent to which this happened was significant and became apparent immediately after the initial evaluation for psychotherapeutic treatment.

A., a Hispanic-American woman, was 44 years old when she first sought help from Dr. O., a psychiatrist in his mid-thirties. She complained of feeling isolated and having a mounting sense of depression and despair; the most recent event she identified as a source of this was having been "dumped" by the man she had thought, finally, was Mr. Right. A. was a successful optometrist in her small community and was extremely sensitive about her reputation, in fact driving a rather substantial distance to see Dr. O.; psychotherapy was "not for our family," said her parents many times. She had never been in therapy before but had probably suffered from a low-level depression for some years. When she finally did enter therapy, it was due to a feeling of panicked helplessness, looking around and noticing that she no longer knew anyone her age who was unmarried and childless.

BACKGROUND INFORMATION

A.'s mother was a housewife and her father a hospital administrator. The central fact of A.'s life was the existence of her sister, one and one half years her senior, who shortly after A.'s birth was diagnosed with mild but significant mental retardation. The parents were, understandably, deeply upset by this and (Dr. O. conjectured) had little emotional energy left for A. A. turned out to be the good baby her parents needed and passed through early childhood with no major illnesses or

problems, meeting developmental milestones in an unremark-
able fashion, or so the family mythology went. A later difficulty
was to follow: the sister developed significant behavior problems in school and after a few years of unsuccessful efforts at
discipline, the diagnosis of ADHD (Attention Deficit Disorder
with Hyperactivity) was made. The parents were preoccupied
with the sister's increasingly complicated needs and paid little
attention to A. A., however, must have been fairly well en-
dowed with ego strength for she manifested no problems,
doing well in school both academically and socially. She was,
to a great extent, left to grow up on her own, for her sister's
problems did not lessen in severity over the years. Nonetheless,
A. graduated from high school and went on eventually to take
training as a doctor of optometry. She attended school in a
distant city, her departure apparently having little significance
to her or her parents.

A. settled in this city having a circle of friends both from
school and from her life and work in the community; she dated
regularly and felt relatively confident that she would be able to
marry and have children if she so wished. All seemed to go
well, with no more than life's usual ups and downs, until one
day when A. was 31. She returned home to a condominium she
had purchased only a year earlier to find that it it had been
burglarized and seriously vandalized. Even after insurance
had replaced the ruined or stolen items, A. found that she had
changed in some profound way. She no longer felt like herself;
she felt exposed, vulnerable. An increasing sense of isolation
developed when even those she had considered to be close
friends became irritated that she could not "just get on with my
life."

At this time, A. learned that her parents had finally arranged
for her sister to live in a protected group home. Her father had
just taken early retirement due to a minor but chronic illness,
and A. told herself that her parents needed her closer to them.
A. thus moved back to her home town, finding a job and a new

condominium easily. Being the "good child" now seemed to her to require demonstrating a high degree of devotion to her parents, in particular to be available to help her father weather the depressive moods to which her mother had become prone in the last five or so years; to Dr. O., however, it was clear that A.'s ego functioning and adaptive balance had been seriously undermined by the trauma she had suffered. Thus began a period in which A. would become more and more restricted in her thinking and her functioning.

TREATMENT

Dr. O. found A. to be bright, engaging, and attractive as she first presented her story to him. She was confused and hurt that no romantic relationships had worked out for her. However, she did describe how she consistently gave priority to her parents' needs, often turning down dates or other social opportunities. To A., there was no choice involved in these matters; her obligations were self-evident. Dr. O.'s gentle challenges to her thinking, such as questions to clarify in his mind the actual severity of her mother's depressions and her father's disability, evoked resistant irritability in the patient. And it was soon apparent that the list of topics that were off-limits in therapy was not limited to this. For instance, beyond the initial description of the isolation she had experienced after the burglary, A. refused to try to recall how she had felt. Nonetheless, A. seemed to have many areas of competence and ego strength and she began once-weekly psychotherapy.

A specific and subtle clinical problem rapidly emerged. A. would arrive at her sessions, report to Dr. O. on minor daily events such as how the traffic had been on the way to his office or how busy her work day had been. She would then fall silent until Dr. O. asked her some question about a current concern or one of the problematic areas of her life. A. would then talk about this issue, but eventually she would exhaust that particular subject and her thoughts would trail off; she would then fall silent and Dr. O. would experience the same pressure to bring up another area of concern. After a few sessions, Dr. O. gently pointed out this pattern to A., asking if she had some thoughts about why she preferred him to introduce topics. She refused to explore her reasons, making it clear to him that these were simply the ground rules of working with her. A.'s inability to engage in even minimal free association represented an *ego inhibition*, a restriction of mental processes resulting from attempts to minimize intrapsychic conflict. Her refusal to discuss the inhibition was an additional defense against the exposure of painful thoughts or affects.

THEORETICAL FORMULATION

Dr. O. felt this to be an embedded characterological defense for which psychoanalysis would be the most effective treatment. A. refused to discuss this, or any other change that might alter her depression—medication, a new job, reducing contact with her parents, joining community activities. There was always a reason why changing her external circumstances or changing herself in such a way that she would be able to feel less frustrated was ruled out. A.'s adaptation had come to be entirely *autoplastic*, that is to say, dependent on molding her own psychological requirements to meet perceived external demands. The very thought of *alloplastic* solutions, which would alter the environment, seemed to intensify A.'s defensiveness. Since nothing in life can ever really change or work out well, A. seemed to be saying, I might as well just change myself so as to fit in better. But isolation, frustration, and depression finally drove her to seek help. In fact, A.'s ego was doing too good a job at adapting to external reality, at the expense of adaptation to the reality of her inner needs.

In sum, A. was utilizing adaptation as a defense against unpleasurable thoughts and affects. Dr. O. saw A.'s behavior in his office in this context as well. She was attempting to adapt to the treatment situation just as she had adapted to the rest of the world for over a decade. She both required the therapist to introduce the topic in the session so that she could adapt to his wishes, yet at the same time his doing so represented a certain newness that provoked resistance. Dr. O. sensed that A. needed to know that he remembered her issues from session to session, that he had a place for her troubles in his mind, but the very fact that he selected the issue also meant that what was on A.'s mind was not given priority. A. insisted, in this enactment, on the very parameters that she feared, and which had characterized her early life. For, Dr. O. realized, A.'s inner life had been ignored, had been left unattended when she was a child. She had had to adapt to the existence of the needy older sister who overwhelmed the parents' emotional resources. What had appeared to be a successful adaptation to life had in fact been rather fragile, and A. had been unable to manage previously unproblematic intrapsychic conflicts after the trauma of the burglary.

THERAPEUTIC STRATEGY

There was no choice for Dr. O. but to accept A.'s rules in order to keep her in treatment. In this sort of situation, the therapist may play along, but with the goal, made explicit to the patient, of attempting to understand why these limitations are necessary (Rothstein 1995). In this case, though, the patient was adamant that any discussion of this was off limits. Therefore, the therapist had to find another way to help A. understand the significance of this enactment, and he did so in a most creative and sensitive way—by gently focusing on A.'s affective responses to the interventions she extracted from him. He would notice with her that she didn't appear terribly interested in what he was bringing up, or that she seemed annoyed by something he had said. After a couple of months of similar comments, Dr. O. said to her that he could sense that a particular issue was not important to her but that in asking *him* to choose the subject she was keeping him in the dark about what was important to her on that day. The combination of gentleness, persistence, and respect for the patient's inner life seemed to have a softening effect, and the patient began to be able to glimpse that what she insisted on might not be what she in fact needed.

What was also crucial was Dr. O.'s personal conviction, which was undoubtedly communicated in nonverbal ways, that understanding A.'s demands was really necessary as part of the helping process. Dr. O. was able, too, to connect A.'s behavior in their relationship to the ways in which she similarly limited herself in her daily life. She made certain assumptions about what people would think of her if, for instance, she came to therapy more often or didn't see her parents several times a week. She would then feel as though she had no choice but to act in such a way as to preclude the possibility of any of these imagined negative consequences, and she expected her therapist not to question any of this. This hyper-adaptiveness was almost certainly a pattern of thought laid down in childhood when A. had learned that the way to thrive was to avoid calling attention to her own needs—because no one was interested anyway. As A. came to understand that this logical progression might be built on faulty premises, she became a bit more curious about how she had come to be this way. After almost a year of indecision and continued gentle interpretation of her resistances to truly taking her own needs seriously, A. agreed to increase the frequency of sessions to twice weekly. The work progressed in a steady fashion—that is to say with continuing pattern of resistance to Dr. O.'s refusal to be intrusive—but at the increased frequency A. was better able to

tolerate the uncomfortable affect that the interpretations elic-
ited in her. It is perhaps a tribute to A.'s ego strengths and to
her capacity to form a relationship with the therapist that she
was able to become curious about herself at all and to begin
what must have seemed to her to be a treacherous journey.

3 MELANIE KLEIN:
THE REPERCUSSIONS OF
AGGRESSION IN THE MIND

Those who have bought or sold a house are likely familiar with the three cardinal principles of determining the value of real estate: location, location, location. Similarly, one might summarize the contribution of Melanie Klein: aggression, aggression, aggression. Klein (1882–1960) took what Freud posited as a metapsychological and philosophical underpinning of human existence, the death instinct, and transformed it into an experiential principle operating from the first day of life (Greenberg and Mitchell 1983). In the United States for a great many years it was controversial to the point of being self-destructive for a psychoanalytic writer to acknowledge an intellectual debt to Melanie Klein. Kernberg, for instance, appears to be brilliantly original, but a certain portion of his work is a restatement of and translation of Klein's ideas into contemporary understandings of psychopathology and infant development. In fact, although Klein's work is far from unproblematic in its theoretical breadth, her clinical contributions form a legacy that has permeated to the very core of modern psychoanalytic thought. And, as with real estate location, it is at once accurate and caricature to limit Klein's importance to her belief in the centrality of aggression.

Melanie Reizes was born in Vienna in 1882, the youngest of four children. Her father was a doctor whose practice was so unsuccessful that her mother opened a shop in order to help support the family. Although Klein remembered her childhood as "mostly serene and happy" (Segal 1981, p. 21) and had a close and warm connection with her mother, she had a painfully distant relationship with her father; two of her siblings died before she was 10, and her colleagues attributed the depressive streak they noted in her personality to this. At age 21 she married Arthur Klein, an engineer, whose work required him to travel and thus prevented her from undertaking the study of medicine. The marriage was unhappy, and Klein derived pleasure from her study of foreign languages, her three children, and her beginning engagement with psychoanalytic ideas when she first read Freud in Budapest. She had an analysis with Ferenczi and remained in Budapest until 1919. The separation from her husband in 1919 was followed by a divorce a few years later. In 1921 Klein moved to Berlin where she was analyzed and encouraged in her psychoanalytic work with children by Karl Abraham. Unfortunately she was to suffer yet another loss when Abraham died in 1925. Without his support, her ideas were attacked by colleagues, and an invitation by Ernest Jones to lecture in England was followed shortly thereafter by her move there in 1927.

INFANCY: LOVE, HATE, PHANTASY

With the therapeutic and research tools of the analyses of children, Mrs. Klein, as she was known, thus embarked on what she portrayed as an extension of Freud's own theories. However, she never treated a child under age 2¾, so it is important to remember that Klein, too, was involved in reconstruction and not observation of the very earliest months of life. Perhaps Klein's most radical proposal was that infants experienced the Oedipus complex in the first year of life. Later research did not support this theory, refuting that infants possessed the requisite cognitive and developmental capacities; however, our current understanding does confirm Klein's belief that even very tiny infants possessed far more sophisticated psychological abilities than her contemporaries thought possible. Greenberg and Mitchell (1983) suggest that we not throw the baby out with the bathwater: "[Klein's] depiction of early object relations provide useful tools for understanding the psychodynamics of older children and adults, whether or not they accurately portray the early months of the newborn's experience" (p. 148).

The model of mental life and motivation from which Klein begins is summarized here by Juliet Mitchell (1986):

> Klein's basic model is that the neonate brings into the world two main conflicting impulses: love and hate. In Klein's later formulations, love is the manifestation of the life drive; hate, destructiveness and envy are emanations of the death drive. The life drive and the death drive are two innate instincts in conflict with each other. From the very beginning the neonate tries to deal with the conflict between these two drives, either by bringing them together in order to modify the death drive with the life drive or by expelling the death drive into the outside world. [p. 19]

So far Klein seems to be turning Freud's metapsychology into the psychological matter of early life — an unprovable tenet then as now. The controversy thickens when we add the next ingredient of her thinking, which was a belief that babies are born with archetype-like knowledge of parents' anatomy and sexual intercourse into which they fit their actual experience with the parents, and that oedipal conflicts begin in the second six months of life (Klein 1946), not in late toddlerhood as Freud had suggested. This drama is mediated through *phantasy*.

One of Klein's earliest renovations of theory was an expansion of the concept of fantasy. When used with her meaning, the term is commonly spelled in her fashion — phantasy. While Freud believed fantasy developed after the dominance of the reality principle had been established, Klein saw in her very young patients evidence that all relations with reality were colored by unconscious phantasy. The main psychological tasks neonates confront is the management of constitutionally determined quantities of the death instinct which, if not expelled, would threaten their survival. The world the infant faces is not universally gratifying, thus the content of the earliest phantasies represents efforts to manage this situation. The breast is thus divided into the good, satisfying breast and the bad, frustrating one, the division being a defensive attempt to cope with otherwise overwhelming aggression. Further, the good breast is seen as ideal and the bad as persecutory, a mark of the baby's projected death instinct. These are known as part objects in contrast to the baby's later capacity to see the good and bad as different aspects of the same whole mother. The baby might say, "I fear the strength of my own urges toward death and self-destruction, so I deny them in myself, as much as I can, and see them in the bad breast which denies me comfort and thus persecutes me." That quantity of the death instinct that is not projected remains in the personality as primary erotogenic masochism. Klein (1936a) wrote, "External reality is mainly a mirror of the child's own instinctual life . . . peopled in the child's imagination with objects who are expected to treat the child precisely in the same sadistic way as the child is impelled to treat the objects" (p. 133).

Two primitive defense mechanisms are used as the baby struggles to maintain his innate destructive tendencies. *Projection*, a familiar concept, involves first the ejection of an intolerable impulse or affect from the self and then the attribution of this to a part of the environment. Conversely, either loving or sadistic elements may be made part of the baby through the process of *introjection* in which the baby takes in the object's loving and gratifying or hurtful functions. The term *identification* refers to a more mature level of becoming like the object, but both are forms of internalization, making something from without a part of the self. Klein also proposed the notion of *projective identification*, in which the baby identifies with the projected sadistic material. Projected material may also be reintrojected. These are the ways and means of establishing object relationships, that is to say, relations with mentally constituted *internal objects*.

Phantasy combined with reality permits the establishment of internal objects, mental representations that give form to the instinct-influenced perceptions of the world. These internalized objects have relations with each other within the mind and their relation to the actual environment is a very complicated one. Freud had theorized that the id expressed the representatives of the drives, and Klein continues this parallel with the notion that drives find their expression in unconscious phantasy. Klein (1930) describes her view of the baby's world:

> The sadistic phantasies directed against the inside of [mother's] body constitute the first and basic relation to the outside world and to reality. Upon the degree of success with which the subject passes through this phase will depend the extent to which he can subsequently acquire an external world corresponding to reality. We see then that the child's earliest reality is wholly phantastic; he is surrounded by objects of anxiety, and in this respect excrement, organs, objects, things animate and inanimate are to begin with equivalent to one another. As the ego develops, a true relation to reality is gradually established out of this unreal reality. Thus the development of the ego and the relation to reality depend on the degree of the ego's capacity at a very early period to tolerate the pressure of the earliest anxiety situations. [p. 98]

REPUDIATION OF PRIMARY NARCISSISM

For Klein, the infant's desires are not only for the specific physical satisfactions but also include the element of the other person, the need-satisfying object. In a sense, there is no need that exists outside of the parameters of object relations. Hence, another important way in which Klein disagreed with Freud: she does not believe in primary narcissism, a period after birth in which the infant is essentially unrelated to objects in the outside world save for their need-satisfying (feeding, etc.) actions. Here Klein (1952) affirms her belief:

> The analysis of very young children has taught me that there is no instinctual urge, no anxiety situations, no mental process which does not involve objects, external or internal; in other words, object-relations are at the *centre* of emotional life. Furthermore, love and hatred, phantasies, anxieties and defences are also operative from the beginning and are *ab initio* indivisibly linked with object relations. [p. 206]

Klein could hardly repudiate the concept of primary narcissism in stronger terms.

Contrary to Freud who dissected each drive into source, aim, object, and impetus, Klein (1959) stresses that the desired satisfaction is inseparable from the object, thus, "Gratification is as much related to the object which gives the food as to the food itself" (p. 141). As an instance of how wide Klein's influence has been, note the similarity of this statement to Kohut's of 1977 cited in Chapter 7, this volume.

THE EARLY SUPEREGO AND THE ONSET OF THE OEDIPUS COMPLEX

If aggression has been underemphasized so far in this summary, it has been in order to point out other features of Klein's contribution. To return to the story she tells of child development, though, is to refocus on the manifestations of the death instinct. One of the most important results of the aggressively toned internal object relations is that the mind develops its structures under this influence. Klein felt that the superego budded much earlier than had previously been thought, and thus that it was not the heir to the Oedipus complex that Freud theorized. Rather, the superego forms at a time when the child still vividly phantasizes being persecuted by bad objects, and the superego derives its relentless qualities from this sadism that had originally belonged to the infant's own death instinct. As Klein (1929) puts it,

> The phase in which sadism is at its zenith in all the fields whence it derives precedes the earlier anal stage and acquires a special significance from the fact that it is also the stage of development at which the Oedipus tendencies first appear. That is to say that the Oedipus complex begins under the complete dominance of sadism. My supposition that the formation of the super-ego follows closely on the beginning of the Oedipus tendencies, and that, therefore, the ego falls under the sway of the super-ego even at this early period, explains, I think, why this sway is so tremendously powerful. For, when the objects are introjected, the attack launched upon them with all the weapons of sadism [e.g., oral, anal, urethral destructive phantasies] rouses the subject's dread of an analogous attack upon himself from the external and the internal objects. [p. 87]

Klein (1928) also stresses the layered quality of the mental structures, which are comprised of "identifications dating from very different periods and strata in the mental life" (pp. 70–71). She traces the biting and devouring qualities of the superego to the early onset of the Oedipus complex with the attendant jealousies and wishes to destroy; the baby's primary weapon at that time would be oral, thus he imagines that others would retaliate in kind and this phantasy of projected oral aggression is internalized as the earliest layer of the superego.

The earlier onset of the Oedipus complex results from Klein's (1928) controversial supposition that children are born with an innate knowledge of parental anatomy. Thus the persecution anxieties of the first months of life also take on a sexualized meaning, with the baby phantasizing, for instance, that the mother retains the father's penis for herself, and that the baby may take refuge from the attacking breasts in the phantasy of the nurturing penis.

> . . . The Oedipus tendencies are released in consequence of the frustration which the child experiences at weaning, and . . . they make their appearance at the end of the first and the beginning of the second year of life; they receive reinforcement through the anal frustrations undergone during training in cleanliness. The next determining influence upon the mental process is that of the anatomical difference between the sexes. [p. 70]

Although some of her specific assumptions are questionable, in fact Klein opened the door to a much more sophisticated view of early childhood as she traces the differential development of the superego in boys and girls and relates it to the central anxiety situations faced by each. For Freud, the Oedipus complex was the bedrock that a thorough analysis was to reach—penis envy for women and castration anxiety for men. Klein causes us to ask again which came first, the penis or the breast? Her answer is that oedipal anxieties are secondary occurrences, defenses against much earlier anxieties. Both girls and boys have from early months of life a strong curiosity about the world, which Klein termed the epistemophilic impulse, and the initial object of this curiosity for both sexes is the mother's body. Babies of both sexes also have a related "wish to *appropriate* the contents of the womb" (Klein 1928, p. 72). What results from this for both girls and boys is an identification with the mother. From here there is a bifurcation of the sexes.

SNIPS AND SNAILS . . .

The boy starts to have genitally based love feelings even as he is still under the sway of strong oral and anal sadistic tendencies directed to the mother who has inevitably frustrated and disappointed him. Thus his sadistic wishes are in conflict with his love. Additionally, he must tolerate his fear of being castrated by his father. The demands on the boy are considerable.

> The degree to which he attains to the genital position will partly depend on his capacity for tolerating this anxiety. Here the importance of the oral-sadistic and anal-sadistic fixations is an important factor. It affects the degree of hatred which the boy feels toward the mother; and this, in turn, hinders him to a greater or lesser extent in attaining a positive relation to her. The sadistic fixations exercise also a decisive influence upon the formation of the super-ego, which is coming into being whilst these phases are in the ascendant. The more cruel the super-ego the more terrifying will be the father as castrator, and the more tenaciously in the child's flight from his genital impulses will he cling to the sadistic levels, from which his Oedipal tendencies in the first instance then also take their colour. [Klein 1928, p. 73]

Klein speaks of a "femininity phase," which is for the boy roughly equivalent to the castration complex in girls—the boy wishes to have an organ such as his mother possesses. At this young age, the boy equates feces with babies and phantasizes feces both as the longed-for baby he cannot have and as potential siblings that he wants to "steal and destroy." The little boy fears retribution from the mother for these phantasies of possession and destruction.

> In this early period of development the mother who takes away the child's feces signifies also a mother who dismembers and castrates him. Not only by means of the anal frustrations which she inflicts does she pave the way for the castration complex: in terms of psychic reality she *is* also already the *castrator*.
> The dread of the mother is so overwhelming because there is combined with it an intense dread of castration by the father. . . .
> The greater the preponderance of sadistic fixations the more does

the boy's identification with his mother correspond to an attitude of rivalry towards the woman, with its blending of envy and hatred; for on account of his wish for a child he feels himself at a disadvantage and inferior to the mother. [Klein 1928, pp. 74–75]

Thus, the boy's high valuation of his penis is in great part a defense against these earlier conflicts, which do not lend themselves to seamless resolution. (Klein also sees these dynamics as explaining the adult male's scorn for women and sense of superiority.) The boy is caught between castrators, as it were, and takes a precarious refuge from the threat of his femininity phase in an identification with his father by the end of the oedipal period, or by about five years of age. Klein made great strides toward an appreciation of the complexities of male development; just because the boy does not change love objects does not mean that he has an easier time than the little girl, for the boy must change object of identification and is thus left with a profound vulnerability against which he must defend.

SUGAR AND SPICE . . .

Klein (1928) begins her understanding of little girls with a departure from Freud:

I am led to conclude that not only an unconscious awareness of the vagina, but also sensations in that organ and in the rest of the genital apparatus, are aroused as soon as Oedipus impulses make their appearance. . . .

In the girl identification with the mother results directly from Oedipus impulses: the whole struggle caused in the boy by his castration anxiety is absent in her. In girls as well as boys this identification coincides with anal-sadistic tendencies to rob and destroy the mother. . . . Dread of the mother, too, impels them to give up identification with her, and identification with the father begins. [p. 77]

Through the intense curiosity Klein called epistemophilic the little girl discovers that penises exist and that she does not have one. Because she learns that at a time when her sadistic wishes toward mother are dominant, it is with aggression that this episode is flavored. She thus imagines that her lack of a penis represents a punishment, a retaliation, from mother. However, Klein (1928) stresses that this all takes place in the context of the loss of the breast, weaning, and that it is this profound disappointment that is at the root of the girl's turn toward father as an object of identification. "Hate and rivalry of the mother, however, again lead to abandoning the identification with the father and turning to him as the object to be secured and loved" (p. 78). There is yet another disappointment in store when the father rejects the girl in favor of her mother. A final complexity of this episode lies in the fact that unlike the little boy who actually has something—the penis—what the little girl has is a potential, an "*unsatisfied* desire for motherhood, and of this, too, she has but a dim and uncertain, though a very intense, awareness" (p. 79). Klein points out the sense of anxiety and guilt in women that results from their one-time desire to destroy their mother. She feels this explains women's preoccupation with physical appearance—a defense against the mother's retribution phantasy in which she will retaliate by destroying her daughter's beauty and physical potential to bear children.

> It is this anxiety and guilt which is the chief cause of the repression of feelings of pride and joy in the feminine *role*, which are originally very strong. This repression results in depreciation of the capacity for motherhood, at the outset so highly prized. Thus the girl lacks the powerful support which the boy derives from his possession of the penis, and which she might find in the anticipation of motherhood. [p. 79]

Klein (1928) also has a different take on the significance of castration for women:

The dread of injury to her womanhood exercises a profound influence on the castration complex of the little girl, for it causes her to over-estimate the penis which she herself lacks; this exaggeration is then much more obvious than is the underlying anxiety about her own womanhood. [p. 81]

There are corresponding differences in the development of the superego in girls and boys. Going beyond Freud who had postulated that women simply had weaker superegos than men, Klein (1928) observed that women have the tendency toward petty jealousy but that they also have a generally greater capacity than men to "[disregard] their own wishes and [devote] themselves with self-sacrifice to ethical and social tasks" (p. 80). (It is noteworthy that this is written in 1928, a half-century before Carol Gilligan published *In a Different Voice*.) Whether a woman's character will be dominated by jealousy or by this transcendence of personal concerns will be determined, Klein says, by whether it is the pregenital sadism of the mother or the "devoted kindness of an indulgent mother ideal" of the genital period that characterizes the resolution of the oedipal challenge. The superego in the little boy also rests on the same mixture of sadistic and benevolent experiences and phantasies of the mother, but its qualities are finally determined by the boy's identification with his father: "He too sets before himself a figure of exalted character upon which to model himself, but because the boy *is* 'made in the image of' his idea, it is not attainable" (p. 82).

Underlying this altered view of the development of the structures of the mind is a subtle but significant revision of the understanding of the mental conflict that constitutes normal states as well as psychopathological ones. For Freud, conflict resulted primarily from the clash between loving and destructive desires and the constraints of society. For Klein, the central human conflict is between the death wishes and the life forces, between the wish to protect/love and demolish/hate oneself and others (Greenberg and Mitchell 1983).

THE PARANOID-SCHIZOID POSITION

The concepts of the *paranoid-schizoid* and *depressive positions* are further elaborations of how Klein reconstructed the first year of life. A position is to be distinguished from a stage in that though a person may achieve the subsequent depressive position, the paranoid-schizoid network of feelings, vulnerabilities, and defenses yet remains. The essence of the notion of the position is described here by Hanna Segal (1981):

> The concept of positions is not comparable to a phase of development of the libido. True, the paranoid-schizoid position precedes the depressive position; nevertheless, the constant fluctuations between the two positions makes "position" a structural concept rather than a chronological one. The term "position" refers to a state of organization of the ego and describes characteristically conjoint phenomena: the state of the ego, the nature of the internal object relationships, the nature of anxiety and characteristic defenses. [pp. 125–126]

Klein's concept of positions encompasses not only psychosexual but cognitive aspects of development and thus the very structure of consciousness.

Klein, like many of Freud's contemporaries and successors, attempted to fill in the blanks in Freud's very schematic outline of the first year of life. Unlike Freud, she felt that a rudimentary ego existed from birth. Like Winnicott, though, Klein (1946) saw the early ego as largely unintegrated and lacking in cohesion: "A tendency towards integration alternates with a tendency towards disintegration, a falling into bits. I believe these fluctuations are characteristic of the first few months of life." Anxiety is one of the earliest functions of the ego and she sees it arising "from the operation of the death instinct within the organism, is felt as fear of annihilation (death) and takes the form of fear of persecution." Note that the infant perceives this to be caused by an object. Other primary anxieties that seem to be caused by objects include birth (e.g., separation) and inadequate gratification of physical demands (e.g., feeding). "Even if these objects are felt to be external, they become through introjection internal persecutors and thus reinforce the fear of the destructive impulse within" (pp. 179–180). Whether or not Klein's reasoning is correct, there is significant agreement about her conclusion—namely that babies use the primitive defense of *splitting* to cope with this quite frightening and overwhelming psychic reality in the first year of life.

Splitting, defined in Moore and Fine (1990) as "the separation of psychological representations according to their opposing qualities" (p. 183), characterizes the paranoid-schizoid position that dominates the first few months of life. The mother is perceived not as a whole person who is sometimes gratifying and sometimes frustrating, but rather as a shifting, vacillating set of mutually exclusive actions. This is embodied by the concepts of the *good breast* and the *bad breast*. In the paranoid-schizoid position, then, object relations are with part-objects, not whole ones. The paranoid quality of this position derives from the fear of "the 'bad' denying breasts, which are felt as external and internal persecutors" (Klein 1936b, pp. 140–141). The underlying paranoid-schizoid anxiety, then, is the fear of annihilation (Segal 1981). Klein's original conception was simply of a paranoid position. Influenced by Fairbairn, she added "schizoid," which refers to the infant's tendency to withdraw protectively from contact with the environment in the face of seemingly overwhelming frustration or aggression.

One of the effects of this process that Klein describes is later emphasized by Kernberg in his work on borderline conditions. As Klein (1946) puts it,

> I believe that the ego is incapable of splitting the object—internal and external—without corresponding splitting taking place within the ego. Therefore the phantasies and feelings about the state of the internal object vitally influence the structure of the ego. The more sadism prevails in the process of incorporating the object, and the more the

object is felt to be in pieces, the more the ego is in danger of being split in relation to the internalized object fragments. . . .

It is in phantasy that the infant splits the object and the self, but the effect of this phantasy is a very real one, because it leads to feelings and relations (and later on, thought processes) being in fact cut off from one another. [p. 181]

THE DEPRESSIVE POSITION

Normally by about 6 months of age the baby has achieved a rudimentary sense of mother as a whole person, with good and bad aspects, who is generally seen as good and need-satisfying. This takes place when the good, pleasurable, satisfying experiences outweigh the bad ones such that there is little credence to the infant's paranoid phantasies of being persecuted and devoured. This is the basis for the depressive position in which the leading anxiety "concerns injury to and loss of the object through one's own aggression" (Segal 1981, p. 127). In other words, the baby is no longer relying predominantly on projection and is thus experiencing his own destructive capacities. These destructive phantasies can be tolerated because the baby also wishes to repair the damage. The attainment of the depressive position is crucial to later development, for a child who is unable to solidify a sufficiently secure whole internal object will be unlikely to achieve personality functioning beyond the borderline level. As Segal (1981) writes, "The shift from the paranoid-schizoid to the depressive position is a fundamental change from psychotic to sane functioning" (p. 136).

Klein and her followers write of what they call "manic" defenses against the pain inherent in the depressive position. This terminology may be misleading, for what they describe seems to be akin to narcissistic grandiosity. For instance, this passage in Segal (1981) recalls Kohut's concept of the vertical split:

Before [the onset of the depressive position] the main defenses against persecutors are splitting of the good and bad objects, idealization, violent expulsion, and annihilation of persecutors and of hateful parts of the self. The depressive person mobilizes additional defenses of a manic nature. In essence, these defenses are directed against experiencing the psychic reality of the depressive pain, and their main characteristic is a denial of psychic reality. Dependence on the object and ambivalence are denied and the object is omnipotently controlled and treated with triumph and contempt so that the loss of the object shall not give rise to pain or guilt. Alternately, or simultaneously, there may be a flight to the idealized internal object, denying any feeling of destruction and loss. Those defenses are part of normal development, but if they are excessive and long-lasting, they impede the growth of a relationship to a good and whole object and the working through of the depressive position. [pp. 79–80]

In this passage we see the first reference to the concept of *ambivalence*. Ambivalence functions as a defensive holding place – less primitive than outright splitting – in which the infant has the opportunity to work through the conflicts that characterize the depressive position. This position does not ever vanish but rather is slowly given up over the course of the first few years of life. It is as reality-testing reassures the child that he can rely on the goodness of the object that he is able to relinquish splitting as the primary defense mechanism. A powerful tendency that aids this process is the wish to undo the effects of one's sadism. *Reparation phantasies* contribute to the child being reassured that his love for the object will outweigh his destructive inclinations:

. . . as the adaptation to the external world increases, this splitting is carried out on planes which gradually become increasingly nearer and nearer to reality. This goes on until love for the real and the internalized objects and trust in them are well established. Then ambivalence, which is partly a safeguard against one's own hate and against the hated and terrifying objects, will in normal development again diminish in varying degrees. [Klein 1936b, p. 144]

The depressive position is never entirely worked through, yet the experiences both in actuality and in phantasy of the first years of life will determine the extent to which an individual is able to cope with dependence, with his own sadism, and whether the self and objects are generally seen as whole or as part-objects. When one recalls that Klein redated the onset of the Oedipus complex to the second half of the first year of life, it is not surprising that this coincides with the beginning of the depressive position, for it is being able to see mother as a whole object that allows triadic phantasy and conflict.

In the depressive position, the child has an overall image of the object, mother, as good and need-satisfying. Therefore, the child fears the effects of his sadistic phantasies, fears for the safety of this loved and needed other. For the first time, gratitude and guilt enter the psychological picture, but the child must find a way to cope with increasing perceptions of his own helplessness and dependence. When the depressive position is achieved, introjection comes to outweigh projection as the primary defense mechanism — the baby wants to take in those needed and good qualities of mother. Klein also adds to the understanding of mourning that Freud (1917) offered in "Mourning and Melancholia" by suggesting that the task of mourning is to restore the inner world of good objects that had been achieved in the depressive position. She also believed, in a departure from Freud, that new object relations in the adult's world could aid in this process, just as it was the goodness of the mother that helped the baby overcome the paranoid-schizoid tendencies.

ENVY, GREED, AND JEALOUSY

Envy of the object's good qualities has its origin in the first months of life in the baby's relationship with the breast. The baby experiences himself as helpless and dependent and has intense envy of the breast, for its capacity to provide both food and comfort.

Envy is one expression of the death instinct and lends its flavor to the phantasized attacks on the breast. By removing its power, by possessing the breast in phantasy, the infant defends against unbearable dependence. Greed, on the other hand, is a less complex concept in Klein's lexicon for it is related to pleasure and to wanting to get unlimited amounts of goodness. Jealousy is a triadic event, related to a conflict over who will possess the loved object, and aggression is directed toward the rival rather than the object.

The developmental progression, then, of these phantasies of possession is from envy to jealousy, with greed possible at any juncture. One can masquerade as another, though; thus for the clinician to determine the developmental levels at which affects originate can be complicated. For instance, jealousy toward the father can be related to rivalry for the breast which the father has been perceived as winning. In this situation, father may be experienced more as a rival like a sibling than a true genital or whole-object rival.

The most famous (or infamous) sort of envy for which psychoanalysis is renowned is penis envy. Unlike Freud, Klein (1956) sees penis envy as secondary to breast envy; when there has been excessive envy of the breast, the little girl turn to the penis as a substitute nurturing phantasy object.

> My observations have shown me that when at any stage in life the relation to the good object is seriously disturbed, not only is inner security lost but character deterioration sets in. . . . If the good object is deeply rooted, temporary disturbances can be withstood and the foundation is laid for mental health, character formation and a successful ego development. . . .
>
> The internalized persecuting object, which is felt to be grudging and envious owing to the individual's envy being projected upon it, is experienced as particularly dangerous because it has the effect of hampering all attempts at reparation and creativeness. Envy interferes most of all with these constructive attempts because the object

which is to be restored is at the same time attacked and devalued by envy. Since these feelings are transferred to the analyst, the incapacity to make reparation, which shows itself as the incapacity to co-operate in the analysis, forms part of the negative therapeutic reaction. [pp. 224–225]

Boys who have less than adequately gratifying experiences with the breast tend to transfer their hatred and anxiety to the female genital, thus putting the man at risk for deeply troubled relationships with women. Klein postulates that for both sexes envy of the breast can translate in later life into a generalized envy of creativity. Again, Klein's (1956) contribution is to point out how the very earliest difficulties can result in profound and lifelong disturbance. The Oedipus, for Klein, is not the bedrock; its contours are determined by what goes before.

KLEIN'S CLINICAL WORK WITH CHILDREN

Klein's clinical genius and originality rested in her work directly with children. Unlike Freud, who reconstructed child development, both normal and pathological, from the psychoanalyses of late adolescents and adults (in the case of Little Hans, Freud was actually a supervisor and consultant to the father who "treated" Hans, and he was the analyst of Hans's mother), Klein pioneered the psychoanalytic treatment of children. It had been thought that children were so bound up psychically in relationships with their parents that they did not have any libido left over, as it were, with which to develop a transference to the analyst. It was also feared that talking directly about their anxieties would prove destructive to children. These were the main grounds on which Klein and Anna Freud, who also worked with children, were to disagree. (What Klein [1955] did realize early in her work with children was that it was necessary to analyze a child in her office; analysis conducted in the home proved too unsettling, for the child needed to be able to regard it as separate from everything else.) Anna Freud also believed that child analysis ought to be primarily educative in order to strengthen the superego and that work with the negative transference was contraindicated (Segal 1981). Another obstacle to analytic work with children was their inability to free associate. Klein sidestepped this problem by regarding all of the child's actions, play and motor activity, as a form of association and thus interpretable. Indeed she believed that the unconscious material was much more accessible in children than in adults when one knew how to listen to it. It is difficult to make a clear differentiation between Klein's theoretical and clinical contributions, for they are intimately linked. For instance in a passage cited above, Klein ties the most metapsychological of concepts, the death instinct, to a clinical phenomenon. The full-blown negative therapeutic reaction, in which a patient's symptoms worsen after therapeutic and interpretive work that ought to contribute to their dissolution, is not seen daily in the practice of psychotherapy but may be rather common in more diluted forms.

KLEINIAN INTERPRETATION

Klein practiced and preached adherence to the strictest standards of orthodox psychoanalytic technique with regard to neutrality, anonymity, and avoidance of gratifying the patient. Her modifications in the work with children, treating play as their associations, greatly enlarged her capacity to understand very primitive material. This made it possible for psychoanalysts to work with borderline and narcissistic pathology within the bounds of the generally accepted analytic techniques. With adults as with children, Klein championed early and deep interpretation of what was most anxiety-provoking to the patient. This is quite in opposition to the standard psychoanalytic principle of beginning with the surface, with the manifest material, and working toward deeper material as it appeared the patient could tolerate it. An additional criticism of the early and deep interpretation is that it runs a great risk of having more to do with what the analyst expects to hear than with what the patient has said. Prominent Kleinians no longer adhere to this technical principle according the report of Hanna Segal. Segal also related this caricature that the Anna Freudian analysts had of the Kleinian ones. A patient was said to have phoned her Kleinian analyst to say she would be late for that day's session. But, she said to the analyst, you can just go ahead and begin without me.

Nonetheless, Klein (1955) did believe that deep interpretations offered relief of anxiety. She describes her route to this practice:

> My first patient was a five-year-old boy [Fritz]. . . . To begin with I thought it would be sufficient to influence the mother's attitude. I suggested she should encourage the child to discuss freely with her the many unspoken questions which were obviously at the back of his mind and were impeding his intellectual development. This had a good effect, but his neurotic difficulties were not sufficiently alleviated and it was soon decided that I should psycho-analyse him. In doing so, I deviated from some of the rules so far established, for I interpreted what I thought to be most urgent in the material the child presented to me and found my interests focusing on his anxieties and the defences against them. This new approach soon confronted me with serious problems. The anxieties I encountered when analysing this first case were very acute, and though I was strengthened in the belief that I was working on the right lines by observing the alleviation of anxiety again and again produced by my interpretations, I was at times perturbed by the intensity of the fresh anxieties which were being brought into the open. [p. 36]

Klein's (1930) general rule was not "to interpret the material until it has found expression in various representations" (p. 106), and in this she remained quite orthodox in technique. She advised the child analyst to be "succinct" and to use the child's own expressions as much as possible, and she felt that, contrary to the contemporary wisdom, children were indeed capable of a high degree of insight and could be helped by interpretation, the making conscious of the unconscious.

> To some extent this is explained by the fact that the connections between conscious and unconscious are closer in young children than in adults, and that infantile repressions are less powerful. I also believe that the infant's intellectual capacities are often underrated and that in fact he understands more than he is credited with. [Klein 1955, p. 46]

Klein kept a separate toy box for each child patient in which she deposited a variety of small, nonmechanical toys. There was a certain neutrality to the toys, for the little dolls were to suggest no particular role or profession. The goal was to enable the child to use these items to express as wide a range as possible of phantasies in the consulting room. The acting out of aggression or destruction with the toys—but not with the analyst's person—was to be tolerated and interpreted. She suggested that the analyst not attempt to repair a damaged toy but rather to allow the child to experience whatever guilt or reparation phantasies emerged.

VIEW OF TRANSFERENCE

For Klein (1952), the interpretation of transference played a central role in the treatment of both adults and children:

> Altogether, in the young infant's mind every external experience is interwoven with his phantasies and on the other hand every phantasy contains elements of actual experience, and it is only by analysing the transference situation to its depth that we are able to discover the past both in its realistic and phantastic aspects. [p. 208]

She believed that past conflicts would be reproduced within the transference, so that the transference came to be of greater therapeutic importance than the reconstruction of the past in the Freudian sense (Segal 1981). From her own experiences as an analysand, Klein had learned how important it was to allow the full expression of the negative transference. Any treatment that was devoid of negative transferential material could not reach the necessary depth of mind to be truly therapeutic, for Klein believed transference to be profoundly determined by the primitive phantasies, which are themselves characterized by the hatred and destruction that represent the death instinct. Following the natural vicissitudes of the death instinct as it is expressed through gradually diminishing splitting in the paranoid-schizoid and depressive positions of normal development, Klein found that the interpretation of splitting in the analytic situation was therapeutic. (This is certainly one of the major ways in which her work influenced Kernberg.) Here Klein (1946) writes of how schizoid patients appear not to experience anxiety and emotion due to an annihilation of parts of the self:

> I have recently found that advances in synthesis are brought about by interpretations of the specific causes for splitting. . . .
> The feeling of being disintegrated, of being unable to experience emotion, of losing one's objects, is in fact the equivalent of anxiety. . . .
> Interpretations which tend towards synthesizing the split in the self, including the dispersal of emotions, make it possible for the anxiety gradually to be experienced as such, though for long stretches we may in fact only be able to bring the ideational contents together but not to elicit the emotions of anxiety. [pp. 196–197]

Klein also widens the concept of transference beyond the sense Freud had defined in which it is essentially seen as the patient's distortion of the analyst based on past relationships. Klein (1952) sees transference as more pervasive and looks for clues to the transference and to the defenses against the experiencing of the transference in the patient's reporting of everyday activities seemingly unrelated to the analytic situation: "From the whole material presented the *unconscious elements* of the transference are deduced" (p. 209).

BIOLOGY AND ENVIRONMENT

Criticisms of Klein often include the accusation that she is insufficiently attuned to the actual environment of the patient, both external and biological. A careful reading, though, may show otherwise. One of the ways in which she measures the success of psychotherapeutic treatment has to do with whether the patient's ability to adapt to reality, to live in the actual world, has improved. Indeed, the move to the depressive position has to do with the strengthening of the ego and the achievement of reality testing as the baby becomes able to experience the mother as other than the feared persecutor.

> At a very early age children become acquainted with reality through the deprivations which it imposes on them. They try to defend themselves against it by repudiating it. The fundamental thing, however, and the criterion of all later capacity for adaptation to reality, is the degree in which they are able to tolerate the deprivations that result from the Oedipus situation. Hence, even in little children, an exaggerated repudiation of reality (often disguised under an apparent "adaptability" and "docility") is an indication of neurosis and differs from the flight from reality of adult neurotics only in the forms in which it manifests itself. Even in the analysis of young children, therefore, one of the final results to be attained is successful adaptation to reality. [Klein 1926, p. 59]

Klein believed that the therapeutic power of analysis lay in the working through of the envy, hatred, and destructive tendencies of the earliest months of life. However, because the quantity of envy and destruction was to a great extent inborn she recognized that there existed boundaries to the effectiveness of psychoanalysis (Klein 1956). These constitutional factors represented the individual's biological environment. What Klein left to Winnicott and others was the exploration of the damage that the environment could impose after birth.

POORLY POSITIONED:
A CASE OF DEVELOPMENTAL FIXATION

S., a 33-year-old white woman of upper middle class background, worked as an assistant to a high-level administrator in the government of the southern state in which she lived. She was always groomed so impeccably that, as with Scarlett O'Hara, men may seldom have realized that she was not unusually beautiful. Unlike Scarlett, though, S. was not the belle of the ball, for men rarely asked her out. It was her confused loneliness and pressured wish to marry to meet her family's expectation that brought her to treatment. It is significant, though, that the wish to marry had less to do with loneliness and more to do with social image; in fact, S.'s smooth appearance and apparent social affability concealed a constant and anxious preoccupation with whether people liked her. S. had sought counseling as a college senior, unable to choose a job, but described the male counselor she saw at the college health service as having been more interested in finding ways to blame her for her problems than in helping her feel cared about. S. called Dr. W., a psychologist in his sixties, after attending a presentation he gave for the state policy-makers in which he was advocating for recognition of the psychological ramifications of family violence. S. experienced Dr. W. to be both benign and empathic as well as charismatically self-confident and influential, qualities Dr. W. would come to understand S. saw in her father. Indeed, the paternal transference would play a central role in the treatment. This presentation focuses on this crucial transference, the unconscious phantasies underlying it, and associated interpretive themes from a five-year psychotherapy of thrice-weekly sessions.

BACKGROUND

S. was the oldest of three children born to an aristocratic southern family; after her birth, the mother suffered several miscarriages and finally, five years later, conceived and bore the patient's twin brothers, triply prized for their gender, number, and for the miracle of their existence after so many failures. Although the family had had a nanny since S.'s birth, it was S.'s impression that her mother took on many of the tasks for the twins that, for her, had been relegated to the nanny. The mother was, as the patient described her, cold, inscrutable, and confusing in ways that were difficult for the patient to describe; she only knew that encounters with her mother left her with the gnawing feeling that there was something wrong with her, that she just couldn't understand at all things that seemed so clear to her mother. For instance, an event that took place when the patient was in her early twenties captures the flavor of the mother's hostility to S. throughout her life. The mother, with the exception of some instances of open hostility and others of tantalizing offers of warmth, was generally coldly polite and uninterested in S. After a family event in which the mother had seemed marginally less icy, the patient telephoned her and tentatively expressed the hope that the two of them could develop an adult friendship; the mother in her elegant Southern style said, "I'd welcome that," was then interrupted by Call Waiting, and simply forgot that S. was waiting on the phone. On another occasion S. told her mother that she had just ended a brief but increasingly abusive relationship with a man. The mother responded, "You're so sensitive to such little slights. How are you ever going to keep a man if things have to be oh-so-perfect for you?" The effect of interactions such as these (which one is tempted to label mind games, or soul murder) was to give S. a sense that her own thoughts, experiences, and judgment were always of less value than those of her mother; indeed, her very capacity to perceive reality had been undermined. It is important to emphasize that it was not only what seemed to Dr. W. to be the mother's "real" sadism that affected the patient, for S.'s phantasies of her mother played a part as well. S. described intense rage at her mother even as the mother performed what sounded to the therapist to be some generally appropriate maternal and spousal functions.

The father, on the other hand, was warm but mercurial. In addition to his inherited wealth, the father earned a substantial income in a highly successful business he developed with great ease, taking advantage of a developing market for a rare product. He seemed to have little sense of how lucky he had been and expected S. to be as perfect as he imagined himself to be. He was an impulsive man who drank excessively at times and ate large amounts of food to satisfy what S. described as gargantuan cravings. He had not completed college but remained nonetheless fiercely loyal to his school, attending each local basketball game and experiencing what approached rage when the team did not do well. In his relationship with S. he alternated between indulgence, at unpredictable intervals buying her extravagant gifts of toys or clothing, and abusive criticism, for instance ripping up a school assignment on which he had discovered some misspelled words. It was likely that these temper tantrums may have served to help the father bind his libidinal impulses as S. grew older, for S. remembered her father touching her, rubbing her legs when she had "growing pains" as a young child, in a seemingly innocent and affectionate manner; these encounters had nonetheless been unsettling in a nameless sort of way until, as an adult, S. was able to recognize that her experience of her father's behavior with her had had strong sexual features, arising from both her phantasies and his phantasies of their relationship.

The parents divorced when S. was 12, the father having had several affairs and finally falling for a very attractive woman of 22 who coddled and indulged him. They married as soon as the divorce was final and later had two daughters who, S. felt, were relatively well-nurtured; her stepmother seemed to have some ability to protect them from the father's emotional storms. The mother did not remarry, and in fact refused to tell S. and her brothers, after they moved away from home, whether or not she dated at all—she had not done so during their teenage years. As far as S. was aware, her mother devoted herself to the volunteer charity work that had for years formed the core of her social and moral existence.

When S. first saw Dr. W., she had been working steadily in the same office for a number of years, and had received promotions based on her ability to keep her wits about her in a hectic government position. This professional competence, though, concealed powerful and contradictory elements in her personality. An identification with her father's commercial success gave S. a certain strength, but there also existed a sense of confusion that Dr. W. attributed to her projective identification of her intelligence and rage into the outside world. S. would generally experience men as being strong and intelligent (that is, she projected these qualities of hers into them), and women she saw with distrust and rage (also by virtue of projective identification). With defenses such as this, it is easy to understand that S. had essentially no social life of any emotional depth; having graduated from a woman's college without making any friends, she had also had but few relationships with men.

S. maintained a rather extraordinary level of physical fitness, exercising daily to a level that could be termed addictive, and she also severely restricted food intake at times (although never to the point of amenorrhea or serious weight loss). Until age 27 S. had been a chain-smoker. The exercise had essentially replaced the self-medicating effect of smoking, although S. would occasionally smoke a pack of cigarettes during particularly stressful work assignments, or when the transference relationship became unusually uncomfortable. Dr. W. came to understand S.'s obsession with fitness as a defense with multiple meanings; being slim and firm allowed S. to avoid identifying with maternal femininity, while it simultaneously served to protect her against imagined attacks from the retaliating internalized material object. A strong body also may have represented a protection against imagined castration as well as an identification with her father. In sum, S. held herself together superficially by keeping herself from knowing the depths of her suffering. Her affect was thus primarily one of confusion, hence the question she presented to Dr. W.: Why were things not working out for her with men?

THE SPECIFIC CLINICAL PROBLEM

Within the first year of treatment Dr. W. became aware of how delicately balanced the therapeutic relationship was. He noticed that S. was intensely sensitive to actual or imagined criticism and that she often reacted to his interpretations or clarifying comments with an instantaneous and searing sense of having been injured. Sometimes this would occur even following remarks that Dr. W. had intended to be supportive (and believed he had communicated in a supportive or warm manner). For example, in one session S. described her detailed and morally agonizing work on a piece of legislation that proposed some restrictions in social services in the face of state budget pressures. Dr. W. summarized S.'s narrative by saying that she seemed to have been carefully analytical in her difficult task without losing sight of the individuals who would be affected by these program cuts. S. responded with fury at the therapist for how he had condescended to her. In her negative therapeutic reaction, S. showed herself to be unable to welcome Dr. W.'s understanding. Positive comments such as these were so threatening because they attempted to integrate the "good" parts of S. with the "bad" (destructive and thus punishable) parts. In other words, S. needed to resist the interpretation of her splitting. After many similar episodes, Dr. W. formulated a narrative to help him understand S.'s reactions. He believed that S. experienced herself as having defeated her mother in the oedipal struggle. As a result, she had intense guilt, which she needed to keep unconscious, over her incestuous longings. S. could not admit to feelings of destructiveness and hostility, and she maintained this freedom from self-knowledge and guilt in the treatment situation by projecting her bad destructiveness and aggression into the therapist. But, when Dr. W. appeared to her to be good, this had the effect of forcing back into her the bad projected material that he had previously contained for her. This integrated state of seeing that she was not all good, that she was bad as well, was, as yet, unacceptable to the patient. She therefore could not accept Dr. W.'s empathy.[2]

The result of encounters such as these was that Dr. W. felt in great danger of hurting S.; he felt that he had in fact damaged her without even knowing that the situation had been potentially dangerous for the patient. He gradually came to under-

2. Patrick Casement (1990) (a current object relations theorist) refers to this phenomenon as the "pain of contrast." A negative therapeutic response to experience that might appear to be "good" seems to be an unconscious attempt by the patient to preserve childhood memories from comparison, particularly when there is a risk of exposing the depth of early deprivation or the true nature of damaging experience in childhood.

stand this, along Kleinian lines, as S.'s having projected her own punishing and hurting self representation into him such that the more Dr. W. attempted to care for her, the more she experienced him as a persecuting object. S.'s reality testing was so compromised, due to the splitting that characterizes the paranoid/schizoid position, that she did not have the ability to compare her phantasy with the reality of Dr. W.'s empathy and concern. Dr. W. closely examined his countertransference responses for many months before he felt certain that this fear of hurting S. in fact represented a projection of her own badness. When this sense of badness is projectively identified into the other, the other is then experienced as persecutory, and it is this fear of persecuting the patient that Dr. W. was experiencing in his containing of S.'s transference.

As in almost all transference encounters, though, there is an anchor in the reality of the situation, at least in the reality as the patient perceives it. S. had known something of Dr. W. from having heard his presentation on family violence and what she "knew" entered into her choice of him to be her therapist. As Salman Akhtar (1994b) has remarked, people do not come to therapy seeking to speak to therapists, rather they are searching for a renewed dialogue with their mothers and fathers. And S. was no exception to this. Perhaps some measure of the seeming intractability of the negative therapeutic response resulted from S.'s belief that Dr. W. was paternal, charismatic, and moody like her father. In other words, the real encounter S. had had with Dr. W. diminished the "as if" quality of the transference, such that his very efforts to interpret her experiences of his "criticisms" themselves functioned as criticisms; S. could not believe that Dr. W. had nothing at stake in their interactions. (One wonders what it must have been like for Anna Freud to be analyzed by Sigmund Freud, a situation in which the illusion that the analyst is not ego-invested in the particulars of the treatment could not possibly have been maintained.) However, Dr. W., although perhaps similar to S.'s father in his authoritative style, was also profoundly different in several important ways; he possessed a high degree of self awareness, sufficient empathy to understand S.'s predicament, a genuine desire to help her out of her excruciating bind, and a keen appreciation of the confounding effects of projective identification.

Theoretical Formulation

In the Kleinian view, normal development involves the progression from the paranoid/schizoid to the depressive position. Necessary to achieve this, though, are adequate experiences in reality that serve to *disprove* the paranoid sense of persecution resulting from the need to project the bad things inside (unpleasure, aggression—representatives of the death instinct) onto the outside objects. For S., it is clear that this did not happen. She learned such profound self-doubt from the intrusive manner of her parents (most likely a form of pathological projective identification on their parts) that she was unable to tolerate the taking on of the depressive position which would have required her to integrate a sense of badness as well as goodness in herself as well as in others. Also unbearable would have been the guilt over her aggressive and sexual wishes that she would have to take possession of in the absence of projective identification of these into her parents and others. The persistence of the paranoid/schizoid defenses of splitting and projective identification maintained her harsh, primitive superego and thus compromised her ego capacities. Recall that Klein posits that the superego develops early in life and that it takes on the characteristics of the early paranoid position. It is thus not surprising that S. suffered from relentless self-criticism and hypervigilance concerning expected persecution and criticism from others.

THE BEGINNING OF WORKING THROUGH THE DEFENSES AGAINST THE DEPRESSIVE POSITION

There is no magic to the process by which a patient works through any characterological position. It is simply a matter of going through the issues again and again as they present themselves, both in the therapeutic dyad and in relation to important others in the patient's life. And it was this excruciatingly slow process that took place with S. The question of what is curative is a vexed one about which there exist no definitive answers. Thinking as Klein might have, though, we can imagine a growth trajectory, never entirely abandoned, that could now proceed in the presence of a good object—the person of Dr. W. For Dr. W.'s patience, understanding, and continuing presence in the face of S.'s projected aggression provided a reality that was substantially different from what she had experienced as a child and thus had imagined relationships to be like ever since. Dr. W.'s ability to contain both the poisonous bad as well as the overstimulating good permitted the patient to take ownership of this material gradually as she was able to tolerate an integrated sense of self as both good and bad. This exemplifies Klein's belief that it is possible for new objects to aid in the mourning process.

To examine S.'s working through, let us compare an episode from rather early in the treatment to a later one. Early on, S. refused to consider the significance of the transference, maintaining a bland, defended attitude in the sessions with only intellectual appreciation of her difficulties. To protect herself from intolerable psychic pain and intense neediness, she could not allow herself to experience a true sense of emotional connectedness within the therapy sessions. She displaced feelings onto other relationships—or into Dr. W., whose countertransference reactions were stormy and disturbing. In a session following one in which S. had felt injured by the therapist, Dr.

W. attempted to point out S.'s displacement of her anger while giving her permission to direct those feelings toward him:

Dr. W.: Expressing such anger in the meeting with your lawyer seemed to give you that chance to say things that don't feel safe to say directly to me.

S.: Just what is it that you want me to do? I did everything I was taught to do in that assertiveness training course I took and now you're telling me that I was demanding, like a . . . like . . . a tantrum-y baby. Whatever I do you find something wrong with.

Dr. W.: I can see that even thinking about having acted in a powerful way fills you with guilt, and you feel assaulted by that feeling as well as by me. Apparently any "show" of power taps into that inner reservoir of frustrated rage and desire for retaliation. Your primitive conscience won't tolerate any sign of strength, power, or force for fear of revealing a very hurt and angry hidden self.

The entrenched and desperate quality of S.'s defenses is obvious. It would have been intolerable for S. to experience any manifestation, however remote, of her wish to destroy her needed object. The narcissistic indignation thus protects her from knowing that it is from her, and not from Dr. W., that the primitive rage emanates. Just as a preadolescent is unconsciously aware of the challenges and conflicts of adolescence even before the struggles become manifest, so too did S. seem to be aware that the demands of the depressive position—the relinquishing of splitting and projection in the name of tolerating ambivalence; the integration of inner objects, the bad as well as the good within herself and others—would have overtaxed her psyche.

Much later in treatment, changes had slowly become apparent. S. was much better able to tolerate transference interpretations, and this generalized to an improved self awareness in other relationships as well. Less relentlessly certain of being criticized, S. must have appeared less distant and men had begun to ask her out. In addition, she was able to see that she not only anticipated that others would treat her as her parents had but also that she, herself, treated others that way as well in order that she could projectively identify with their helpless confusion. Here, S. is struck by the possibility of an entirely new way of seeing herself as she seems to appreciate Dr. W.'s empathy for the first time:

S.: You know, I have this heavy, terrible feeling that I really hurt Joe by not calling him, but I don't know why I can't really feel sorry, . . . no, not sorrow, remorseful. It's so much easier just to hit *myself* over the head with a big stick.

Dr. W.: I wonder whether feeling so bad makes you feel guilty, and that's a feeling we know you always try to protect yourself from experiencing.

S.: . . . I just had the most peculiar . . . it's as though I could see myself not as I've seen myself all my life, but differently. . . . Like for an instant I can truly believe that you can listen to me and not need to lash out at me.

This vision that Dr. W. can see her in a positive light as well as being able to recognize deficiencies within herself signifies functioning characteristic of the depressive position—mental functioning *not* characterized by splitting but rather by the integration of good and bad aspects of self and object, a symbolic space in which to experience relationships, as well as a sense of gratitude to the rescuing Other and a wish to repair any damage done by the self (reparation).

Shortly after this exchange, S. learned that her boss would be receiving a political appointment in Washington, D.C., and she agreed to follow him there. She had little time to end treatment and Dr. W. was unsure that she would be able to consolidate these gains on her own. She did not accept a referral to another therapist, citing the undoubted pressures that would accompany the new job. However, Dr. W. understood that S. needed to defend herself from the risks of an intense relationship with an unknown, and possibly dangerous, person. Perhaps there was an element of good judgment and accurate appraisal of reality in that S. had learned in treatment more than a little about her own fragility and her tendency to find bad objects. Too, politics being what they are, S. did indicate that her stay in the nation's capital might not be lengthy and that she could return to Dr. W. in the future.

4 WINNICOTT: THE INFANT'S EMBEDDEDNESS IN THE ENVIRONMENT

Just as Freud's psychoanalytic career was developing in Vienna, Donald Woods Winnicott (1896–1971) was born in the town of Plymouth in Devon, England. He was the youngest of three children in a happy family. (Indeed, some have speculated as to how a man with such a happy childhood could end up in the field of psychoanalysis, and there is some information recently emerging that perhaps casts some doubt on the completeness of the happiness of Winnicott's early life.) He had not one but several "mothers"—his biological mother, two older sisters, and a nanny to whom he remained devoted for years. His father, a business-man who was later knighted, was twice mayor of Plymouth and wanted his son to follow him into his business. While at boarding school as an adolescent, Winnicott acknowledged a profound and long-held wish to become a doctor, and did obtain his father's permission to undertake these studies. After a stint in the Navy during the war, Winnicott opened a practice in pediatrics and simultaneously undertook a personal analysis and began psycho-analytic training.

METAPSYCHOLOGICAL POLITICS

Winnicott's central contribution to the field of psychotherapy and psychoanalysis was a focus on the infant's embeddedness in the environment from (and before) the first days of life. The psycho-analytic environment in which Winnicott established himself in the 1920s had become very complex indeed. Melanie Klein, whose work focused on the fantasy life of infants and children and who posited the existence of an innate death-drive derived aggression, dominated the psychoanalytic scene in Britain until Sigmund and Anna Freud moved to London in 1938. There then rapidly developed a split in the British Psycho-Analytical Society between the Kleinians and the Anna Freudians, both groups claiming to be the true disciples of Sigmund Freud, who had died in 1939. Anna Freud, who also worked with children, explored the area of the ego and its defense mechanisms in contrast to Klein's preoccupation with id impulses—the drives of libido and aggression, Eros and Thanatos, self-preservation and death. With a certain acrimony, the institute split into three training tracks, the third being the so-called middle or British school of which Winnicott and Michael Balint were the luminaries. Winnicott dealt with this split between Klein and Sigmund Freud (as represented by Anna) by misinterpreting the work of both in such a way as to present himself as theoretically continuous with each (Greenberg and Mitchell 1983). He had strong intellectual and personal ties to both camps: his first analyst, James Strachey, was a Freudian, and his second, Joan Riviere, a Kleinian; he was taught by Klein and analyzed one of her sons; he made the first referral to Anna Freud's war nursery (Winnicott 1989) and expressed pleasure in her professional contributions and growth.

WINNICOTT'S THEORY OF EARLY CHILDHOOD

Winnicott's stress on the infant in the environment took him in a different direction from both Klein, who believed tiny babies to be motivated by drives and drive-derived intrapsychic fantasies from the beginning, and Sigmund Freud, who had posited a postbirth state of primary narcissism in which the baby was essentially unconnected to the environment and sought only the satisfaction of physical needs. One of Winnicott's (1960a) most often quoted remarks was, "There is no such thing as an infant. . . . Whenever one finds an infant one finds maternal care, and without maternal care there would be no infant." Stated less dramatically, "The infant and the maternal care together form a unit" (p. 39). Winnicott also believed, in part through motivated misreadings of Freud and Klein, that he was laying claim to an area of adult psychopathology that neither of them had touched, namely the psychotic and borderline states. Freud (and Anna Freud) had explored the neuroses, and Klein the depressive states. However, at times Winnicott stated that the neuroses did not truly represent pathology (clearly a departure from Freud) and that intrapsychic problems or symptoms related to conflicts over drives were secondary in severity to the primitive dyadic disturbances he treated. In other words, in Winnicott's view the Oedipus complex, the triadic situation, could not satisfactorily explain all psychopathology—a monumental revision of extant psychoanalytic theory. (Kohut would echo this position.) Klein had tried to elucidate early childhood problems by extending oedipal conflict into the first months of life; it is questionable, to say the least, to assume that a baby younger than 1 year of age has the cognitive knowledge of anatomy and relationships that con-stitute oedipal desire, envy, and anxiety. This new view of psy-chopathology led Winnicott to a reformulation of the nature of psychoanalytic treatment.

Just as Freud's ethos has permeated modern culture to the point that, for better or worse, we now live in a Freudian society, so have many of Winnicott's ideas become common parlance in the popular literature on child rearing through "disciples" like T. Berry Brazelton. This includes such concepts as the *good-enough mother*, the *holding environment*, the *false self*, and the *transitional object*, which Winnicott derived from experiences in his pediatric and psychoanalytic practices. Unlike many psycho-analytic theorists and practitioners, Winnicott observed and treated not only the well-to-do but also the less fortunate whom he saw in his large clinic practice, thus regularly observing children raised in less than optimal circumstances (James Grotstein as reported in Greenberg and Mitchell 1983). An earlier example of a study of a lower socioeconomic population can be found in August Aich-horn's *Wayward Youth* (1925). Aichhorn allowed adolescent delinquent boys to act out to their hearts' content within the confines of a residential school setting and supervised by a psychoanalytically educated staff of teachers. Following Aich-horn who studied and found meaning in the delinquent acts (i.e., the symptoms) these boys displayed, Winnicott (1961) also saw seemingly antisocial acts as attempts at self-cure, as expressions of hope:

> The antisocial tendency represents the S.O.S. or *cri de coeur* of the child who has been at some stage or other deprived, deprived of the environmental provision which was appropriate at the age at which it failed. The deprivation altered the child's life; it caused intolerable distress, and the child is right in crying out for recognition of the fact that "things were all right, and then they weren't all right," and this was an external factor outside the child's control. [p. 65]

THE TRUE SELF AND THE
GOOD-ENOUGH MOTHER

The hope inherent in antisocial acts, Winnicott believed, was an expression of what he came to call the *True Self*. In all cases of delinquency, Winnicott discovered a history of early childhood trauma, that is of an environment that consistently or profoundly did not meet the needs of the developing infant and toddler. The stealing or other transgression expressed the (accurate) conviction of the child that he had not received something to which he had been earlier entitled. What is the mechanism by which this occurred? Winnicott believed that it was due to a failure on the part of the mother. He described how *good-enough* or *ordinarily devoted* mothers generally become deeply preoccupied with their infants from several weeks before giving birth to some time afterwards, reaching a level of absorption that in other situations would be deemed an illness. He termed this *primary maternal preoccupation*. In Winnicott's (1960a) words:

> It seems to be usual that mothers who are not distorted by ill-health or by present-day environmental stress do tend on the whole to know accurately what their infants need, and further, they like to provide what is needed. This is the essence of maternal care.
>
> With "the care that it receives from its mother" each infant is able to have a personal existence, and so begins to build up what might be called a *continuity of being*. On the basis of this continuity of being the inherited potential gradually develops into an individual infant. If the maternal care is not good enough, then the infant does not really come into existence, since there is no continuity of being; instead the personality becomes built on the basis of reactions to environmental impingement. [p. 54]

The True Self cannot develop without a mother free enough from narcissistic concerns (whether of intrapsychic or environmental origin) to be able to identify with her baby and thus accurately assess and respond to his needs. (Note that Kohut would later describe this phenomenon, referring to it as empathy.) Winnicott (1960b) states:

> It is because of this identification with her infant that she knows how to hold her infant, so that the infant starts by existing and not by reacting. Here is the origin of the True Self which cannot become a reality without the mother's specialized relationship, one which might be described by a common word: devotion. . . .
>
> At the earliest stages the True Self is a theoretical position from

which come the spontaneous gesture and the personal idea. . . .
Whereas a True Self feels real, the existence of a False Self results in
a feeling unreal or a sense of futility. [p. 148]

THE FALSE SELF

This is the essence of the *False Self*, one of Winnicott's most well
known concepts, the (partly inevitable) personality structure that
results from excessive early demands that the infant respond to
the needs of the environment. The notion of "excessive" is key
here, for one might well ask whether Winnicott requires heroic
self-sacrifice and perfect attunement from mothers for extended
periods of time. But recall the concept of *good enough*, for in fact
good enough is more perfect than perfect. It is from mother's
well-timed and incremental failures (Kohut's "optimal frustration") that the baby learns to perform certain functions for
himself. The false self describes "a defensive organisation in
which there is a premature taking over of the nursing functions of
the mother, so that the infant or child adapts to the environment
while at the same time protecting and hiding the true self, or the
source of personal impulses" (Winnicott 1950s, p. 43). (Note that
"impulses" refers to needs and creativity, and not to Freud's
drives and the search for instinctual gratification, a distinction
that characterizes Winnicott's thinking.)

What does the False Self defend against? How does it protect
the developing baby? The primary anxiety, in Winnicott's view, is
that of psychological annihilation, the fear that the True Self will
be exploited or done away with. (Again, this is a central element
in Kohut's understanding of anxiety.) This is the damage that
maternal or environmental impingements or attacks can cause.
Thus, even a psychosis was seen as a defensive formation prefer-
able to a state of intolerable anxiety and psychological death. The
politeness and social pretending that we all practice represents an
adaptive version of the False Self, with a true False Self (so to

speak) defined by a pervasive compliance, lack of spontaneity, inability to play, and sense of unreality.

THE HOLD

The mother's care is part of what Winnicott termed the *holding environment*, those qualities of the infant's surroundings that permit a complex group of psychological and physical developmental events to occur. Included in this group are the development of the ego from unintegrated to increasing integration (carrying the attendant fear of disintegration) such that the infant attains the status of a person in his own right; the coordination of sensory and motor experiences with this sense of being; the understanding of the skin as "limiting membrane" and hence of the boundary between self and not-self; the partnering of motor abilities with pleasure seeking or erotogenic senses; and the beginnings of memory, dreaming, intelligence, secondary process — in general the beginnings of the mind (Winnicott 1960a).

Holding, which is an absolute requirement of an absolutely dependent baby, enables the baby to relate in a less dependent way to mother and then to include father in the mental picture, what Winnicott (1960a) calls "living with":

> The alternative to being is reacting, and reacting interrupts being and annihilates. Being and reacting are the two alternatives. The holding environment therefore has as its main function the reduction to a minimum of impingements to which the infant must react with resultant annihilation of personal being. [p. 47]

Winnicott often wrote of paradoxes. One, closely related to the concept of good-enough mothering, is what he termed the capacity to be alone. Aloneness refers to a psychological rather than a physical state, and the paradox is that this capacity develops through an experience of being together. It is through the mother's satisfactory hold and through liking, or ego-relatedness (as opposed to loving, her id-relatedness), that the baby first learns to be alone in the presence of the mother who is also alone. Being alone is crucial for it is when one is psychologically alone that the sense of personhood, the sense of being, can develop. To allow oneself safely to feel unintegrated permits a state of alertness focused within the self. And it is from within that the feelings that constitute personhood emerge. Without satisfactory mothering that frees the baby from the necessity of reacting, the capacity to be alone will be severely compromised (Winnicott 1958). The important clinical implications of this and of the concept of holding will be discussed later.

TRANSITIONAL SPACE AND MATERNAL "FAILURES"

The well-nurtured baby, then, is insulated from environmental impingements and the resulting traumatization and loss of personal being. But eventually babies grow up and need to learn to venture out into their surroundings. How do they accomplish this? For many, the first step toward a psychologically safe engagement with the world is demonstrated by the development of an omnipotent relationship with an illusion—the *transitional object*. This object is "found" by the infant (usually in the second half of the first year of life) and inhabits the space between the infant and the mother. Usually the object bears characteristics of the mother, such as softness or smell, and it becomes necessary to the baby as a defense against anxiety, for instance at bedtime. Sometimes there is no concrete item and instead the baby will engage in other transitional phenomena, such as singing or gurgling. The function, though, is the same—to help the infant achieve the illusion of control over aspects of reality; it is thought that the accompanying fantasy is associated with the maternal object or its functions.

Perhaps the first bit of reality to which the infant must learn to adapt is the failure of his mother to anticipate his needs:

> *If all goes well* the infant can actually come to gain from the experience of frustration, since incomplete adaptation to need makes objects real, that is to say hated as well as loved.The consequence of this is that *if all goes well* the infant can be disturbed by a close adaptation to need that is continued too long, not allowed its natural decrease, since exact adaptation resembles magic and the object that behaves perfectly is no better than a hallucination. Nevertheless *at the start* adaptation needs to be almost exact, and unless this is so it is not possible for the infant to begin to develop the capacity to experience a relationship to external reality, or even to form a conception of external reality. . . .
>
> *The intermediate area to which I am referring is the area that is allowed to the infant between primary creativity and objective perception based on reality-testing.* [Winnicott 1951, pp. 12–13]

Good-enough parents respect the baby's need for the transitional object and do nothing to question its effectiveness, to change its characteristics (such as by washing it), or to remove it from the child's control. Indeed many exhausted though good-enough parents rely on this object almost as much as do their infants! The case illustration later in this chapter provides a vivid example of the effects of an interrupted transitional experience.

The importance of the transitional space for all babies cannot be underestimated whether or not the child has a classically intense relationship with a blanket, for it is this area of illusion, of fantasized objective experience that constitutes the first use of a symbol—something that represents something else. Thus Winnicott (1951) theorized that transitional phenomena form the basis for art and culture. But transitional experiencing for the baby depends on the parents' ability to pretend along. As Greenberg and Mitchell (1983) state:

> The transitional object is neither under magical control (like hallucinations and fantasies) nor outside control (like the real mother). . . .

Transitional objects help the baby negotiate the gradual shift from the experience of himself as the center of a totally subjective world to the sense of himself as a person among other persons. Transitional experiencing is not merely a developmental interlude, but remains a cherished and highly valuable realm within healthy adult experience. . . . Transitional experience is rooted in the capacity of the child to play; in adult form it is expressed as a capacity to play with one's fantasies, ideas, and the world's possibilities in a way that continually allows for the surprising, the original, and the new. [pp. 195–196]

CLINICAL APPLICATIONS

Winnicott as a pediatrician had ample opportunity for direct observation of infants and mothers. From this as well as from the analyses and psychotherapeutic encounters with children he developed his convictions about the crucial features of early childhood. He applied his findings to his consultations with both adults and children—or, as he might have said, children of all ages, for he stressed the continuing importance of play, an outgrowth of the transitional space, throughout life. "Play is the 'work' of childhood, and for some it becomes the work of psychotherapy" (Moore and Fine 1990, p. 206). Games, art, culture, and psychotherapy occur in what Winnicott (1971) describes as having originally been a playground, "a potential space between the mother and the baby or joining mother and baby" (p. 55). At birth, baby and mother are merged, are as one. They then move forward as the baby rejects then reaccepts the mother and gradually begins to have an objective perception of the object; play facilitates this process. Next comes the capacity to be alone in the presence of the mother—the child has developed a sense of basic trust in the safety of the environment. Finally comes a time when the baby becomes capable of playing mother's games, when their two play areas may overlap. "Thus the way is paved for playing together in a relationship" (Winnicott 1971, p. 56).

Winnicott's clinical work demonstrated how he utilized his theories of early child development. He shifted the focus of treatment from the purely oedipal conflicts of the patient to an appreciation of the profound influence of the early mother–child relationship on all later functioning. While he did not completely do away with the notion of drives or instincts as motivating forces, he relegated them to secondary importance. Winnicott's notion, at the end of his career, was that neurotics were basically healthy and that the single most important factor in the diagnosis of psychopathology was the elucidation of the False Self; earlier in his working life he had divided the three domains of pathology more or less evenly: neurosis belonged to Freud, depressive states to Klein, and the psychotic and borderline states to Winnicott.

CLINICAL USE OF REGRESSION

A number of clinical strategies resulted from this weighting of the preoedipal period. First, probably, was the desirability and therapeutic necessity of a deep regression during the course of a psychoanalysis. Winnicott (1950s) re-defined regression in object-relations terms as

an adult's or a child's state in the transference (or in any other dependent relationship) when a forward position is given up and an infantile dependence is re-established. . . . The term "regression" is also used to describe the *process* that can be observed in a treatment, a gradual shedding of the false or caretaker self, and the approach to a new relationship in which the caretaker self is handed over to the therapist. [p. 44]

Winnicott stressed that the therapist must be prepared for the depth of the regression and must anticipate the need to be trustworthy, reliable, and consistent to an unusual degree while working with a very troubled and regressed patient. With particular patients the setting itself (the therapist, the office, the predictability) becomes more therapeutic than interpretations. In the following vignette the therapist skillfully provides an interpretive narrative for the meeting of a regressed patient's demand.

> The patient, a woman in her early thirties who met the criteria for borderline personality disorder, was in twice-a-week psychotherapy. She developed a dislike for a particular decorative object in the therapist's office and finally, one day, virtually exploded with her irritation and asked the therapist to remove it. The therapist pointed out to her how encouraging it was that she had reached the point at which she could make such a demand, could ask such a thing of him (in other words, he was finding the element of hope and potential for healthy growth in a seemingly outrageous and inappropriate request). He responded that he liked that item and thus would not banish it from his office entirely, but as he understood how much she disliked it he would remove it from her view before each of her sessions. And he did so, reliably, for months until the patient told him not to bother any longer.

Winnicott (1964) states:

> It is because of the development in the patient that there is this gradual demand for a specialised environmental provision. In the kind of case I am talking about it is never a question of giving satisfactions in the ordinary manner of succumbing to a seduction. It is always that if one provides certain conditions work can be done and if one does not provide these conditions work cannot be done and one might as well not try. [p. 97]

> So in the end we succeed by failing—failing the patient's way. . . . I must not fail in the child-care and infant-care aspects of the

treatment until at a later stage when *she will make me fail* in ways determined by her past history. [Winnicott 1963, pp. 258–259]

TRANSFERENCE AND THE HOLDING ENVIRONMENT

This view of the importance of regression implies a shift in the conception of the place of the analyst in the therapy. From a position outside the patient where the therapist was supposed to be able to identify and interpret distortions in reality-testing as expressed through transference manifestations, the therapist now becomes a sort of transference partner—an active participant in the patient's experience of the therapeutic encounter, which amounts to a reenactment of the traumatogenic phenomena. The reliability and predictability of the therapist contribute to the development of a holding environment for the patient, the necessary condition for regression.

When Winnicott speaks of holding we understand it metaphorically, and we recall his reference in the citation above cautioning against providing undue gratifications to the patient. Nonetheless it must be told that the master himself occasionally held patients in the literal sense and at times bought them groceries or wrote to them when they were hospitalized (Little 1990). Despite these modifications he used with borderline and psychotic patients, Winnicott otherwise held to a classical analytic technique. He preferred to give a patient no more than one interpretation per hour, although it could be given in several parts, and cautioned against the analyst slipping into a teaching mode: "Moreover, in my view an interpretation containing the word 'moreover' is a teaching session" (Winnicott 1962, p. 167). Winnicott (1971) further speaks of the importance of timing in the clinical setting: "Interpretation outside the ripeness of the material is indoctrination and produces compliance" (p. 59). The impression of Winnicott the clinician is of one extremely sensitive to the level of regression in patients, a restrained and modest interpreter, and one who appreciated the importance he held for his patients. Lest this seem an idyllic view of treatment, Winnicott (1971) also writes, it should be noted, of the importance of hate in the transference and the countertransference (related to the hate he believed each mother felt for her child). This serves to emphasize Winnicott's belief that cure rested not entirely in self-knowledge, as Freud had held, but in the capacity to feel real.

> Psychotherapy is not making clever and apt interpretations; by and large it is a long-term giving the patient back what the patient brings. It is a complex derivative of the face that reflects what there is to be seen. I like to think of my work this way, and to think that if I do this well enough the patient will find his or her own self, and will be able to exist and to feel real. Feeling real is more than existing; it is finding a way to exist as oneself, and to have a self into which to retreat for relaxation. [pp. 137–138]

CASE ILLUSTRATION

Among the most important concepts in object relations theory are the false self and the transitional object. The process of attaining object- and self-constancy requires the young child to negotiate a veritable emotional minefield. The child may indeed have an innate striving to be as related to others as possible, but developing this capacity requires appropriate responsiveness in the environment; most important, says Winnicott, is the good-enough mother. The following case, assessed and treated in a style heavily influenced by Winnicott, illustrates the importance of the transitional object and how a false self develops in response to a mother's inability to permit her daughter to retain and rely on her transitional object.

BACKGROUND INFORMATION

C., an 18-year-old white woman, began treatment with Dr. T., an elderly white clinical social worker, saying she wanted to "come and talk to you about how to get my life together and not feel as bad about my mother." C. was about 75 pounds overweight and quite unhappy about this. She had made many efforts to diet but felt that her family wanted her to stay fat. This would undermine her determination. Having just become interested in dating, she wished to lose weight to make herself more attractive to men. C. was then living with her mother, a 60-year-old AA-affiliated sober alcoholic, and her 23-year-old brother, unemployed and with an alcohol problem. The brother's twin lived abroad and was a successful businessman. C.'s father, a 72-year-old semiretired lawyer, left home and returned many times during C.'s life; he had a serious problem with alcohol. The family was extremely wealthy, C.'s grandfather having made money as a clothing manufacturer, and C. was thus easily able to finance her weekly therapy, which lasted for five years. She never missed an appointment, except on rare occasions of illness, and always paid her bills promptly; in these respects she was what she tried very hard to be—an ideal patient.

The event that prompted C. to seek help was her father's return home. This seemed to disrupt the relationship C. had strived to achieve with her mother; "I'd been *her* mother since my father left and now he wants to come back and take over." Dr. T. initially credited C. with what seemed like a significant level of insight into the family dynamics despite the obvious enmeshment with her mother. Later, though, when insights such as this did not lead to any change in behavior (weight loss, moving away from home, or completing school), it became clear that the patient presented what Dr. T. came to think of as a "pseudo-mature posture." C. possessed a lively intelligence, although she had never finished high school; during the early part of therapy she read (and made reference in sessions to) many of Freud's works; indeed, she presented herself as highly competent, always well-groomed and dressed and composed in manner. It was only after some time that Dr. T. began to experience the impenetrable quality of the impeccable surface.

In this first stage of treatment, C. tried to give Dr. T. an easy hour—in other words, she was replicating with Dr. T. the way in which she had had to limit the expression of her own needs in order to make sure that her caregiver was intact. C. went further than this, though. She tried to make herself attractive, physically and intellectually, to Dr. T., fearing that he would not be emotionally available to a less-than-ideal C.; in fact C.'s childhood illness—a failure to be perfect—did give occasion for her mother to lose the capacity to take care of her. Thus, feeling undeserving of care, she came to Dr. T. for help, presenting herself as a person with no needs of her own, with all the essential ingredients of a false self.

C. was an unplanned baby ("I believe I was an accident"), born to middle-aged parents. She was said to have been a "perfect baby" until the age of 18 months when she almost died of meningitis. Her mother, from that time on, lived in terror that C. would die and began a pattern of overprotectiveness and overindulgence. C. recalled feeling "overloved and overcuddled," thus learning that she had a frightening (to her) ability to control her mother. She also sensed her mother's vulnerability, likely a result of crippling guilt; C. began at a very young age to take care of her mother. The enmeshment was so strong between mother and daughter that, when Dr. T. asked early in the initial assessment whether C. had ever considered moving away from home, she instantly developed an asthma attack.

In normal, healthy adults, this capacity to put one's own needs temporarily on hold is supported by a sufficient maturation and, above all, by experiences of having been adequately nurtured and satisfied oneself. In C., this ability to be a caregiver had to develop prematurely at a great cost to her own development. Incidents in which C. literally rescued her comatose inebriated mother by calling an ambulance were counterbalanced by episodes in which she continued to have violent temper tantrums long after toddlerhood. The family mythology C. related held that by latency she had become a tyrant. From age 8 through puberty she would raid the refrigerator in the middle of the night, slamming doors to wake people up when she couldn't find anything she wanted to eat. As in other areas, her mother had been unable to deny C. much as far as food was concerned, and by age 12 C. outweighed her mother. Limit setting in general was a problem during these years; for instance, C. often chose to stay up watching television until 2 in the morning. During this time, C.'s father lived with the family only sporadically. She remembers his time at home to be full of conflict; in their many arguments the father seemed to this young girl to be authoritarian and harshly critical. Dr. T.'s impression was of an intrusive and inappropriate parent who was consistent only in his emotional unavailability. Dr. T. believed that C. had been school-phobic, probably out of the need to make sure her mother was all right. She dropped out of school at age 16, but it was not until a year later that her mother finally got to AA. In sum, this was a family in which poor self–other differentiation and psychological intrusiveness were the norm.

TREATMENT

Dr. T. nonetheless felt that C. would be able to enter into an adequate therapeutic alliance for productive work to occur; he sensed a survivor mentality in C., an intelligence and solidity even stronger than the false self. Another telltale sign of strength was that C. was able to recall a transitional object – a teddy bear—that her mother could not tolerate. When C. was 4 ½, her mother put the teddy bear in the trash compactor. C. recalled this: "She said, 'Why do you need this thing any more, you've got me?,' only I didn't have her." She reported what Dr. T. saw as a transference dream in which an older woman asked, "What will make you happy?" C.'s response: "To eat anything I want and then to have my teddy bear." Dr. T.'s formulation was that C. must have gotten from her mother in her first 18 months if perhaps not a sense of being good enough then at least a sense of the possibility that one day she could be good; she had survived a severely traumatic childhood and yet was able to begin to respond to a good-enough therapist. In fact, Dr. T. was an unusually sensitive and gentle individual and thus an excellent match for C.'s particular vulnerabilities.

C. spent most of the first year of therapy talking about her parents, putting them down for not having done better by her. She was particularly angry at her father for returning home just when her mother seemed to have reached a precarious stability in her functionings. C. began to lose weight and was frightened about what this would mean for her; she experienced great anxiety upon feeling her pelvic bones for the first time since childhood. In the following dialogue, she and Dr. T. discuss her ambivalence about the weight loss:

C.: Well, I've lost about 27 pounds.

Dr.T.: What's that like for you?

C.: It doesn't make any difference because no one can tell. I'm still the same.

Dr. T.: Is that good or bad?

C.: Well, in a way I want to keep it; it's mine and I own it. If I gave it up then everybody else would win.

Dr. T.: Does "everybody" include me?

C.: Well, if I lose weight everyone will think therapy is a big success.

Dr. T.: Would that be so bad?

C.: Well, I'd be like everybody else, I'd have knuckled under. The me I knew would disappear.

Dr. T.: Perhaps you're worried that if you let the weight go you'll disappear here, too.

C.: Yeah, if I'm thin I'll be well, and you won't want to see me anymore.

Dr. T.: So I'll disappear, too.

C.'s weight clearly had been part of her identity; but this identity had defined a false self. C. was afraid that if she relinquished this characteristic that had served for so long to stabilize her family that she would lose not only the only self she had ever consciously known but also the only intense relationships to external objects she had ever known. Notice in particular C.'s third remark in the dialogue in which she speaks of her weight as though it is a discrete object. Food and weight were transitional phenomena for C. as she struggled to grow up in an environment that denied her appropriate transitional experiences. She felt as possessive of her weight as she did of her teddy bear and accordingly had intense anxiety about relinquishing it.

In the second year of treatment C. continued to play out her wish to give Dr. T. an "easy hour." In the dialogue below, the therapist attempts to make this desire part of the subject matter of the session, to talk about it rather than to enact it. But C. continued to play the role of the perfect patient, habitually sitting with folded hands, maintaining eye contact, and reporting many dreams; in fact, Dr. T. came to look forward to C.'s sessions. He was aware, though, that C. must have been struggling to control her affect as she blandly reported violent fights between her parents. Dr. T. thus considered that the first time C. cried in a session constituted a turning point in treatment. In this interchange C. reacts to her crying:

C.:   This is stupid, I can't do this.

Dr. T.: Why not?

C.:   It must be hard, seeing me, wondering how to help me.

Dr. T.: Can you say a little more about that?

C.:   You must get so burned out. It must be so draining to listen to other people's problems day in and day out. . . . Some people just dump it on you. Me, I think about it and try to pull it all together so you won't feel so overwhelmed.

Dr. T.: You worry that I'll feel overwhelmed.

C.:   (laughs) I kind of see myself as your easiest patient, you know, the kind you read about that tell dreams and all. . . .

Dr. T.: And if you're not easy . . . ?

C.:   Well, you might get uncomfortable or start to be tired and fall asleep.

Dr. T.: So you need to make sure you keep me awake.

C. had developed enough trust in Dr. T.'s ability to tolerate her that she was able to cry and to express her fears about how that might affect the therapist. She had previously acted as though it were necessary to treat Dr. T. as no more competent than her own mother. C.'s ability to work in the transference was becoming quite good, particularly in the context of a once weekly frequency when she would have to work to maintain a sense of continuity from session to session.

During the second and third years of therapy, C. lost an additional 20 pounds and made gains in other areas of her life as well. She received her high school equivalency certificate, took a job as a receptionist, and bought a car. However, each gain seemed to entail some kind of regression, for instance, going on disability for two months to treat a constant backache. In the following year, the fourth, C. regained all her weight and more. Dr. T. had been most enthusiastic about C.'s achievements, and C. experienced this as an empathic failure: "I have to lose weight at my own speed. When you helped me lose weight it was like you took something I needed away from me." It felt to C. as though Dr. T.'s enthusiastic acceptance of the many significant concrete gains was becoming a repetition of her early life.

C.'s mother had been unable to tolerate any signs of independence and differentiation in her daughter. C.'s healthy attachment to a transitional object threatened her mother's obviously precarious sense of self-confidence. When her mother destroyed the teddy bear in the trash compactor, C. learned that object ties *of her own choosing* were dangerous. She retreated to using food and her body as a kind of precursor to a real transitional object; C. had been forced into a regression. In C.'s choice of her own body she had found a private sphere in which her mother could less easily intrude. In other words, although use of one's body as a transitional object is clearly less healthy than use of an external object, perhaps on the level of the two mental representations (of the body and the external object) it represented a sidestep rather than a total retreat into schizoid unrelatedness or a regression to a pretransitional position. (However, Winnicott [1953] does define "transitional object" as the actual physical item collected by the child rather than the mental representation of that item.) C.'s quest for relatedness and for transitional space was not entirely thwarted by her mother's violence and intrusions. In the treatment this was apparent in C.'s ability to benefit from Dr. T.'s help and to engage in a therapeutic relationship.

C.'s weight gain led to a dramatic rise in her blood pressure, and Dr. T. began to doubt the wisdom of having undertaken long-term dynamically oriented therapy; however, he doubted that C. would be able to sustain any weight loss achieved through behavioral or medical intervention. The patient consulted an internist and, fortunately, her blood pressure responded to the removal of salt from her diet; so the psychological regression that led to the weight gain could be allowed to continue. Other unhealthy behaviors, though, ensued; C. became rather promiscuous and did not use any form of birth control.

In the fifth and final year of therapy C. lost most of her excess weight and seemed to settle at a comfortable level. She was also able to verbalize her anxieties, such as "disorientation" upon feeling her pelvic bones again, and work them through in therapy sessions. She moved to her own apartment and applied to various colleges. During this final year C. continued to relinquish her need to take care of her helper. On one occasion she expressed anger that Dr. T. was slim: "You can't understand." (Ironically, Dr. T. could understand quite well as he had struggled with his own weight since adolescence; he had thus had some disturbing countertransference during this long encounter with C.)

Termination took place in a less than ideal fashion when Dr. T. announced with some trepidation that he was planning to retire from his practice of psychotherapy. C. was distraught, and her response demonstrates both how far she had come and how much she could yet have achieved in therapy. She did not regain any weight—a considerable achievement considering the number of years she had used her own body as a transitional object. C. had relinquished the intense need she had had for almost constant daily transitional eating that had brought her into treatment. She was also able to continue living independently and began to study for a college degree. Nonetheless it cannot be said that the impending termination was only a minor difficulty for C. Dr. T.'s retirement did not constitute what Winnicott called an "inevitable nontraumatic frustration" but rather a narcissistic injury too severe for C. to risk repeating. Despite a carefully arranged referral to a younger and very talented colleague C. decided not to continue treatment. The colleague would later report to Dr. T. that C. had telephoned to cancel the first scheduled appointment saying,

"This was too much; I can't do this again." It is a measure of C.'s strength that she was able to undertake at least some anticipatory mourning with Dr. T. and did not flee from treatment before the scheduled ending date.

As she prepared to terminate, C. became preoccupied with Dr. T.'s behavior and facial expressions and was able to realize that she was searching for evidence that Dr. T. loved her. Dr. T. felt that C. was trying to "fix" him in her mind, to find a way to make permanent a mental image of him, when the following interchange occurred.

C.:   I had a dream that your answering service called during our session and that you had to leave for a few minutes to handle some kind of emergency. While you were out of your office I looked around to find something to take with me.

Dr. T.:   What are you thoughts about this?

C.:   (Blushing) Well, I guess I wanted to steal something. You know, you have that paperweight that looks like a crystal ball. Maybe I could put it on my bed table.

Dr. T.:   You mean take it to your own territory.

C.:   Well, it feels so crazy, when I'm sitting on the bed and talking on the phone to my family, that the ball would be something stable, something that belongs here with us.

Dr. T.:   And why the paperweight?

C.:   (Laughs) It's crossed my mind that you use the crystal ball to figure me out. It would always let me know what was going on inside me.

C. showed just how much she had gained from treatment in this exchange in which her poignant wish is for a transitional object that represented the analyzing and understanding function of the therapist.

CONCLUSION

Treatment based on the writings of Winnicott aims, as this case demonstrates, to provide the patient with a stable therapeutic relationship (holding environment) managed by a healthy and competent therapist (ordinarily devoted mother). The therapist's goal is to be optimally gratifying—establishing and maintaining the positive transference—as well as optimally frustrating—not providing support that the patient can generate for himself. In this setting the patient can regress to the point when the false self first came into being and can resume a healthy course of development.

5   MARGARET MAHLER: THE QUANDARY OF PSYCHOLOGICAL CONNECTION AND INDEPENDENCE

Margaret Mahler (1897–1985) was a child psychoanalyst known primarily for pioneering work on the early development of children. Of Hungarian birth, she trained in Vienna originally as a pediatrician and then as a psychoanalyst before coming to the United States where she practiced in New York City. Mahler was among the first clinicians to regard the severe disorder of childhood—infantile psychosis—as a pathological variant of what she would come to describe more elaborately in her later work as a normal stage of development—symbiosis. Like other post-Freudian analysts, Mahler stressed the very great extent of psychological development that takes place before the oedipal period; by contrast, Freud saw the working through of the oedipal crisis as the major task of childhood. This chapter outlines Mahler's developmental schema (which is already, deservedly, well known in the field) and presents a case that illustrates separation-individuation pathology in an adult.

MAHLER'S THEORETICAL NICHE

Although Mahler claimed allegiance to (and is generally seen as belonging to) the school of ego psychology, her work is not easily categorized. For one thing, unlike most psychoanalytic writers, Mahler bases much of her work on systematic studies of the observable behavior of children and their mothers; she does not base her theories only on the intensive examination of a few analytic cases. In addition many writers have drawn conclusions about childhood development and experiences as they are expressed by troubled adults (in the form of dreams, memories, or transference behaviors). Mahler has studied normal as well as troubled children. Finally, although the subject matter Mahler addresses is essentially that of object relations, she does not affiliate herself with the school of object relations theorists. Paradoxically, while Mahler's research clearly indicates the importance of the relationship between infant and mother in the first days and weeks of life, she espouses the notion of primary narcissism — "a Freudian concept to which I find it most useful to adhere" (Mahler 1968, p. 10).

In the state of primary narcissism the infant is believed to be unaware that stimuli have sources outside himself; moreover, there is a lack of orientation toward the outside environment for at least the first few weeks of life. According to this perspective, object relations are motivated solely by the drive to satisfy physical needs; there is no other pressure to relate to the environment. However, at times Mahler makes statements that seem to throw into question her adherence to the concept of primary narcissism. For instance, she postulates that severe autism has its roots in the first week of life:

Because of the infant organism's lack of autonomous somatic defense functions as well as because of the disorientation to what is inside and what is outside of the organismic self, even the most primitive orientation and coping must be promoted and helped by the mothering partner. We are inclined to assume that in cases of early autism, organismic distress of such magnitude affects the organism at such an early stage of maturity that it certainly *destroys the perception of the mother as functioning on his behalf.* [Mahler 1968, p. 64, emphasis added]

Mahler seems to be implying that at least a primitive sense of mothering-person-as-helper exists just about from birth, that is to say during the period supposedly characterized by primary narcissism. Mahler (1968) also suggests that this inability to accept mothering may be nonpsychological in cause:

If [this turning a deaf ear toward mother and to the entire world] is an acquired somatopsychic defense, it develops so early (at or after birth) that psychic content and meaning are open to question. . . . Perhaps there exist severe intrauterine physiological incompatibilities between fetus and mother which result in this negative autistic reaction. . . .

In contrast, the symbiotic psychotic child has some awareness of the mothering principle. [p. 65]

THE VULNERABLE NEWBORN

Mahler vacillates between a view of the ego as strong and adaptive — prewired with what Hartmann would call autonomous ego apparatuses — and a view of the infant's psyche as fragile, again lending doubt to her espousal of primary narcissism, which implies that the infant possesses a certain ability to protect itself from external stimuli. Ego psychologists hold that the emerging ego is relatively strong and adaptive. Object relations theorists tend not to believe that there exists a state of primary narcissism, and thus see the infant as vulnerable to damage from the environment (as well as from internal impulses) from birth.

In *The Psychological Birth of the Human Infant* (subtitled

"Symbiosis and Individuation") Mahler and her colleagues (1975) stressed the great variability in the combinations of infant disposition and mothering style that can result in normal development. In her earlier work, *On Human Symbiosis and the Vicissitudes of Individuation* (subtitled "Infantile Psychosis") (1968), she reported the clinical observation that children are unable to integrate (even primitively) the good and bad aspects of themselves and their mothers until the second year of life; surely this leaves a baby prone to serious emotional damage in the first year of life (as Mahler indeed demonstrates). Note that Mahler's clinical observations with regard to the developmental timetable are in step with these of other writers; for instance, Melanie Klein labels and interprets similar data from a different metapsychological perspective when she writes of the development of the depressive position.

It should be stressed, however, that, although they sometimes use similar language, Mahler and Klein (and later, Kernberg) may be describing different phenomena. Mahler is not addressing herself primarily to the question of how libido and aggression are articulated in the infant's developing world of mental representations. In other words, her concern is not to specify the ways in which young children come to have positively and negatively valenced representations of themselves and their important early objects, although her work does have some bearing on this. Rather, she is telling the history of a parallel developmental process by which the child comes to understand the fact of separateness from mother and by which the maturational thrust toward individuation takes place. A further clarification is also needed here, for the terms Mahler uses are confusing. *Symbiosis* used accurately in its original biological sense refers to a two-way dependence between two organisms that need each other in order to survive; both benefit from the relationship. Mahler does not use the word in this way. For her, symbiosis denotes only the mental experiencing of the infant, the *dual unity* in which, she believes, the baby assumes himself to be embedded. (*Autistic*, too, is a poor way of describing the early weeks of life; both terms emerged from Mahler's earlier work on childhood psychosis.) Mahler's dual unity is not very distant from Winnicott's assertion that there is no such thing as a baby but only babies-and-mothers.[1] Although Margaret Mahler is generally seen as being an ego psychologist, in some respects she partakes of and helps engender an object relations perspective. Where she does not waver theoretically is in her adherence to the drive satisfaction model to explain the child's motivation.

PSYCHOLOGICAL BIRTH: THE SEPARATION/INDIVIDUATION PROCESS

Mahler's main thesis, as expressed in the title of her best-known work, is that infants are psychologically born not at the moment of emerging from the mother's body but instead during a very gradual process that occurs during the first three years of life. She terms this the *separation/individuation process*, and proposes that it is comprised of several phases and subphases of learning and development, with the adequate experiencing and working through of each as the necessary (but not sufficient) condition for the unfolding of the next.

NORMAL AUTISM

Normal autism, the first phase, occurs during the first few weeks of life. In this period, the infant is in a state of "absolute primary narcissism" (Mahler 1968, pp. 10–11). In other words, the newborn is only very minimally aware of the world beyond his body, and, indeed, has the ability to ignore most outside stimuli. Mahler and colleagues (1975) are correct in saying that "physi-

---

1. I am grateful to Henri Parens, M.D. for these clarifications.

ological rather than psychological processes [dominate this period]" (p. 41); however, other clinicians and writers (mainly from the object relations school) as well as many parents would hold that Mahler underestimates the psychological capacities and vulnerabilities of the newborn. Indeed, it has been reported that Mahler came to feel that "the word 'autistic' does not well describe what we now know about the neonate" (Bergman and Ellman 1985, p. 240). As later infant researchers such as Stern would describe, the newborn is quite attuned to the external world and has an astonishing array of abilities to perceive and discriminate. It is, however, unclear how "psychological" rather than "reflexive" these functions are. There is likely very little, if any, "self," in the sense of intentionality or agency, in these very early ego functions. Henri Parens (1994), for instance, has pointed out that a newborn is capable of hostile destructive urges in the first days of life; an infant who is repeatedly pinched will develop a rage reaction. But it cannot be said with any degree of certainty that this infant hates the pincher or has any accurate notion of the existence of another being who harbors sadistic intention.

The psychopathology associated with the inability to move beyond this early phase is obviously profound. Mahler (1968) calls it the *autistic syndrome*, or *early infantile autism*; she characterizes the autism as a psychotic defense against "the lack of that vital and basic need of the human young in his early months of life: symbiosis with a mother or a mother substitute" (p. 21). It is an axiom of psychodynamic thought that too much difficulty or dissatisfaction at a new, more mature level of functioning will lead to a return—regression—to a previously achieved and more comfortable level. Similarly, too much satisfaction at a particular phase of development can inhibit the unfolding of that maturational process and the push toward greater accomplishment and more differentiated mental functioning. In either case, failure to acquire more complex modes of relating to the environment places a restriction on the quality and quantity of satisfaction that can be attained. In other words, when it is impossible for the baby to receive nurturing from a mother (or mother substitute), the baby will be stuck in a pathological autistic mode. The next level of development, an articulation and definition of the relationship between baby and caregiver, will not occur. The crucial beginning of the specific attachment between this baby and this mother will be inhibited.

THE SYMBIOTIC PHASE

The onset of the normal symbiotic phase is marked by the infant's growing (but still dim) awareness of a need-satisfying or mothering agent who relieves those tensions that the infant cannot take care of alone. At about one month of age the infant's neurological system undergoes a surge in development, thus making the baby more sensitive to the environment, more vulnerable to overstimulation, and in more need of protection by the mother. (Parents and pediatricians know this to be the time when colic can develop.) Mahler and colleagues (1975) chose the term *symbiosis* to convey their impression that the infant at this stage "behaves and functions as though he and his mother were an omnipotent system—a dual unity within one common boundary" (p. 44). It is the specific smiling response that signifies that symbiosis has been established.

The symbiotic phase is crucial to healthy psychological development. The infant will either feel rewarded by this beginning engagement with the environment or will revert to autistic functioning. It is necessary for the baby to develop what Therese Benedek (1938) termed "confident expectation" (Mahler uses this phrase as well) that his needs will be met. During this phase (as well as later ones) confident expectation and the ability to trust the environment can be encouraged by providing appropriate and consistent satisfaction of those tensions the baby is unable to reduce on his own. Constant inappropriate satisfying of needs— such as feeding a baby who is not hungry, trying to satisfy a need the baby does not experience — can give rise to serious psychopathology in later life: an impaired sensitivity to the status of one's own needs. Such faulty ability to discern the feeling states of one's baby is strongly suggestive of narcissistic pathology in the caregiver. (Daniel Stern addresses this issue with his concept of the RIG [see Chapter 8], the vehicle through which psychopathology may be passed from one generation to another.) The concepts of tension reduction and homeostasis, which Mahler treats as central to this process, reflect Freud's belief that the basic struggle of the infant was to restore and maintain psychological and physical equilibrium in the face of increased tension (excitation) caused both by external, environmental stimulation and by internal, instinctual, drive-based needs.

Normal autism and symbiosis are both phases of nondifferentiation, with autism being "objectless" and symbiosis "preobjectal." Mahler and colleagues (1975) call these stages the "forerunners of the separation-individuation process" (p. 41). In the most serious psychopathological condition, autism, symbiosis is never achieved, probably due to either a poor "fit" between mother and infant or some inborn deficiency in the baby. In the case of symbiotic child psychosis, the ego regresses to the symbiotic state defined as a "hallucinatory or delusional somatopsychic *omnipotent* fusion with the representation of the mother and the delusion of a common boundary between two physically separate individuals" (pp. 44–45).

The Subphase of Differentiation

The first subphase proper, *differentiation*, ranges approximately from 4 or 5 months to 10 months. Differentiation is marked by the following behavioral changes: the infant no longer "molds" to the mother when she holds him but instead holds himself more upright; the infant no longer has times of being "tuned out" even while awake; and the infant begins to reach out to explore physically the body and accessories of the mother (or other caregiver). Mahler uses the word *hatching* to describe this early part of differentiation. Later on the baby will express interest in the not-so-immediate environment, using what Mahler called the "checking-back pattern" to glance back at the mother from time to time, learning that there is a difference between "mother and other." The successful achievement of this is marked by the appearance of stranger awareness. Mahler believes that adequate "confident expectation" allows the baby to experience curiosity rather than anxiety, although this is a statement of the ideal rather than the usual.

This first subphase is called "differentiation and the development of the body image." By this Mahler is referring to the critical developmental task of boundary definition, which she sees as beginning during this phase. The baby is now able to distinguish internal from external sensations and thus can begin to develop "a clear sensory discrimination between self and object" (Greenberg and Mitchell 1983, p. 275). The ability to know mother from others in the environment is a refinement of this.

The Subphase of Practicing

The next subphase of the separation-individuation process is called *practicing*; it begins during the end of the differentiation period. Early practicing takes place when the infant first becomes physically capable of moving away from the mother in all ways except by walking. The practicing subphase proper requires "free, upright locomotion," to use Mahler's words.

At least three interrelated, yet discriminable, developments contribute to the child's first steps toward awareness of separateness and toward individuation. These are the rapid *body differentiation* from the mother, the establishment of a *specific bond* with her, and the growth and functioning of the *autonomous ego apparatuses in close proximity to the mother* (Mahler et al. 1975). At this stage it is important for the mother to remain available to the baby for what Mahler calls "emotional refueling" as the baby engages in experimenting with physical separation. Also during this time babies increase their interest in and knowledge of the world of inanimate objects; this may be expressed by the choosing of a transitional object, an inanimate object having qualities that resemble some characteristic or attribute of the mother, such as softness. (See Chapter 4 for a fuller description of the transitional object.)

Mahler dates the phenomenon of *psychological birth* to the practicing subphase proper, the time when the baby has learned to walk. The baby is in love with himself as well as with the world, at the height of feelings of omnipotence. For the child to have a successful practicing period, the mother must be able to allow the child to begin assuming ownership of his body and its capacities; the mother is used as a kind of "home base." Despite the repeated leaving and returning, though, the practicing child does not truly appreciate that the mother is separate.

The Critical Subphase of Rapprochement

The *rapprochement* subphase usually begins between the fifteenth and the eighteenth months. The child's sense of himself achieved during the practicing subphase as a separate person with unlimited abilities changes; the realization dawns that he in reality is a small and quite vulnerable person in a big world. Separation anxiety thus will increase at this time. The toddler is coming to see the mother as a separate person—and one who is sometimes unavailable to or incapable of meeting the toddler's every need.

Mahler and colleagues (1975) stress that while "the need for closeness had been held in abeyance" during the practicing subphase, the issue of closeness is central to the emotional life of the rapprochement-subphase toddler. One sees in the behavior of the toddler a desire for "intimate bodily contact" as well as a fear of it; the toddler will vacillate in the protection of his hard-won "autonomy." Mahler used "shadowing" and "warding-off" to describe the behaviors that reflect what she calls the child's "wish for reunion with the love object and his fear of re-engulfment by it" (p. 77). Verbal communication attains importance equal to the physical relationship during rapprochement as the toddler tries to engage the mother in his activities; the child has developed a beginning awareness of separateness.

The *rapprochement crisis* (from about 18 to 24 months of age), in which the child learns to balance the need to be separate, the need to be involved with mother, and the fear of being re-engulfed by mother, is a pivotal point in development. Mahler believes that the child's emotional life at this time is characterized by great ambivalence, which is expressed by the "terrible twos" behavior syndrome of alternating periods of clinginess and battling. Also, the child's major anxiety is undergoing a transformation. More accurately, a new fear is getting layered on top of the previous one. The toddler no longer only has the fear of losing the object, but now comes to fear losing the love of the object. (This progression represents the move to the next of the danger situations that Freud had identified in his writing on anxiety.) The child is struggling to integrate the love and the rage he feels toward the mother; it is a struggle to be able to see mother (and self) as possessing good and bad qualities. The defense mechanism associated with this struggle is splitting. Normal at this age, splitting becomes extremely inefficient as an adult coping mechanism.

Borderline personality organization, which is characterized by the use of splitting, is thought by Mahlerians to result from the failure to negotiate the rapprochement crisis successfully. This crisis presents challenges for both baby and mother. It is crucial for the mother to remain emotionally available to the toddler throughout this time. If she cannot do this, as will be shown in the case illustration, the child will learn powerful and dangerous lessons about separation and individuation. The father becomes quite important during this period as an alternate object, a source of relatedness untainted by the same struggle that characterizes the relationship with the mother. An appropriately available father can compensate to some extent for compromised mothering. (Although Lacan does not speak of the separation/individuation process as such, his theory does address the central role of the father and of language in breaking open the mother–child dyad. Thomas Wolman, M.D., explores the interdigitation of Lacanian and Mahlerian theory in his as yet unpublished essay, "Separation/Individuation Viewed Through a Lacanian Lens.")

The Subphase That Never Ends . . .

The fourth subphase Mahler has named "consolidation of individuality and the beginnings of emotional object constancy." Note that "object constancy" is to be distinguished from Piaget's "object permanence," an earlier phenomenon that refers to the recognition that an object does not cease to exist when it is no longer in view. Mahler stresses that we struggle to attain emotional object constancy throughout our lives. In this effort one must develop a sense of oneself as constant as well as a stable sense of the other; this is impossible if one is still relying on the rapprochement phase defense of splitting. One must recognize simultaneously one's own individuality and the separateness of the other.

Also important to grasp is the distinction between separation and individuation:

> Separation and individuation are conceived of as two complementary developments; separation consists of the child's emergence from a symbiotic fusion with the mother . . . , and individuation consists of those achievements marking the child's assumption of his own individual characteristics. They are intertwined but not identical developmental processes; they may proceed divergently, with a developmental lag or precocity in one or the other. [Mahler et al. 1975, p. 4]

Individuation in particular is a lifelong process but, as Mahler has shown, it cannot take place if most of the crucial emotional development — attaining a sense of psychic separateness — is not accomplished in the first three years of life.

CASE ILLUSTRATION

Mahler's major contribution was the development of a theory of a separation-individuation process that seemed to explain the data she and co-workers gathered in their observations of small children and their mothers; separation and individuation are lifetime tasks central to healthy psychological functioning, and the failure to achieve an adequate degree of psychic separateness from one's mother in the first two years of life will predispose an individual to serious psychopathology. The following case shows the centrality of these issues in an adult with borderline personality organization. Mahler's theory can be used as a guide — a metaphor — for understanding the patient, for we are not looking at a troubled toddler but at a child's troubles magnified and distorted by the years of life she navigated through without adequate emotional resources.

M., a 30-year-old single Jewish woman, came to a community mental health center suffering from panic attacks so severe she thought she was going crazy. Several months earlier her first and only sexual relationship had ended; she had been living with her lover, a Catholic woman, for almost three years. This woman left M. "with no warning," leaving only a brief note saying that she had not been happy with M. for some time. In the course of treatment, it turned out that there had, indeed, been many subtle and not-so-subtle indications of the lover's intentions that M. had not been able to allow herself to understand. M. worked as a technician in a research laboratory and reported no difficulties there; her job entailed minimal contact with people, and the quality of her work was so outstanding that her boss seemed to tolerate the periodic manifestations of her difficulties in getting along with others. Before coming to this agency she had sought and received counseling for three months at a center for sexual minorities; dissatisfied with what she had perceived as propaganda and empty support from her counselor there, she now said she was looking for more "serious" treatment.

In her initial session with Ms. J., a clinical social worker in her forties, M. presented two interconnected areas she wished to address. First, she wanted to understand what she called her "sexual preference conflict": was she really a lesbian or could she relate to men? She was 30 at the time and she anticipated the ticking of the proverbial biological clock, the life-cycle pressure of whether she would ever have children. Second, she talked about a Jewish identity conflict. Her lover had been Catholic and M., ever since leaving home to go to college, had been very involved with Catholics; indeed, some of her friends were nuns. These presenting complaints are suggestive of the phenomenon of identity diffusion, a typical feature in borderline personality organization.

M. was the second of two children; her sister was two years older. The parents, both children of immigrants, were in their late thirties before they began having children. The father had achieved moderate success in his career as a librarian, directing a large branch of a city library. The mother worked as a secretary to the president of a medium-sized company until her first pregnancy. Having tried unsuccessfully for years to have children, they had resigned themselves to childlessness and were therefore stunned when their first daughter was conceived. The difficult road to parenthood may well have contributed to some of the problems that M. experienced as she grew up; it had taken so long to get these children that the mother could not easily let them go. M.'s parents were approaching 70 years of age at the time she began treatment.

M. did not have detailed knowledge of her early development but believed that she had attained the various milestones of development on a normal timetable. There had been no childhood illnesses of more than routine severity. M.'s trauma was not related to any specific episode but instead to the cumulative effect of her mother's manipulative possessiveness. M. described her father as being passive, uninvolved, and aloof, seemingly oblivious to the intense and conflictual relationship between M. and her mother. The older sister, to M.'s envy and bafflement, appeared to be untouched by the mother's histrionics. M., on the other hand, was never able, even as an adult, to dismiss her mother's complaints. She recalled that her mother would pretend to be ill (to be choking or having a heart attack) whenever M. tried to engage in an activity away from her (e.g., joining the Girl Scouts or sleeping over at a friend's house); this behavior, which continued through the present and had begun when M. was about 8, demonstrated an extraordinarily pathological and pathogenic (for M.) inability to tolerate separation from her child. Although M. did not recall any specific memories from the rapprochement period, it seemed fairly clear to the therapist that these dramatic threats probably represented an exacerbation of trends that had earlier been expressed in other ways. M.'s latency-age interest in teachers and peer friendships led to panic in the mother who accurately perceived M.'s attempt to attenuate their relationship. For M., school provided the first sustained opportunity for experimenting with separation and individuation. Although she did well academically and developed a few good friends, she was not popular; she was able to describe to her therapist a kind of constant tentativeness, an inability to immerse herself in the activities of her peers and of the school.

Thus M. grew up with a primary caregiver who punished separation and urges to individuate and who rewarded dependency, lack of individuation, and (later) regression. In any family it is ideally the father who provides an alternate object for the child who is learning to separate from the mother. In M.'s case, though, the father was emotionally unavailable.

Therefore, M. formed a close bond, characterized by admiration but tinged with envy, with her sister, which persisted through the years. M.'s sister had developed a counterdependent style of dealing with her mother. This made her the "bad girl" in the family; M., who retained her dependent and passive relationship with her mother stayed the "good girl," but at great cost.

M. remained at home while she attended college, doing well academically but taking no part in extracurricular life on campus. This bright but emotionally impoverished young woman had no trouble finding the job that she still had upon entering therapy. She moved away from home only when her parents, under the financial pressure of retirement, moved into a relatively small apartment. M.'s mother was unhappy with the situation (her husband had essentially made the decision to move), and telephoned M. several times a day. M. had not told her parents that the girlfriend with whom she lived was in fact her lover. Although the very fact that M. had a lover might appear to represent a capacity to separate, it is important to bear in mind how M. reacted to the termination of this relationship; psychologically, the relationship may well have represented an attempt at symbiosis. The panic attacks M. suffered were similar to the panic her own mother had experienced in the face of M.'s maturation; M., however, was healthy enough not to somatize her suffering but to create a psychological symptom. M.'s presenting complaint translates easily into Mahler's terminology and frame of understanding: she was telling the therapist she needed help coping with separation.

TREATMENT

This information about M. and her family background is presented here as though it had been available to the therapist in this form before treatment started. In fact this was not the case. Most of these facts emerged not during the initial assessment but during the course of a treatment that lasted over three years. Ms. J. began treating M. with once weekly psychotherapy, but it soon became clear that one session was inadequate to help M. deal with either the presenting anxiety or the underlying difficulties. M. became better able to enter the treatment process as the frequency of sessions was increased to two and then three times per week.

During the the first eight months of therapy, M.'s behavior escalated as she demonstrated to the therapist just how severe her problem with separation was. At the end of the session she would dissolve into tears and curl up on the floor in front of the door, refusing to leave the office; this constituted a truly malignant inability to leave the therapist. Patients' separation difficulties do tend to appear in the way in which they manage the end of sessions as well as other breaks in the treatment, such as vacations or cancellations by the therapist. (It should be noted that a therapist with unresolved separation conflicts may find it difficult to perceive the patient's actions as an expression of conflict.) M.'s reaction, though, was extreme. M. made a strong attachment to Ms. J. very early in the treatment such that the early months were characterized by this acting out of the separation issue in the transference arena. This suggests that this was truly a transference phenomenon representative of borderline functioning in that there had not been time for a genuinely close relationship to develop such that one might expect some sort of difficulty with ending—not that such a severe reaction would ever be expected in an adult. In other words, M. was not reacting to the actual qualities of *this* therapist but rather to a projected fantasy she had of Ms. J.

After M. collapsed on the floor she would complain to J. that the mental health center was "cruel and mean for forcing people to leave, for setting an arbitrary limit." She felt the center to be "an inhumane place." After leaving the office she would sit down in the hall outside. Note here how the patient splits the badness off from the good therapist—it is not the good therapist but the bad mental health center that makes her leave. By attributing all the responsibility for the perceived cruelty to the center instead of to Ms. J., M. displayed her reliance on splitting as a defense—she could not integrate the satisfying and the frustrating sides of Ms. J. (For a discussion of splitting, see Chapter 6.) Ms. J. understood M. to be splitting off the bad mother, the mother of separation, while experiencing the therapist as the good mother who surely would have allowed her to stay. Empathic interventions only served further to reinforce the split between good and bad "mother," even though the appropriate therapeutic goal was to try to help the patient heal the split, to help M. integrate and experience good and bad in a single person. Ms. J. was often provoked into raising her voice and saying firmly, "M., you have to leave." By this insistence she hoped to communicate that she had no doubts about M.'s ability to function outside of the office. But the provocative and aggressive nature of these daily occurrences should not be disregarded; the therapist felt drained, exhausted, and on edge after each session.

A RAPPROCHEMENT-LIKE TRANSFERENCE

Mahler emphasizes that the resolution of the rapprochement crisis depends to a great extent on the mother. Children have ambivalence about separating and doubt about their as-yet-untried capacity to function successfully outside of the mother's protective presence. The most deeply empathic intervention for a mother or therapist at this point may be to give as lovingly strong a "shove" as the child may need; appropriately empathic interventions do not always sound "nice" or "understanding." This clinical situation represented a crisis, though, because M. was behaving in such a way as to re-create what she remembered happening to her. The therapist became a participant in the enactment by virtue of the provocativeness of the infantile and clinging behavior that forced her to set limits and to be the rejecting "mother" that M. desired and feared. But M. was also confused: If Ms. J. was going to be like a good mother, why didn't she reward M.'s clinginess?

M. had learned that a "good mother" rewards dependence and regression while simultaneously punishing efforts to be independent; a "bad mother" sets limits to dependence. By her behavior in the therapeutic relationship, M. revealed how she had been treated as a child, acting out the unconscious assumption that Ms. J. would have to act like her mother if she was really to be a good therapist. When Ms. J. stood for separation, she stirred up all the associated painful affects. The bind for Ms. J. was that M. experienced as strange and frightening the therapist's ability to manage separation. Perhaps the most emotionally salient feature of the reenactment was the role reversal that M. had created and that the therapist effectively addressed. M. had unconsciously so identified with her mother's fear of separation that she threatened the therapist, using almost the same words her mother had used in her threats, when she said she was sure she would die if she were forced to leave the office. She was shocked when, one day, Ms. J. pointed out, "You are doing to me what your mother does to you." Role reversals in enactments are common: the patient may play either part. Either way, the task for the clinician is to understand the evoked countertransference experience as a way in which the patient is communicating an aspect of her affective history and present fears or wishes.

After about two years of intensive treatment M. understood enough about this wish to separate—and her fear of separation—that a therapeutic alliance developed. She was beginning to be able to talk about what she was feeling rather than act it out, and the end-of-session dependency behavior diminished. M. struggled with increasing success to understand and believe, affectively and intellectually, that her therapist was not like her mother and that the goal in therapy was to support M. in her desire (albeit an ambivalent one) to become an adult. Ms. J. came to feel that this extended phase of extreme dependence could have been averted if she had managed the session endings better with earlier interpretations like the one above; she was, at the time, a young clinician. However, enactments take place for a reason, and it is not clear that the patient would have been open to accepting interpretations any earlier; very likely, the patient needed to discover that the therapist was not like her mother, that neither she nor the therapist would react with illness or abandonment when the patient left. It was the therapist's reliability and the fact that both she and the patient survived the separations that perhaps allowed the patient enough distance from the affect storms to be able to make use of an explanatory interpretation. In effect, this therapist had permitted a rapprochement crisis to develop.

As M. began to be able to consider her feeling and behavior more objectively in the treatment, her acting out of separation conflicts continued to dissipate—to be replaced by a deep and suicidal depression. And, unfortunately, just as she was becoming fully aware of the critical nature of her difficulties with separation, her father died. She was thus faced with a genuine loss as well as with the crisis of abandonment she was experiencing in the transference. The immediate danger of her father's death just as M. was making the commitment to separation was that it further reinforced for M. the "fact" that separation incurred punishment.

Also during this time M. had been trying to sell the small condominium she and her lover had jointly owned. Although the sale had gone through and settlement rapidly approached, M. was unable to face the prospect of moving; in therapy sessions she exhibited an avoidance of reality in the face of this additional separation. After her father died, she moved back into her mother's apartment where she had not lived for many years. It was a sign of M.'s fear of independence that she had not been able to entertain the idea of moving to a place that would truly be her own, yet there were also some opportunities that she created for herself by this seeming step backward. Although this might seem an opportunity of dubious value, it did give M. the chance to work through the relationship with her mother *in vivo*. Ms. J. strongly suspected that this return to the mother was an acting out of transference wishes (or fears), but it was not possible to address this in treatment. Nonetheless, Ms. J. did feel it a significant measure of M.'s strength that she had not fled treatment entirely upon the death of her father.

The next months of treatment focused on coping with M.'s suicidal depression and on helping her mourn her father. It should be stressed that, during all of this, M. was continuing to function at her job without problems, thus underlining the many ego strengths she did possess as well as how successful the treatment was in restricting the expression of conflicts to the therapist's office. At home, M. began to confront her mother's habitual manipulative style as she again bombarded M. with constant complaints about her health (the complaints had in fact continued by phone while M. did not live there). The emotional insight and cognitive understanding achieved in therapy helped M. separate the reality of her mother's manipulations from her previous perceptions, which had been so influenced by her own fears and by her mother's panic in the face of "abandonment" by her daughter. M. gradually was able to leave the apartment even at times when mother declared herself to be near death. And with the support and insight gained in treatment, M. persevered, even reporting that her mother's behavior to her improved a bit as every whim was no longer gratified.

A NECESSARY TERMINATION

Although the focus in this case report has been primarily on the vicissitudes of separation, M. had been able to further her individuation during treatment. She had had herself tested and diagnosed as learning-disabled, she looked into going to graduate school for a master's degree, her identification as a Jew became stronger, and her friendships were becoming qualitatively better. But these quite considerable accomplishments were to be all that M. would achieve with Ms. J., for an insurmountable transference–countertransference crisis developed.

The final months of treatment became centered on the relationship between M. and Ms. J. M. moved out of her mother's home after a great deal of difficulty in finding a place she liked. The "only" apartment she found suitable turned out to be across the street from Ms. J.'s residence, which M. had seen on Ms. J.'s posted professional license; and following the move M. became very active in community events. The town being very small, it was common knowledge that Ms. J. was also involved in these very same activities. The result of this was that the two, therapist and patient, were now participating in the very same small group social events that took place almost on a weekly basis. Needless to say, the therapeutic relationship had become extremely complicated as M. had changed it, in great part, into a real relationship. The aggression toward Ms. J. in M.'s actions scarcely needs to be pointed out. Ms. J. felt intruded upon and attacked, yet was able to understand that M. had chosen this action because she had little capacity to express her enormous rage toward her mother. So terrified was M. about her destructive wishes, that she had been unable to acknowledge her anger at her mother, who had so effectively thwarted her development. Ms. J. believed that M.'s resistance to expressing this rage derived from her fear of becoming a dominant, aggressive woman like her mother, that is, the killer of her father.

One of the strongest forces in M.'s life had been her sister to whom she had turned as an alternate love-object during rapprochement. And Ms. J. saw elements of this in M.'s move from her mother's apartment to Ms. J.'s neighborhood. Ms. J. had become the main "other" in M.'s life, M. having had no lover and having shown no interest in getting one during the course of therapy. Ms. J. felt that M. had either fallen in love with her (this implying that M. was no longer able to maintain the "as if" quality of the transference) or was using her attachment to Ms. J.–as-therapist as a resistance, as a way of avoiding the psychosexual conflicts she feared in a relationship with a real lover. M. adamantly refused to discuss any sexual or romantic feelings she had for Ms. J. At the same time, her identification with Ms. J. was very strong, leading Ms. J. to believe that in the process of incorporating Ms. J.–internalizing her as a positive introject–M. had perhaps also begun to confuse their identities. Ms. J. saw this as a repetition of M.'s relationship with her older sister.

It was clear to Ms. J. that she could no longer be of help since M. refused to deal with the most pressing issue–the transference elements in their relationship. In acting out this transferred rage/love toward her therapist, M. created an intolerable situation for the therapist, and thus a situation in which her fear/wish would come true. Unable to interpret M.'s fusion fantasy, Ms. J. responded to M.'s euphoric declarations of how well she was doing by suggesting that perhaps it was time to terminate treatment. M. was no longer presenting ego-dystonic material and Ms. J. felt that the most responsible action, given her own anger at the patient, was to suggest to her that she continue treatment with a colleague if she felt it necessary in the future.

The ending phase of this case is very unusual. The normal therapeutic strategy would be for termination to be agreed upon by both therapist and patient instead of unilaterally proposed. For Ms. J. to have continued seeing M., though, would have meant reinforcing M.'s regression, her refusal to deal with issues verbally rather than through actions. Despite its unusual features, this case demonstrates how Mahler's concept of separation may function as a central issue around which the clinical data can be organized. The concrete difficulties with separation this patient displayed are indicative of severe psychopathology. Recall that Mahler's separation/individuation theory is not simply a story of how children relate to actual, physical people but about the mental representations of objects. Like children, though, M. expressed things in literal terms. The same issues, however, are present in more subtle ways in higher-functioning patients as they struggle to separate self from other and to individuate in their psychic representations of themselves.

6   OTTO KERNBERG:
CLINICAL AND THEORETICAL
UNDERSTANDING OF
BORDERLINE PHENOMENA

Otto Kernberg (born 1928) is no doubt best known for his pioneering work on the treatment of patients with borderline personality disorder, but his contribution to the field extends far beyond this specific clinical entity. Because he was educated for the most part in Chile, Kernberg's development as an analyst was influenced (more than would have been likely in the United States) by the Kleinian branch of the British school that had flowered in South America. As he himself describes, the borderline condition had been identified but not remotely understood during the 1950s. Clinicians and theoreticians were unsure whether it was in fact a form of psychosis, termed pseudoneurotic psychosis or "prepsychotic." Should treatment be supportive or exploratory? Kernberg's work with this population, which included leadership of the psychotherapy research project at the Menninger Foundation, led to significant clinical refinements and contributions as well as to metapsychological revisions as theory expanded to include previously unexplainable phenomena. Kernberg's treatment of borderline conditions has thus influenced the way in which we understand the assessment of psychopathology for all patients. Although Kernberg readily acknowledges his debts to the thinking of others, such as Edith Jacobson and Melanie Klein, it is perhaps not generally understood that much of his brilliance lies in his reorganization, refinement, synthesis, and applications of previous work.

PSYCHOANALYTIC-HISTORICAL CONTEXT

The obstacle to understanding borderline phenomena was rooted in the then-predominant view of all psychopathology, the model of psychosexual developmental phases proposed by Freud (1905b) in his "Three Essays on the Theory of Sexuality," which had essentially stood unmodified (Parens 1991). Borderline patients displayed clear oral stage–derived problems and yet also demonstrated pervasive problems with aggression (a trait that was associated with the anal phase) particularly in their sexual behavior. Kernberg (1980) states:

> Borderline patients, in short, defied all efforts to hypothesize the origin of their psychopathology in the usual manner—that is, by situating it along the line of libidinal development and its stages. To make matters worse, although clinical observation detected the presence of ego weakness, the examination of defense-impulse constellations often afforded no clear delineation of which agency within the tripartite structure (ego, superego, or id) was defending against which impulse from which other agency. [p. 4]

Today it seems difficult to imagine that era in psychoanalytic thinking when clinicians did not have the concept of psychological deficit we now take for granted, of psychopathology associated not with structural conflict but with deficits in the ego and in the formation of the structures of the id, ego and superego. But to appreciate the scope of Kernberg's contribution we must see it as addressing this deficit in theory. (Kohut, too, attempted to fill in this gap in the conceptualization of profound personality problems in his work on narcissism.)

Kernberg began his conceptualization of borderline functioning with a series of clinical observations that brought into clearer focus the diagnostic considerations and the theoretical unknowns. He argued that it made better sense to focus on the depth features of the syndrome than on the superficial descriptive features, which, because many of them were associated with other types of pathology, both neurotic and psychotic, have historically confused the issue. He nonetheless lists some of the "presumptive" diagnostic features of what he terms *borderline personality organization*. Patients with borderline personality organization typically present clinically with such other symptoms as chronic, diffuse, free-floating anxiety; multiple phobias; conversion or dissociative reactions; hypochondriasis; paranoid trends; polymorphous perverse sexuality (either in action or in fantasy); prepsychotic states, such as schizoid personality; problems with impulse control, which may be manifested in eating, sexual activity, or drug addiction; and the so-called low-level personality disorders described as infantile, narcissistic, "as if," and antisocial. In addition, there are other personality disorders that exist in a continuum, from relatively mild to much more severe; the lower level forms of hysterical and depressive-masochistic character problems are to be included with the borderline states (Kernberg 1975). It is one of Kernberg's greatest contributions to the field that he helped remove the focus from symptoms and psychological mechanisms as primary diagnostic indicators to a more sophisticated consideration of the enduring personality structures, which can create a shifting or confusing constellation of symptoms.

SPLITTING

Central among the characteristics of borderline patients Kernberg studied was their use of the primitive defense mechanism of splitting. What Kernberg observed in the clinical setting was a puzzling tendency for these patients to display what he came to call contradictory ego states. The patient could, seemingly without conflict, manifest both positive and negative reactions to a person or event. In other words, the patient would not be aware of or would not have affective memory of the opposing feelings. Kernberg (1976) was able to observe this starkly in the transference behavior of his patients and here describes one patient who

> remembered having bad periods in which absolutely opposite feelings to the present ones occupied his mind, but this memory had no emotional reality to him. It was as if there were two selves, equally strong, completely separated from each other in their emotions although not in the patient's memory and alternating in his conscious experience. . . .
>
> One other feature of this patient was that any effort on my part to question his idealization of me during the time he had only good feelings and to remind him of how critical and angry he had felt with me at other times would bring about intense anxiety. [p. 23]

The contradictory ego states described here constitute a split[1] in the ego (a situation not unrelated to the syndrome of multiple personality disorder). The patient's anxiety resulting from the attempted interpretation of this split signifies that the splitting is an ongoing process of defense that serves to protect the patient from an affective state that would threaten to be overwhelming. Associated with these shifting ego states were a lack of impulse control, weakened reality testing, and most of all the inability to integrate rage and guilt—the motivating affects of the opposite states.

---

1. It is important to note that "split" may be used to refer not only to the defense mechanism but also to other areas of mental structure and function. Salman Akhtar (1994a) lists as many as eight different usages (e.g., splitting of the ego in the defensive process, Kohut's vertical and horizontal splits, etc.).

The theoretical question implied in this description of border-line personalities is whether this pathological use of splitting represents the persistence of what was once a normal state of affairs; we are here assuming the point of view integral to psychoanalytic thinking that disorders have their roots in early life. To put it another way, we assume that it makes sense to extrapolate backward to reconstruct the early childhood of these patients, but was it ever normal to function with such a predominance of splitting and other primitive defenses? Kernberg develops a theory of development that accounts for both the normality of splitting and the potential for it to become pathological and persist into adulthood under certain circumstances.

Splitting, he postulates, originates in the infant in order to manage early anxiety associated with the experiencing of the object as alternately good/satisfying and bad/frustrating. The infant first experiences pleasure and unpleasure as separate qualities because they are associated with distinct events. Kernberg (1976) believes that early affect in the tiny baby is of an "intense, overwhelming nature" and that it has an "*irradiating* effect on all other perceptual elements of the introjection" – introjection being that first step in the development of connection to and identification with caregivers. The positively and negatively "valenced" affects, originally kept apart because they occur at different times, will tend to come together because of the baby's tendency toward integration and organization of disparate elements. When this occurs, it causes great anxiety and thus stimulates splitting, the keeping apart of these oppositely valenced affective states, as a defensive measure. Kernberg theorizes that the baby attempts to retain the good/pleasurable and to reject and project the bad/unpleasurable as that which is "not me," in an attempt to preserve what has been called the "purified pleasure ego." These introjections, positive and negative, become the core elements in the internalized object relations the baby is developing. As Kernberg summarizes, "This active separation by the ego of positive and negative introjections, which implies a complete division of the ego and, as a consequence, of external reality as well, is, in essence, the defensive mechanism of *splitting*" (pp. 34–37).

The psychic consequences of splitting are severe; this is a inefficient way of maintaining homeostasis for an adult.

> The main objective of the defensive constellation centering on splitting in borderline personality organization is to keep separate the aggressively determined and the libidinally determined intrapsychic structures stemming from early object relations. The price the patient pays for this defensive organization is twofold: the inability to integrate libidinally and aggressively invested self-representations into a self-concept which more truly reflects the actual self and to integrate libidinally invested and aggressively invested object-representations and so to understand in depth other people. Together, these characteristics determine the syndrome of identity diffusion. [Kernberg 1976, p. 67]

Kernberg's conclusions seem to have an almost commonsense sort of logic; it cannot be possible to experience oneself or others in anything approaching an accurate or realistic way if one cannot experience both love and hatred, the good and the bad, with at least some areas of gray. Ego functions such as reality testing, perception, and the synthetic tendency (the capacity to integrate disparate elements of the personality) will naturally be highly compromised under these limitations to what an individual can tolerate. Neurotic functioning, on the other hand, is characterized by repression, which, although it banishes conflictual material from consciousness, leaves reality testing and the synthetic function of the ego essentially intact. Kernberg (1976) follows Klein (see Chapter 3) when he points out that "*Splitting, then, is a fundamental cause of ego weakness. . . . Since splitting requires less countercathexis* [e.g., the control of impulses] *than repression, a weak ego falls back easily on splitting, and a vicious cycle is created by which ego weakness and splitting reinforce each other"* (p. 46, italics original). Kernberg departs from Klein, though, in that he does not believe that the ego, as Klein envisions it, exists from birth. While Klein postulates that introjection develops from oral-incorporative fantasies, Kernberg follows Hartmann's conception of the conflict-free functioning of the ego and holds that it is the "primary autonomous apparatuses of perception and memory" (p. 39) that give rise to the infant's capacity to develop mental representations of self and other and then internalized object relations. Klein dates these processes to the first six months of life, while Kernberg has them occurring throughout the first two to three years.

Kernberg also points to another common feature of borderline personality organization, namely the prevalence of polymorphous perverse sexuality. The explanation for this follows logically from his understanding of the patient's inability to outgrow splitting in a normal way. Most children attain what Klein called the depressive position—that is, they achieve ambivalence, the ability to integrate the good and bad (loving and angry, libidinal and aggressive) aspects of themselves and others. Kernberg and others, from Freud to Stoller, have outlined the ways in which normal sexuality is comprised of pleasurable experiences and fantasies—including the aggressive and so-called perverse ones—that derive from all stages of psychosexual development and all the erotic zones of the body. If one has been unable to integrate and neutralize the aggressive/destructive with the loving urges, then it follows that borderline sexuality would be colored by elements from the earliest psychosexual stages and the fantasies associated with them. The residuals of the splitting process are primitively idealized and persecuting objects, the defensive purpose of the former being to ward off the toxicity of the projected destructive wishes. The toddler is overwhelmed by these paranoid distortions of the early mental representations of the parents, which derive from projected oral-sadistic and anal-sadistic impulses. Therefore, both parents (first mother and then father by fantasized contamination) come to be experienced as sources of danger. The child may take defensive refuge from his preoedi-pal no-win situation in an earlier than usual arrival at the Oedipus complex; however, because of the existing predomi-nance of aggression, this is unlikely to be a successful solution in the long run (Kernberg 1992).

AFFECTS AND THE PSYCHE — A REVISED METAPSYCHOLOGY

From this brief and incomplete overview of the clinical descrip-tive features of borderline personality dynamics, let us move to a consideration of Kernberg's metapsychological statements. The essential thesis (to follow the real estate "rule of three" — location, location, location) can be summed up in these words: affects, affects, affects. Although Kernberg writes in the language of classical psychoanalysis, he departs from Freud in his under-standing of the motivational system. Drives, he feels, are not instinctual in the sense of existing from birth. Rather, they develop as a result of the variety of early positive and negative affective experiences. As such, they serve as organizers rather than as true motivational forces in the Freudian sense (Greenberg and Mitchell 1983). Kernberg (1992) considers affects to be the central motivating force that fuels psychic life:

> In my view, affects are the primary motivational system in that they are at the center of each of the infinite number of gratifying and frustrating concrete experiences the infant has with his environment. Affects link the series of undifferentiated self/object representations so that gradually a complex world of internalized object relations, some pleasurably tinged, others unpleasurably tinged, is con-structed. . . .
>
> Eventually, the internal relation of the infant to the mother under the sign of "love" is more than the sum of a finite number of concrete loving affect states. The same holds true for hate. Love and hate thus

become stable intrapsychic structures in the sense of two dynamically determined, internally consistent, stable frames for organizing psychic experience and behavioral control in genetic continuity through various developmental stages. By that very continuity they consolidate into libido and aggression. Libido and aggression, in turn, become hierarchically supraordinate motivational systems, expressed in a multitude of differentiated affect dispositions under different circumstances. Affects are the building blocks, or constituents, of drives; they eventually acquire a signal function for the activation of drives.

Again, it needs to be stressed that drives are manifest not simply by affects but by the activation of a specific object relation, which includes an affect and in which the drive is represented by a specific desire or wish. [pp. 19-20]

Kernberg thus rewrites the most basic classical psychoanalytic principle of the drives. He also takes exception to a less well accepted proposal of Freud's, but one that Melanie Klein used as a central element in her metapsychology, namely the death instinct; "I am not aware of any evidence from psychoanalysis or any related science which would justify calling libido and aggression 'life' or 'death' instincts" (Kernberg 1976, p. 109). Instead, libido and aggression form out of early affective experiences that Kernberg also stresses, can be overwhelming; gratification and frustration are truly powerful experiences for the infant. As Eissler (1958) said, the infant might well wish to correct Descartes and say, "I experience pleasure, hence I exist" (p. 239). A Kernbergian version of this would be extended, no doubt, to encompass the negative valence as well: "I feel, therefore I am."

AFFECTS AND INTERNALIZED OBJECT RELATIONS

Kernberg found a clue to the centrality of affects in his work with borderline patients when he observed their tendency toward splitting and the resulting separation of ego states. These ego states, he claims, are associated with incompatible affective experiences. And the final building block in this metapsychological understanding is that of object relations, which Kernberg (1976) sees as intertwined with affects. The baby is born prewired to experience pain and pleasure. The context in which these states first occur is in the relationship with the mother (or other primary caregiver). Thus, the earliest memories (rudimentary remembering being another of the infant's prewired capacities) consist of the physical sensations and the associated perceptions of the environment. "All of this leads to the fixation of memory traces in a primitive, 'affective memory' constellation or unit incorporating self components, object components, and the affective state itself" (p. 104). Kernberg (1992) also hypothesizes that there exist "peak affect states" characterized by intense experiences of self and object that facilitate the internalization process. In contrast to these are the quiescent or low-level affect states in which perception and cognitive learning are relatively free of affective influence. Here he states his theory succinctly:

> I propose that the units of internalized object relations constitute subsystems on the basis of which both drives and the overall psychic structures of ego, superego, and id are organized as integrating systems. Instincts (represented by psychologically organized drive systems) and the overall psychic structures then become component systems of the personality at large, which constitutes the suprasystem. In turn, the units of internalized object relations themselves constitute an integrating system for subsystems represented by inborn perceptive and behavior patterns, affect positions, neurovegetative discharge patterns, and nonspecific arousal mechanisms. [Kernberg 1976, p. 85]

The implications of Kernberg's revised metapsychology are vast. Both ego and id, he says, have their origins in experience; they consist of the residues of affect/object-relating episodes.

This constitutes a major departure from the classical view that all motivation and energy in the infant are produced by the drives in an already functioning id. Kernberg's theory can be seen, despite his dense language, as less distant from experience and therefore more parsimonious in the sense that he minimizes the number of theoretical constructs he calls on as explanatory devices. The conceptual leap of faith that he requires us to make, though, is that pleasure and unpleasure become transformed into the libidinal and aggressive intrapsychic motivational forces (Greenberg and Mitchell 1983).

In a sense, much of psychoanalytic theory can be said to be a theory of object relations, a theory of how the mind is structured from birth and how the individual comes to relate to the environment as it exists and as the mind fantasizes it to be. Kernberg (1976) proposes a more specific usage of "object relations" to distinguish what is unique to his particular refinement of the object relations school. What he stresses is "the buildup of dyadic or bipolar intrapsychic representations (self- and object-images) as reflections of the original infant–mother relationship and its later development into dyadic, triangular, and multiple internal and external interpersonal relationships." There is a "simultaneous buildup of the 'self' (a composite structure derived from the integration of multiple self-images) and of 'object-representations' (or 'internal objects' derived from the integration of multiple object-images into more comprehensive representations of others)." In this view, it is the units of self-image, object-image, and affect disposition that become the "primary determinants of the overall structure of the mind (id, ego, and superego). Affect in the infant is defined as "the earliest experience of pleasure or unpleasure" (pp. 57 and 62).

DEVELOPMENTAL STAGES

Kernberg lays out a model of development that follows Mahler's general structure. There is during the first month of life a Primary

Undifferentiated Stage, also referred to as Normal "Autism," in which the infant does not yet possess a quorum of experiences around which to begin to organize self and object images. From the second to the eighth to tenth month comes Normal "Symbiosis," which Kernberg (1976) characterizes as the Stage of the Primary, Undifferentiated Self-Object Representations. (Note that this is *not* the Kohutian selfobject to which Kernberg is referring.) He theorizes that this stage is marked by the development of a "basic 'good' self-object constellation, which will become the nucleus of the self system of the ego and the basic organizer of integrative functions of the early ego." Excessive unpleasure at either of these early stages would lead to psychopathology of a psychotic dimension. The second stage comes to a close "when the self-image and the object-image have been differentiated in a stable way within the core 'good' self-object representation" (pp. 60–64). Cognitive maturation, too, depends on the successful unfolding of the relations with the world; pleasure and minimal levels of frustration serve to reinforce the infant's curiosity and the urges to experiment and to explore. Kernberg posits that it is approximately between the fourth and ninth months that the good and bad representations are differentiated and that, correspondingly, the associations between good-libido and bad-aggression occur.

In Kernberg's (1976) third stage, Differentiation of Self-from Object-Representations, this process continues and results in an integration of a self concept and of object-representations; the approximate timetable for this is from about the sixth to eighth to between the eighteenth and thirty-sixth months, thus corresponding to Mahler's separation-individuation phase. Failure to negotiate this period of development will result in psychopathology in the borderline range. "The differentiation of self and object components determines, jointly with the general development of cognitive processes, the establishment of stable ego boundaries; there is not yet an integrated self or an integrated conception of other human beings (so that this is a stage of 'part' object-relations)" (p. 64–65). The connection to the clinical-diagnostic idea of identity diffusion follows clearly from this description. (The reader may note, in passing, that Kernberg treats the self not only as a mental representation but also as an entity that functions as a separate structure within the mind; this is yet another break with classical metapsychology [Greenberg and Mitchell 1983].) Gradually during this stage, the child begins to clarify the self and the nonself. This achievement is fragile, though, and there is likely to be a regression to part-object mental representations if the child experiences severe frustration. Splitting may be a helpful defense at this time, as it serves to protect the fragile good self-and object-representations from "contamination" by the bad self- and object-representations. Under normal circumstances, splitting as a predominant defense will gradually diminish; when it does not it will compromise the future development of the ego, in particular the capacity for reality testing.

The fourth stage is the Integration of Self-Representations and Object-Representations and Development of Higher Level Intrapsychic Object Relations–Derived Structures. Corresponding to Mahler's "Beginnings of Emotional Object Constancy," this begins toward the end of the third year and lasts through the oedipal period. It should be noted that, for many individuals, this is a lifelong task; this accounts for the commonplace existence of "higher level" character pathology and neuroses, the pathology associated with difficulties in this stage. Kernberg sees narcissistic pathology deriving primarily from this time; there is a stable identity but a distortion in the qualities therein and an intense pressure to defend against painful affects, leading to the grandiosity and devaluation so characteristic of narcissistic patients. The id comes to be "an overall psychic structure containing the sum of these internalized object relations which are unacceptable because of the dangerous, anxiety and guilt-producing experiences involved in the respective intrapsychic and interpersonal interactions" (1976, p. 70). The superego, which also begins to have a life of its own as a mental structure at this time, has its roots in the "internalization of fantastically hostile, highly unrealistic object-images reflecting 'expelled,' projected, and reintrojected 'bad' self-object representations" (pp. 70–71). The ego ideal, that collection of ideas in the superego that represents what we strive to be, results from the "condensation of such magical, wishful, ideal self and ideal object representations" that come into being as the libidinal and aggressive mental representations of self and other are being integrated. As Freud pointed out, the superego must repeat that very internalization process by which the ego itself was formed, taking its content from external objects. However, Kernberg (1976) offers yet another reconceptualization of the classical point of view in which the superego is seen as the heir to the Oedipus complex; clearly, he is arguing that the superego is well on its way to developing its character long before the oedipal period. An additional implication of this revision of superego formation (combined with Kernberg's clinical observations) is a de-emphasis on "the overriding importance given penis envy in both sexes" (p. 195) in classical psychoanalytic theory. In other words, castration anxiety is not seen as the single motivator for the development of internalized moral standards.

The final stage Kernberg names Consolidation of Superego and Ego Integration. Kernberg's (1976) understanding of border-line pathology, specifically of the splitting process, gives him a fresh and rich outlook on the development of superego pathology, and reinforces the conviction that there is true continuity between borderline and neurotic pathology. In this last stage of maturation (which, again, not all people will attain) the conflict between ego and superego so characteristic of neurosis gradually diminishes. In a synergistic fashion, the greater this eases, the more integrated and solid the ego becomes. And as self-concept changes so, too, does the individual's capacity to relate to the environment:

> An integrated self, a stable world of integrated, internalized object-representations, and a realistic self-knowledge reinforce one another.

The more integrated the self-representations, the more self-perception in any particular situation corresponds to the total reality of the person's interactions with others. The more integrated the object-representations, the greater the capacity for realistic appreciation of others and reshaping one's internal representations on the basis of such realistic appraisals. A harmonious world of internalized object-representations, including not only significant others from the family and immediate friends but also a social group and a cultural identity, constitutes an ever growing internal world providing love, reconfirmation, support, and guidance within the object relations system of the ego. Such an internal world, in turn, gives depth to the present interaction with others. In periods of crisis, such as loss, abandonment, separation, failure, and loneliness, the individual can temporarily fall back on his internal world; in this way, the intrapsychic and the interpersonal worlds relate to and reinforce each other. [p. 73]

Kernberg departs from the classical psychoanalytic perspective in more ways than in the reworking of the development of drives. For in his hypothetical conception of the neonate there is no longer the need to postulate a stage of primary narcissism; he sees the infant's disposition as social, as object-directed from the start. In the Freudian construct, the object, to be sure, is seen as one of the constituents of the drive, along with source, aim, and impetus. But for Kernberg drives do not come first; instead, they are shaped by the relationship with an external object (albeit a relationship in which self and other are undifferentiated) in which the infant is embedded. From this theoretical reworking, it also follows that the structures of the mind can no longer be defined in the original manner. For instance, how can the id— supposedly the primary stuff of the mind—be thought of as the representative of the drives if those drives, according to Kernberg, have not yet been structured? Instead, the id is the precipitate of these early object relations.

If the syndrome of identity diffusion lies at the core of borderline functioning, it is because of the failure in maturation of the process of internalization. This process of identity formation constitutes a thread running through Kernberg's outline of development. Beginning with the process of introjection and moving to identification and then to ego identity, this could be called the line of development of the process of internalization—obviously central to this theory of internalized object relations in which the infant *becomes* an individual through the building blocks of affect-laden relationships. Kernberg (1976) clarifies that these terms (introjection, identification, ego identity) refer both to the processes as well as to the mental structures they create.

KOHUT VS. KERNBERG

Although this is not the place to explore the controversy so heated a few years ago over who was "right," Kohut or Kernberg, I will offer a few comments. First, it is not at all clear that they can be compared in any simple way, for they may well have been writing about different patient populations. I think it also almost certain that their personalities and styles of working were so different as to elicit different data even from similar patients. Kohut made valuable contributions to the field in the description and clinical management of narcissistic transferences; however, his metapsychology perhaps oversimplifies the narrative of the creation of psychopathology, laying it almost exclusively at the doorstep of unempathic parents. What Kernberg and Kohut share, though it can be difficult to see because of Kernberg's use of the classical psychoanalytic lexicon, is a view of humans as deeply social and profoundly in need of interactions; Kernberg, I think, may be as radical as Kohut in his turning away from classical drive theory. When Kernberg holds that the self is not only a mental representation but also a supraordinate psychic structure, perhaps, he, too, can be said to have developed a psychology of the self.

TECHNIQUE

Probably the most influential effect of Kernberg's work in the clinical setting has been the revolution in the way we understand symptoms. No longer are the phobias and the obsessions, for instance, diagnostic of a neurosis. Instead the overt psychopathology and the patient's complaints are evaluated within the context of the total character, level of self-concept, and quality of object relations. (Note that Kohut, too, emphasized the unreliability of superficial symptoms as diagnostic anchors.) However the clinician chooses to accomplish it (and the simplest way is just to ask the patient to describe their relationships with friends, spouse, children, co-workers, boss), the emotional constancy and durability—or lack—of important relationships will reveal crucial diagnostic information. For the first step in evaluation and treatment recommendation is to determine whether the character structure suggests psychotic, borderline, narcissistic, or neurotic functioning. Kernberg (1984) stresses that it is only an understanding of the character that can teach us about the significance of the symptoms, and can tell us which kind of treatment could be effective in relieving suffering. His own procedure of evaluation he terms *structural interviewing*; utilizing this technique, he believes it possible to develop a sophisticated preliminary understanding of the patient's dynamics, structural development and object relations.

Kernberg is not alone in recommending that the clinician treat the transference as perhaps the most valuable diagnostic tool. Transference reactions that are very intense or chaotic and that occur very soon after treatment begins are strongly suggestive of borderline personality organization.

A 32-year-old woman sought treatment for persistent mourning for her alcoholic father who had died (of an unrelated physical illness) three years earlier. In the initial session she gave some background information, which included a history of being one of many children and feeling lost in the shuffle. She proclaimed her adoration of her mother and her next thought was of her mother's failure to call when she (the patient) had been hospitalized after a car accident. She went on to describe difficulties in making real friendships with women and also how pressured she felt by herself as well as her family since she was the only unmarried sibling. The patient showed no hesitation about revealing a great deal of quite painful material; the feel of the communication between therapist and patient seemed easy and comfortable. As she was getting up to leave, though, the patient began to cough and complained that there was something in the office that was triggering her allergies. The therapist suspected immediately that this represented the negative side of a splitting defense; indeed, at the following session, the patient said she had nothing to talk about. After a few sessions of increasing tension and some overt verbal aggressiveness (on the part of the patient) both therapist and patient agreed that treatment could not proceed. While negative transference material may be expected from almost every patient in some form, the almost immediate emergence of such a strong reaction would not generally occur in a neurotic patient.

TREATMENT MODALITIES: RECOMMENDATIONS

For neurotic patients or those with higher level personality disorders Kernberg recommends a classical psychoanalysis. For patients with borderline personality organization (recall that this does not refer to a *DSM* diagnosis but rather to an appreciation of ego weaknesses) he recommends a modified psychoanalysis. Supportive psychotherapy, he says, will be ineffective with this population, which follows logically from his understanding of borderline psychopathology. The purpose and technique of supportive treatment is to strengthen and bolster defenses while minimizing any insight into the motivation for the defenses or working through of the underlying conflicts. If, however, we agree that splitting is a continuing defense in these patients and one that continually undermines ego strength, it would be a mistake to support this. What would also compromise the effectiveness of supportive psychotherapy is that the negative transference may be so immediate and overwhelming as to prevent the development of a realistic working relationship between patient and therapist as in the vignette just presented (Kernberg 1975). Kernberg feels very strongly that splitting must be interpreted. The more integration of opposing ego states there is, the more integration there can be; to paraphrase Freud, where splitting was, there integration shall be. The therapeutic process may be difficult for the borderline patient, and Kernberg believes strongly in the use of inpatient treatment to protect the patient and the treatment at times when there are serious threats to safety. (In this day and age of managed care, the treatment-oriented hospitalization is, sadly, a rare thing.) Another modification of classical psychoanalytic technique that may be called for is a structuring of the treatment sessions and possibly of the patient's environment. Although Kernberg writes primarily about psychoanalysis, his diagnostic understanding and the treatment strategies he derives from it are clearly applicable to psychotherapy as well. Indeed, many borderlines are so wary of closeness that they have almost insurmountable resistance to sessions as frequent as required to conduct analysis. Perhaps it is a mistake to label this reluctance resistance, though; for in a person whose object relations have been so fraught with aggression, pain, and fear of merger, it may be a mark of good judgment that they wish to titrate carefully the level of intimacy.

Kernberg (1976) also transcends psychoanalysis's traditional undervaluation of social issues as in this caveat about the significance of analytic neutrality, which he sees as depending on the patient's and analyst's shared assumptions:

The problem of a woman's position in society may be one area in which the analyst has to be particularly attuned to the possibility of his identification with a traditional cultural outlook that places women in an inferior role and supports their acceptance of that role. Therefore the analyst must be especially wary of an implicit stand that overvalues the conventional adjustment of women to society or underestimates a woman's potential to develop new, nonconventional patterns of adaptation. [p. 237]

In the clinical setting, the moment-to-moment understanding of internalized object relations can be a dizzyingly complicated task. Here is Kernberg's (1976) description:

The final outcome of pathological identification processes is character pathology. The more rigid and neurotic the character traits are, the more they reveal that a past pathogenic internalized object relation (representing a particular conflict) has been "frozen" into a character pattern. Psychoanalytic exploration and resolution of character traits as they become transformed into active transference dispositions consistently reveal the activation of units of self- and object-representations linked by a particular affect disposition. At some times, while projecting a parental object-representation onto the analyst, the patient reactivates a self-representation in the interaction with that transference figure; at other times, while projecting the self-representation onto the analyst, the patient identifies himself with the corresponding parental representation. In addition, psychoanalytic exploration of character pathology frequently reveals that the internalized object relation is expressed not so much in the relationship of the patient with the analyst as in the intrapsychic relationship that arises between the patient's ego and superego. [p. 79]

Although it is Kohut and not Kernberg who seems to have patented the use of the term *empathy*, I would like to stress that an empathic appreciation of the patient's experience is a clinical "must" for Kernberg, as should be clear from the above passage. Kernberg's language is often dense and his concepts are certainly complex, but in his later writings a more overt empathic style seems to emerge as, for instance, when he addresses the concept of intersubjectivity:

> Intersubjectivity, whether incorporated in the self experience or rejected by projective mechanisms, is therefore an inseparable aspect of the development of normal identity. The psychoanalyst, too, by means of "concordant identification"—that is, empathy with the patient's central subjective experience—and "complementary identification"—that is, empathy with what the patient cannot tolerate within himself and activates by means of projective identification—may diagnose the patient's world of internalized object relations, which is a part of his ego identity. [Kernberg 1992, pp. 18–19]

Implicit in this and all of Kernberg's technical recommendations is an attitude that may be hidden sometimes behind complicated formulations but which he states explicitly (1976): "It is important to stress the human, personal element in the therapeutic process. The therapist . . . cannot help the patient grow as a human being without authentic respect and concern for him" (p. 264).

CASE ILLUSTRATION: THE PATHOLOGY OF INTERNALIZED OBJECT RELATIONS

W. was 24 years old and single when he entered treatment with Dr. A., a female psychologist in her early thirties. A psychiatrist referred him after a two-year treatment that had been increasingly characterized by silence and discomfort in the sessions with interaction only about the continuing need for anti-anxiety medication (Xanax); the patient was also seeing an employee assistance program (EAP) counselor weekly for support. This splitting of the treatment, which he would continue with his new therapist, immediately raises the suspicion of a borderline personality organization. W. was living alone and had an unsatisfying job as a legal clerk doing what felt to him to be routine and thankless work. He presented initially as a seemingly poor case for insight-oriented work with poor eye contact and a limited ability to describe his experiences. The patient was unable to describe to Dr. A. why he had been unable to talk to his doctor. The patient gradually reduced and then ended his use of the anxiolitic medication during the first year of treatment with Dr. A. After an extended evaluation, Dr. A. recommended psychoanalysis at a frequency of three times a week.

The central problem W. presented was a history of physical ailments (including chest pains, headaches, and backaches), which had come to mean that he was experiencing almost constant pain. Intensive medical workups revealed no organic disorders and the original referral to a psychiatrist came from the family physician whose reassurances that there was nothing wrong were ineffective in relieving the patient's anxiety. W.'s pain and regular visits to his physician started at age 18, six months after the death of his mother. Since that time he had also been seeing a chiropractor for weekly treatment of chronic back pain. It should be noted that each of the physical symptoms the patient experienced had also been symptoms his parents had suffered, which culminated in their premature deaths (father from cancer and mother from a heart attack). W. experienced worsening of his pain when he contemplated changing his job or dating, and thus found it impossible to improve his lonely and frustrating condition. His fear of abandonment was so intense as to outweigh his sense of isolation and desire for human contact.

In the first interview W. exposed what would be a prominent theme in the treatment—that he was reluctant to feel better and do better in life because "my parents couldn't get ahead, so why should I?" When he did something that might lead to his doing better this would make him feel "nervous." He tried to lead a healthy life but felt restrained by the physical pain he experienced. Dr. A. hypothesized that there was an unconscious sense of guilt at work in W. and asked him whether the pain felt like a kind of punishment. This formulation, to which the patient tearfully agreed, was the start of a therapeutic alliance, and the patient responded with an affectively charged memory from about age 11. He proudly showed his father a test on which he had scored 99, only to be asked what had happened to the other one point. He said that he had realized from this exchange that his father did not want him to do well. On another earlier occasion his parents had given no response at all when he showed them a crafts project; he then ripped it up and was soundly scolded, "yelled at." He told Dr. A. that, though he had not meant to "be bad," he preferred being reprimanded to being ignored. Father would feel such remorse for his anger outbursts that they would invariably be followed by warmth and apologies, which W. found deeply, if temporarily, gratifying. Thus began a cycle of provoking his father's wrath. With his mother, too, W. learned that being in pain, helpless, and needy were surefire ways to evoke kindness and warmth; he remembers that it was only when he was sick that she would shower him with affectionate attention.

The patient, despite his severe symptoms that might lead one to doubt his suitability for an expressive insight-oriented psychotherapy, was able to respond to this trial interpretation with affective presence and adequate cognitive distance—and with obvious relief at having been understood. The initial impression of the psychodynamics of W.'s pathology was of an internal persecutor that had been transformed into "the pain"—the patient did not have the awareness that the intruder was of his own psychological making. His childhood had clearly involved a parodox in that masochistic behavior on his part was the only sure route to parental attention. Even as early as this first encounter with the patient, Dr. A. was alert to the possibility that the transference might be colored by the patient's efforts to repeat a sadomasochistic relationship. Indeed, W. expressed relief that Dr. A. was easy to talk to and that she had not been like his sister, "always peeved about something."

BACKGROUND INFORMATION

W.'s father owned a well-located retail business that was surprisingly shaky, and the family life was characterized by a sense of financial anxiety, incipient failure, and confusion about why things never seemed to get better. Despite the family myth of a great romance between the parents, W.'s impression was that his parents were not deeply attached in a sexual or loving way. One sister, nine years his senior, was consistently jealous of any attention the parents gave to the patient. The two siblings shared a room until W. was 10. The family situation was additionally stressed by the presence of the paternal grandmother who had joined the household after the death of the grandfather when W. was an infant. An early memory contributed to W.'s tenuous sense of belonging to the family: he awoke from a nap to hear his mother comment to a girlfriend of hers that W. was "so pretty he would have made a beautiful girl." (It should be noted that incidents such as these almost invariably occur in the childhoods of men who later become transsexual; the potentially profoundly pathogenic effect of a mother's conscious and, particularly, unconscious fantasies about her children's gender identity cannot be underestimated.)

W.'s development was notable for his difficulty with toilet training. Bed-wetting continued until age 9. It was particularly acute from ages 4 to 5 when his mother went to work as the bookkeeper in the father's business—an early indication of the patient's sensitivity to abandonment. As he poignantly described it, "I thought that my parents stopped loving me when

I was 4. . . . I went into my own little world." With his daily needs being taken care of then primarily by his grandmother and sister, W., facing the onset of his school years and the requirement that he leave whatever sense of safety he had at home, withdrew into a persistent anxious state exacerbated by the sense that no one cared how he felt. W.'s tenth year added even more trauma with the loss of his sister, who left home to marry, and the even further attenuation of the relationship with his parents, who instituted evening shopping hours at the store. W. began to overeat, and in fact gained a significant amount of weight. His father, who apparently was the only one even to notice, continued the pattern of reinforcing his son's self-destructive behavior by devising several demeaning nick-names that W., even as he craved the attention, experienced, silently, as deeply upsetting. "I never knew if he was kidding or if he wanted to hurt my feelings." He told Dr. A. how much he had longed for guidance from and camaraderie with the only male figure in his household.

When W. was about 12, his father began to spend more time at home and W. felt tremendous pleasure and gratification in watching ball games together on TV and sometimes actually going to a live game. What W. was not told was the reason for this reduction in his father's work hours: the father had been diagnosed with melanoma and died when W. was 14. W. was not aware of the diagnosis until a matter of days before his father's death. Thus this closeness, which W. so treasured, amounted to yet another instance in which he had been kept out of the loop regarding the truth of the situation. He did have a few friends — but mostly he turned to food, and was almost 90 pounds over his ideal weight by age 18. In this impossible situtation, W. was unable to complete the tasks of adolescence. The father's death and the mother's turning to her son as "the man of the house" represented a realistically terrifying oedipal victory that he had unconsciously desired. W., then, entered adolescence with a precarious male identity, with no immediately available male figure to turn to and then away from – and all this layered upon the preoedipal heritage of an identity shaped by masochism.

Mother contributed to this nightmare-come-true in the following years. Unable to cope with her grief, she began to use alcohol heavily, and was, Dr. A. gathered from W.'s description, sexually promiscuous. W. recalls her being drunk and tearfully telling him how much he reminded her of his father; often these encounters would be followed by her requesting that he help her get undressed as she was too drunk. Other seductive behaviors also occurred and were quite difficult for W. to recount in treatment, so guilty did he feel for having felt some sexual interest, albeit infused with anxiety, in his mother. Before his father's death, however, his mother had been a strict disciplinarian, rigidly forbidding the discussion of sexual matters or the use of curse words. W. missed this clarity of roles and fought with his mother almost constantly when she was not drunk, begging her to help him with his homework and to "act like a mother." The grandmother, too, openly disapproved of the mother's behavior. It was after one of these fights with W. that his mother heatedly left home, and then suffered a fatal heart attack. Although W. knew that his mother had neglected her health, he nonetheless blamed himself for her death, which took place just before he was to graduate from high school.

With this final "refusal" by his mother to witness a success, W. began the end of his adolescence. He enrolled in college, but dropped out before the end of his first year to take the undemanding job he held at the time he met Dr. A. He had tried to cope with the trauma of his mother's death by immersing himself in academic work; when the stress of college proved too great, he resorted to daily exercise at a gym and lost all of his extra poundage over about two years. He was left alone and isolated in the family home at that time when his grandmother died after a series of heart attacks.

Not surprisingly, W. had tremendous conflicts about sexual matters; the very thought of dating would lead to an exacerbation of his somatic complaints. His one attempt at sexual intercourse, with a willing young woman, was unsuccessful; both she and he were able to blame it on the fact that he had been drinking, but he refused any further contact with her. As a preadolescent he had engaged in sex play with both girls and boys, and with great difficulty reported to Dr. A. that he had enjoyed the contact with boys more. W.'s fantasy life, though, showed none of the inhibition of his actual sexual life; he had many incestuous and aggressive fantasies about the various women in his family who had functioned as auxiliary mothers to him. Dr. A. assumed that his actions were inhibited precisely in order to prevent the actualization of these forbidden but pleasureable fantasies. One of the main tasks of adolescence is indeed to transcend and finally repress the oedipal drama; quite clearly W. had not been able to accomplish this. In the sexual arena, too, W. felt as though his father had let him down, as his father had never kept a promise to tell W. about the facts of life. To the patient this would come to mean that his father had never given him permission to grow up.

PSYCHODYNAMIC ASSESSMENT

Perhaps the foremost component of W.'s psychodynamic personality structure was his severely compromised superego. W. had been an oedipal victor (permitted against his father's wishes to sleep in the parental bed) even before the unconscious patricide that his father's actual death would come to represent. With such a weak father there was little in the way of appropriate prohibitions for him to internalize; what he was left with was his father's harsh condemnation. (Lacan's concept of the "name of the father" would be germane here.) W. could thus be excessively demanding of himself as expiation for his fantasized crimes. But his unconscious guilt was so great that he could not contain it within the personality structure and he projected it onto imagined harsh and heartless beings, such as God who had taken his parents because he had been a bad boy. Indeed, he enacted this in the treatment setting, in his attempts to maneuver Dr. A. into the position of condemning his thoughts and behaviors. His grandmother, though punitive, did represent an island of consistency and appropriateness in this otherwise chaotic family. But the harshness of W.'s super-ego did not entirely manage the incestuous fantasies and the acting out of impulses, such as overeating.

Ego functioning was also impaired. For instance, normal levels of aggression and hostility that might be sublimated into effective assertiveness were impossible to regulate, given the additional burden of the projected superego prohibitions; this led to compromised reality-testing as W. could not tell what came from him and what from outside. Accordingly, object relations were fraught with anger, and W. seldom left his uncomfortable but safe isolation. Also notable were W.'s failures to manage affects such as sadness and anxiety. Prominent defenses included avoidance, conversion, projection, projective identification, reaction formation, and turning against the self.

In terms of psychosexual development, Dr. A. saw him as regressed to a stage of oral dependency as a defense against the overwhelming demands of his unresolved oedipal situation. As a child, W. had "solved" an impossible situation by becoming physically sick and thus needy of his mother and by becoming the instigator of sadomasochistic encounters with his father that evoked some semblance of affection. In this family without solid sexual limits, this dependency became the only route to libidinal gratification—and one in which suffering and pleasure became a necessary pair. Thus W.'s presenting symptom, pain, represented a complex compromise formation, a relic of a young boy's desperate attempt to get what he needed from seductive and sadistic parents.

The pain stood for many things, primarily, perhaps, an identification with his dead parents; he had, after all "chosen" their symptoms. By being in pain, he could, in fantasy, hold onto them. The pain, too, represented a cry for help, a wish to be taken care of sympathetically. And it simultaneously expressed aggression against the self—as long as he was in pain he could not succeed (date women, get a better job, etc.) and he hence perpetuated the restrictions his parents had laid down for him. With his fears of being overwhelmed by affects, the pain also served as an external focus, a distraction from the chaotic feelings inside his mind, as a binder of anxiety and anger. W. also experienced the pain as deserved punishment for the sexual fantasies he had had about his seductive mother as an adolescent; notably, the pain began not immediately after mother's death, but upon his eighteenth birthday when "I became a man." Finally, the pain at times acted as a measure of the negative therapeutic reaction—that is to say of W.'s attempts to punish himself for trying to feel better and grow up into a man.

TREATMENT

Dr. A.'s position of neutrality, not favoring either side of W.'s conflicts, resulted in the development of a working alliance in which the patient began to experience the analyst as his "partner" in helping him to feel better. An early interpretative sequence centered around pointing out that W.'s pain semed to occur as he tried to stifle the mental anguish he experienced as he described losing his parents. This effort to understand the pain, this analytic attitude of curiosity, was intended to (and in fact did over a long period) help the patient develop an observing ego; gradually W. became equally curious about the meanings of his pain. But the exploration of this symbolic meaning took place within the context of the therapeutic relationship, and understanding the meanings of the relationship with the analyst took on equal importance.

By the end of the first month of treatment the first transference enactment had occurred. Note that the precocity of this confirms the initial diagnostic impression of borderline personality organization. W. had been unable to reach Dr. A. by telephone between sessions to report an "urgent" need, an increase in anxiety that occurred in connection with an anniversary of a death. Sullen in the following session, W. reluctantly admitted that he felt angry that they had not been able to speak. This resulted in the valuable insight that the patient feared his anger might be destructive to Dr. A. but that in reality she had survived this onslaught of hostility. The patient also feared that he might destroy himself, and Dr. A. further established an analytic atmosphere by her response to W.'s first request for reassurance that his pain would not harm him: "My reassurance would probably help only for a short while, just as you found with the reassurances you've gotten from your doctors and your counselor. Perhaps what will be helpful in the long run is for you to believe this for yourself. Your pain seems to be giving you a message. Let's try to understand what it is."

An issue closely related to W.'s fear of the toxic effects of his anger was his pervasive sense of himself as a "complainer." Analytic exploration of this in the context of the transference revealed W.'s feeling that his own needs, however legitimate, were selfish and would drain and weaken Dr. A. as they had his mother, at least according to her account. W.'s feeling responsible for taking care of his mother after his father's death was much confused by the mother's requests for sexually tinged helping, for example asking him to hug her when she was wearing revealing nightgowns. And as W. revealed more and more of the history of the mother's sexually inappropriate behavior, the same pattern emerged; after each session in which the patient explored the events and his own fantasies about them, his pain would get worse.

In the following example of the interaction from this period of the treatment, W. struggles to separate past from present concerns. Dr. A. works at clarifying his feelings:

Dr. A.: You've been feeling very hurt and angry for a long time. I wonder if you're afraid to let me see how angry you are.

W.: Probably . . . I'm afraid to let you know when I'm angry.

Dr. A.: Why is that?

W.: If I'm angry at you, I'm afraid that I could lose you. . . . You might not forgive me for being angry. Maybe you'll leave. . . . When I get angry I think of all of these things.

Dr. A.: Maybe you're afraid that if you express your anger toward me I might die as you *felt* that expressing your anger toward your mother killed her.

W.: It feels like that was the only time I really let out my anger. . . . (Begins to weep.) When I went to see her in the hospital for the last time she said something to me. She was weak and it was hard to hear her but I think she said, "It's not your fault." It's hard to remember. I was too caught up seeing her like that, with all those tubes and on a heart machine.

As the therapeutic relationship strengthened and W. began to gain some insight about the function of his pain he began to widen his sphere of activities. As he spent more time with peers and friends of both sexes, he noticed that he felt guilty afterward, and he connected this feeling with the occurrence of headaches. "It's like my pain reminds me not to have such a good time." But as Kernberg points out, increased ego strength leads to even greater ego strength, and W. continued to be less and less socially isolated and inhibited. He even allowed friends to fix him up with women, usually limiting the risk to casual double dates for a weekend lunch. At about this time he reported the first dream he had had since treatment had begun, and he gradually was able to make use of this new access to his inner life. He also started to use a pen that had belonged to his father, suggesting both that the mourning process had resumed and that he had managed to achieve a certain masculine identification with his father. Carrying his incestuous wishes into the therapeutic relationship, he asked whether Dr. A. ever dated her patients; but Dr. A.'s gentle refusal and explanation did not seem to hurt the patient and served to reinforce the safety of the therapeutic situation.

Dr. A. had observed that despite the many contacts W. had had with other helping professionals, he had been unable to derive significant benefit from them. This, she suspected, was because advice and reassurance, albeit well intentioned, had been offered as substitutes for serious listening. It was about a year, though, before W. was able to relinquish his use of medication and monthly psychiatrist appointments as well as his weekly contacts with the EAP counselor (who had communicated to Dr. A. that her role was limited to advice about work-related problems). During this time these other relationships served as alternative paths for acting out feelings engendered by the increasingly important relationship with Dr. A. and thus diffused the intensity of the transference. Stopping medication seemed to happen almost naturally, with W. feeling in control of the process. Relinquishing contacts with the EAP counselor was more difficult, but it took place in an interesting manner. W. had had the courage to take a vacation on his own for the first time ever. He had some anxiety about how he would do without the regular contact with Dr. A. Dr. A., though, indicated that she was confident that he could go away without feeling he had to call her, but that if he did she would be available. The EAP counselor, on the other hand, insisted on setting up telephone sessions (belying her statement that her "turf" was limited to the worksite) and insisted that W. take medication along with him. W. realized that he no longer found her help so helpful. It should be stressed that with a lower-level borderline character, the relationship with the counselor that Dr. A. had tolerated would have proven to be fertile ground for splitting of a truly pathological nature; if this had occurred, it would have required firm limit-setting by the therapist. After ending this relationship he began expressing some irritation that Dr. A. was not more like the counselor, that she did not hug him after a session and did not give reassurance upon demand. But he did not try to see the counselor again and was able to withstand the anxiety caused by these negative feelings about Dr. A.

By the end of the second year of treatment W. had developed a steady dating relationship with a woman of about his age. Although she was a virgin and sexually unaggressive – and thus unlike W.'s mother – she did seem to like to take care of W.; this was uncomfortably similar to his mother. Likewise these conflicts began to appear in the transference. W. experienced Dr. A. as alternately seductive and protective, and there was a sadomasochisic flavor to his narrative. When she would interpret resistances, he tended to experience this as a command to continue to reveal uncomfortable material. He did not know how to understand Dr. A.'s inquiries about his sexual fantasies. But her withholding of advice he felt to be overprotective, reminding him of how his parents had withheld both mundane as well as vital information from him.

Resistance was expressed by such devices as delay of payment, feeling his mind to be empty in session, or literally turning his head away from an unwelcome interpretation. (Dr. A. understood this as a projective identification with W. making her feel as shut out as his parents had made him feel.) Particularly dramatic was his reliance on his pain and crying as a protective shield. When Dr. A. found herself reacting to W.'s tears with annoyance rather than empathy, this signaled to her the resistive nature of his plaints. Conversely, what had signified resistance early on had come to be an expression of growing autonomy; W.'s periodic silences of several minutes' duration seemed to permit him to integrate the process of the sessions and to establish firm interpersonal boundaries. At times W.'s silences contained rage toward Dr. A. that he felt guilty about "because you really don't do anything to make me so angry." What they came to understand was that this anger served to distract W. from his sexual thoughts about the analyst. A slight weight gain also indicated a regression to a dependent, needy, childlike state as a safer alternative to the confusing, adult, sexual warmth he felt toward Dr. A.; at times W. would even ask if the actual temperature in the office had risen. When Dr. A. interpreted W.'s use of anger as a defense against sexual feelings, she realized that two months had elapsed since W. had complained of any physical pain. When she commented on this W. said that he had hoped that she wouldn't notice, "If I don't have my pain that means I'm better and I don't have to be here." Thus the onset of pain was intertwined with the experience of loss, as the loss of pain would inevitably mean losing Dr. A.

Despite W.'s conscious fear of object loss, he nonetheless displayed greater security in the therapeutic relationship as demonstrated by his less than idealizing fantasies about Dr. A. No longer regressed in a state of oral dependency, he experienced her next vacation not primarily as a deprivation of a needed object but as a possible threat of castration and punishment for his having kept his progress—that is to say, his emerging male power—hidden. Likewise, Dr. A.'s note-taking he now saw as an opportunity for her to record and share with others the details of his "ridiculous hang-ups"; earlier, note-taking had comforted him as it had signified the therapist's involvement and caring. Outside the treatment, though, improvement continued. W. had internalized the analytic progress to a considerable extent; on the increasingly rare occasions when he would experience somatic symptoms he undertook to analyze them on his own. He continued to fear the effects of his wishes for closeness with Dr. A. Note in the following excerpts the increase since the earlier dialogue in W.'s self-awareness and ability to stay with his internal experience:

W.: I'm afraid to feel closer to you, I'm afraid you'll leave. That's what my life has been. As soon as I got closer to my father he died. Then I got closer to my mother and she died. Then I got closer to my grandmother and she died. That's enough.

Dr. A.: You seem to see a connection between your getting close to them and their deaths.

W.: I know it's not my fault. Nobody has that kind of power.

Dr. A.: Yet you seem to believe you have such power because you're frightened to let yourself feel closer to me and want to protect me.

W.: I don't know. In a way it doesn't make sense because I have a girlfriend and I'm close with her. I'm too confused. . . . I'm afraid to learn more in here.

After this session, the pain returned. But W. was not terrribly frightened by it, understanding that it resulted from the "hot" topic of his fantasies about Dr. A. As he said, "I'm the one who punishes myself." W. used the ego strengths gained in the analytic process to contain the anxiety, to treat it as the signal that it was rather than the ego-dystonic end point it had been. He continued to work this issue through as, for instance in the following excerpt:

W.: You don't want to hear about how I'm growing. All you want is to hear about what's bothering me, like my parents.

Dr. A.: I wonder if you feel you have to hide from me how much you've grown.

W.: Nobody ever cared when I was doing good. All that sticks out in my mind is that my parents paid attention when I was sick or got into trouble. If I show you I'm growing, I won't need to come here. Somehow I have to show you I still need this.

Dr. A.: I wonder if you try to show me by talking about your pain.

W.: It's like I have to show you that I feel helpless. Now, I'm more uncomfortable showing you when I feel better . . . when I'm having a good time.

Despite the intense fear that his growing up could harm Dr. A., W.'s ability to articulate his thoughts strengthened and he did not succumb to the regressive pull toward childlike helplessness and pain. The very fact that this patient was able to sustain an observing ego—and that affective insight was so therapeutic in such a relatively short treatment—speaks to the potential for ego growth that had been present even behind his severe presenting pathology; his character disorder was not of a lower level, initial appearances notwithstanding. What cannot be left out of the equation, too, is that the match between patient and therapist was obviously a good one.

Dr. A.'s theoretical understanding of this case rested on Kernberg's description of pathogical internalized object relations. What W. initially experienced as an ego-alien symptom, his pain, Dr. A. understood as the projection of his punitive and sadistic superego. It is difficult to know what constitutional endowment W. brought to his family situation, whether he had a strong inborn tendency toward aggression. Note, for instance, the deeply empathic remark by the dying mother that W. barely recalls: "It's not your fault." This does suggest that W. may not have been able to experience whatever healthy elements did exist in his parents.

Nonetheless, as the patient experienced his history, his parents had no ameliorating effect on whatever hostility he did have. Just the opposite—his parents evidenced for the most part punitive and dehumanizing qualities. His mother's ambivalence about his gender and his father's affection-only-as-remorse-for-punishment were profoundly pathogenic. W. internalized these elements into the very structure of his personality in the way in which Kernberg has so vividly outlined.

7   KOHUT: A NEW VIEW OF
NARCISSISM AND THE SELF

Heinz Kohut (1913–1981) began his psychoanalytic career in a traditional manner; he took his medical degree from the University of Vienna and completed a residency in neurology and psychiatry at the University of Chicago, continuing on to receive analytic training at the Chicago Institute for Psychoanalysis. The respect he had gained in the conservative, ego-psychological establishment is evidenced by his election as president of the American Psychoanalytic Association in 1964–5. A few years later, though, Kohut had become one of the blackest sheep in the analytic fold due to formulations distinctly at odds with the tenets of ego psychology.

Through treating psychoanalytically what had been seen to be untreatable problems, narcissistic personality disorders, Kohut modified his theories and his techniques and challenged many widely held assumptions about psychopathology and normal development. Like Hartmann, Kohut tried to create a theory useful in helping us understand the social field wider than the analytic consultation room. It is important to keep in mind, though, that Kohut, like many other analytic theorists, developed his ideas out of the analytical material provided by adults rather than through the study of infants and children. To begin this overview of Kohut's contributions consider the way in which the Freudian concept of mental health as the ability to work and love is altered and expanded:

> Within the framework of the psychology of the self, we define mental health not only as freedom from the neurotic symptoms and inhibitions that interfere with the functions of a "mental apparatus" involved in loving and working, but also as the capacity of a firm self to avail itself of its talents and skills at an individual's disposal, enabling him to love and work successfully. [Kohut 1977, p. 284]

Kohut's stress on the self and its capabilities at first glance may seem not too far removed from Freud and Hartmann. But the difference lies in how Kohut thinks of the self and in how a "firm self" develops. The self is more than a mental representation—it is the center of experience.

THE BIRTH OF A HEALTHY SELF

Kohut (1977) holds that an infant is not born with a sense of self, that is to say, he is born without the awareness of being "a unit, cohesive in space and enduring in time, which is a center of initiative and a recipient of impressions" (p. 99). He proposes that the self begins to develop as parents and others respond not only to the baby's actual characteristics but also to his "innate potentialities" (p. 100). Indeed, the infant requires that the mother respond to his whole (potential) self as a condition for growth. While previous theorists emphasized the importance of satisfying the infant's instinctual demands, they stressed the primacy of physiological discomfort as a possible pathogenic factor. They also see the need for physical needs to be met as the motivating factor for the infant to seek object relations. Kohut sees the physical need as part of a larger picture.

It is not, we will say, the child's wish for food that is the primal psychological configuration. Seen from the point of view of the psychology of the self, we will affirm instead that, from the beginning, the child asserts his need for a food giving self-object—however dimly recognized the self-object might be. (In more behavioristic terms we might say that the child needs empathically modulated food-giving, not food.) If this need remains unfilled (to a traumatic degree) then the broader psychological configuration—the joyful experience of being a whole, appropriately responded-to self—disintegrates, and the child retreats to a fragment of the larger experiential unit, i.e., to pleasure-seeking oral stimulation (to the erogenic zone) or, expressed clinically, to depressive eating. It is this fragment of psychological experience that becomes the crystallization point for the later addiction to food. [p. 81]

The child that is to survive psychologically is born into an empathic-responsive human milieu (of self-objects) just as he is born into an atmosphere that contains an optimal amount of oxygen if he is to survive physically. And his nascent self "expects"—to use an inappropriately anthropomorphic but appropriately evocative term—an empathic environment to be in tune with his psychological need-wishes with the same unquestioning certitude as the respiratory apparatus of the newborn infant may be said to "expect" oxygen to be contained in the surrounding atmosphere. [p. 85]

Thus Kohut speculates that the newborn from birth requires need-meeting others who, via appropriate empathy and responsiveness, affirm the infant's emerging sense of wholeness. The emotional environment is as important as the meeting of physical needs (indeed René Spitz [1945] demonstrated this in his landmark studies of what would today be termed *failure-to-thrive infants*). The "self" is seen as the center of experience and action that exists primarily as the newborn's potential.

Kohut (1977) uses several terms in the above passages that require definition. *Empathy* he conceives of as "vicarious introspection" (p. 306) and he believes that the ability to understand another person empathically, that is through the temporary suspension of one's own frame of reference, is a sort of sixth sense. Infants and young children depend on their caregivers to provide sufficient and appropriate understanding of their feeling-states. It is not necessary, though, for the parent to be perfectly in tune with the child at all times; indeed such a process would be harmful. And here Kohut's thoughts parallel Winnicott's. The parents' unavoidable *failures in empathy* (Winnicott: "inevitable non-traumatic frustrations") allow the child to begin the process of internalizing the functions that had previously been provided by the adequate and appropriate parent. Kohut terms this process of structure-building *transmuting internalization* and believes that it occurs under situations of *optimal frustration*. Optimal frustration is to be distinguished from chronic or severe failures in empathy that impede the development of a *cohesive self*. Correspondingly, Kohut's conception of anxiety is based on the need for a cohesive self; fears of disintegration or of annihilation (rather than fear of loss of object, of loss of love of the object, or of castration) are the basic components of anxiety.

SELF-OBJECTS AND EMPATHY

Another unfamiliar term in the above citations is *self-object*. In studying the transference reactions of his adult patients, Kohut drew important conclusions about their object relations. What seem to be intense relationships with other people are in fact qualitatively different from healthy or neurotic object relations in that narcissistically disordered patients do not perceive objects as having wishes, thoughts, or needs of their own. These patients depend on other people to fulfill psychological functions (such as the regulation of psychic tension) that higher-functioning people are normally able to do for themselves. Hence, Kohut created a revised conception of the notion of other-directed strivings and coined the term *self-object* to describe this form of object relations.

Kohut postulated accordingly that infants and children relate to their objects in a similar fashion. In clinical work with narcissistic disorders, interpretations generally focus on the empathic failures the patient perceives in the therapist (transference interpretations) or other current objects or failures that are remembered in important early relationships, usually with parents (genetic reconstruction). These two areas are related in that the patient carries the mirror image of the parents' empathic failures into the transference. The presumption is that the patient must have the opportunity to experience an appropriately empathic self-object, in the person of the therapist, in order to have the opportunity to repair the deficits in the self. Kohut (1977) describes the foundations of self-pathology and the basic clinical rationale:

> The importance of the two-step sequence – step one: empathic merger with the self-object's mature psychic organization and participation in the self-object's experience of an affect signal instead of affect spread; step two: need-satisfying actions performed by the self-object – cannot be overestimated; if optimally experienced in childhood it remains one of the pillars of mental health throughout life and, in the reverse, if the self-objects of childhood fail, then the resulting psychological deficits or distortions will remain a burden that will have to be carried throughout life. . . . Every interpretation, in other words, and every reconstruction consists of two phases; first the analysand must realize that he has been understood; only then, as a second step, will the analyst demonstrate to the analysand the specific dynamic and genetic factors that explain the psychological content he had first empathically grasped. [pp. 87–88]

Kohut (1977) believes that a wide variety of affective disorders can be traced to inadequate or inaccurate empathic responsiveness from important self-objects. He postulates that the child experiences this empathic attunement as a kind of empathic "merger with the omnipotent self-object" (p. 86). When it does not take place, the necessary developmental progression of narcissistic satisfactions is disrupted. For instance, if the self-object is largely unable on a regular basis correctly to perceive the child's needs, the child will lose the experience of regularly feeling affects wax and wane in a manageable and predictable way. When self-objects overreact (psychologically or hypochondriacally) to a child's mild anxiety, this will tend to produce more intense anxiety in the child.

> The end-result in all these instances is either a lack of normal tension-regulating structure (a weakness in the ability to tame affects — to curb anxiety) or the acquisition of faulty structures (the propensity toward active intensifications of affect — toward developing states of panic). [p. 89]

Faulty empathy usually results from parents' own deficiencies in the self; however, Kohut (1977) also cautions that "a mother's faulty empathy can rarely be judged in isolation; in most instances it has to be evaluated as a failure vis-à-vis an unusually difficult task" (p. 29). Such cases as an adopted child, a prematurely born infant, or a colicky baby might constitute a poor match between a child's needs and even a normal mother's abilities. This description of good self-object responsiveness echoes Winnicott's concept of the "good enough mother":

> What a child needs is neither continuous perfect empathic responses from the side of the self-object nor unrealistic admiration. What creates the matrix for the development of a healthy self in the child is the self-object's capacity to respond with proper mirroring at least some of the time. What is pathogenic is not the occasional failure of the self-object but his or her chronic incapacity to respond appropriately which, in turn, is due to his or her own psychopathology in the realm of the self. [pp. 187–188]

Kohut has also emphasized that the need for self-object mirroring ideally becomes less constant as the child grows but never actually disappears; he believes that the need for empathy, mirroring, and admiration persists throughout the life cycle.

NARCISSISTIC TRANSFERENCES

Kohut distinguished several forms in which people require empathic responsiveness as he examined the various types of transferences his narcissistic patients seemed to develop, and thus proposed a multipolar developmental schema. Mirroring responses from the self-object (therapist or parent) permit one to develop a sense of importance, value, and goodness leading to ambitiousness and the ability to take pleasure in living; in a *mirror transference* the patient looks to the therapist to provide recognition of his or her worth. The well-known grandiosity of some narcissistic patients is an expression of this need. Children also need to idealize their self-objects, to grant them the power to soothe, calm, and protect the child's developing and vulnerable sense of self; if a parent is able to allow himself to be idealized, the child will be able to annex the parent's strength and develop for himself a sense of self direction and of personal goals; in an *idealizing transference* the patient will try to maintain an image of an all-powerful or perfect therapist in order to be able to partake of those qualities. Finally, children have what Kohut calls twinship or alter ego requirements, the wish to feel a sense of sameness with other human beings; adequate fulfillment of these needs (by joint activities with trusted parents) allows a child to utilize his or her own individual combination of talents and skills to make achievement of goals and ambitions possible; in a *twinship transference* the patient will have difficulty perceiving and then tolerating the therapist as a separate individual. Kohut stressed that parents need not be perfectly empathic in all these ways in order to bring up a healthy child. Indeed, he believes that the child has several chances to develop a cohesive self in this tripolar scheme; adequate fulfillment of needs in one area may compensate for even serious failures in another (Baker and Baker 1987).

Kohut (1971) describes the importance of the two most important narcissistic needs in the child for mirroring and idealizing responses:

> The central mechanisms ("I am perfect." "You are perfect, but I am part of you.") which the two basic narcissistic configurations employ in order to preserve a part of the original experience of narcissistic perfection are, of course, antithetical. Yet they coexist from the beginning and their individual and largely independent lines of development are open to separate scrutiny. Under optimal developmental conditions, exhibitionism and grandiosity of the archaic grandiose self are gradually tamed, and the whole structure ultimately becomes integrated into the adult personality and supplies the instinctual fuel in our ego-syntonic ambitions and purposes, for the enjoyment of our activities, and the important aspects of our self esteem. And, under similarly favorable circumstances, the idealized parent image, too, becomes integrated into the adult personality. Introjected as our idealized superego, it becomes an important component of our psychic organization by holding up to us the guiding leadership of its ideals. [pp. 27–28][1]

RESPONDING TO NARCISSISTIC TRANSFERENCES

The fundamental psychopathology in narcissistic personality disorders, then, concerns an impaired ability to regulate and maintain self esteem independently. While a patient's superficial presenting symptoms (such as phobias, obsessions, compulsions, or conversions) might seem to suggest a discrete neurotic disorder, "the crucial diagnostic criterion is to be based not on the evaluation of the presenting symptomotology or even of the life

---

1. In the *Analysis of the Self* (1971), the earlier of Kohut's two major works, he had not yet given up the language and metaphors of ego psychology.

history, but on the nature of the spontaneously developing transference" (1971, p. 23). There do exist, however, some diagnostic
indicators of narcissistic disorders. These include either perverse
fantasies or lack of interest in sex, work difficulties, poor relationships, antisocial tendencies, lack of humor, evidence of little
empathy for other people, inability to modulate anger, pathological lying, somatic symptoms, and hypochondria (Kohut 1971).
Many of these elements obviously will affect the therapeutic
relationship as well. Even though narcissistic patients often have
trouble with the sort of suspension of disbelief needed to engage
in the quasi-reality of a therapeutic relationship, the therapist
must not act in such a way as to prevent this "defect from
unfold[ing] freely so that its analysis may be undertaken" (p.
212). Kohut terms antisocial behavior (such as lying, not paying
therapist's bills, etc.) "acted-out communication" (p. 209), and
cautions therapists against using moral pressure, condemnation,
prohibition, or anything beyond pointing out the fact of the
behavior. Winnicott indeed saw an element of hope in the very
audacity of the antisocial behavior. However, this kind of behavior from patients necessitates that the therapist have a high level
of awareness of his countertransference; in general, diagnosing
according to a patient's transference also signifies that one is
diagnosing according to one's own countertransference.

Kohut (1971) proposes an interpretation of the concept of
analytic neutrality radically different from the orthodox understanding as he describes how to go about allowing the spontaneous transference to develop. The neutrality of the analyst must be
composed of "average, expectable humane responsiveness. To
remain silent when one is asked a question, for example, is not
neutral but rude." (p. 89). Far from endeavoring to be as minimally responsive as possible, the therapist should offer:

> the responsiveness to be expected on an average from persons who
> have devoted their life to helping others with the aid of insights
> obtained via the empathic immersion into their inner life. . . . Lack

of emotional responsiveness, silence, the pretense of being an inhu-
man computer-like machine which gathers data and emits interpretations, do no more than supply the psychological milieu for the most
undistorted delineation of a person's psychological makeup than do
an oxygen-free atmosphere and a temperature close to the zero-point
supply the physical milieu for the most accurate measurement of his
physiological responses. Appropriate neutrality in the analytic situation is provided by average conditions. [Kohut 1977, pp. 252–253]

It is important, though, to be sensitive to the needs of specific
patients. A patient whose parents were chronically unresponsive
may require more activity on the part of the therapist, while the
classical neurotic's fantasies of childhood seduction (which Kohut believes is caused by parental overstimulation) call for an
analytic "attitude of emotional reserve and muted responsiveness" (Kohut 1977, p. 256). It is interesting to recall some of the
history of the controversy about the issue of analytic neutrality,
specifically that Freud himself was much more responsive to
patients' actual needs than he advocated in his technique papers.
Kohut as a psychoanalytic phenomenon was perhaps an inevitable and needed reaction to the overdevelopment in the United
States of the notion that the ideal analyst ought to be far removed
from the consideration of the patient's responses to the analyst
and needs within the therapeutic relationship.

A general principle of self-psychological treatment is to focus
on the patient's transference as a reaction to actual events in
treatment, to actual characteristics of the therapist and actual or
perceived empathic failures; the goal in doing this is not to gratify
the needs the patient expresses but to analyze them. Although
Kohut (1971) does sometimes see transitory needs for "*reluctant
compliance with the childhood wish,* the true analytic aim is not
indulgence but mastery based on insight, achieved in a setting of
(tolerable) analytic abstinence" (p. 291). Thus the therapist's
empathic failures, actual or perceived, are the stuff of treatment,
the royal road to an understanding of the patient's pattern of

deficits in the cohesive self. Kohut (1977) addresses the question of how to handle a patient's reaction to an empathic failure:

> It may be advisable to stress here that there is no connotation of guilt or blame involved if the analyst acknowledges the limitations of his empathies. Empathy failures are unavoidable—indeed they are a necessity if the empathy-craving analysand is ultimately to form a firm and independent self. It is nevertheless of crucial importance to state to the patient that he too, is not to blame—at least not in the sense of having manifested some nuclear consciousness—but that his rage was a reaction to a move from the side of the analyst that he experienced as a narcissistic trauma. [p. 115]

CURE, MENTAL HEALTH, AND THE PLACE OF THE OEDIPUS COMPLEX

Kohut's priorities in psychoanalysis also differ from Freud's, for the founder of the field saw the therapeutic outcome as a side effect rather than, strictly speaking, the goal of analysis. Kohut (1977) believes that Freud

> never elaborated—at least not in scientific seriousness, i.e., in theoretical terms—his conviction of the wholesome effect of analysis in the form of the claim that psychoanalysis cures psychological illnesses, that it establishes mental health. Freud's values were not primarily health values. He believed in the intrinsic desirability of knowing as much as possible. [p. 264]

Kohutian analysis is first and foremost a therapy aimed at developing a cohesive self; its end is not a complete-as-possible knowledge of oneself. The emphasis is on growth of missing functions of the self rather than on knowledge of the content of intrapsychic struggle; that is to say, the stress is on deficit instead of conflict. One implication of this is a different view of what is therapeutic about psychoanalysis. Another result is that Kohut's "cured" patient may retain many areas that analysis has not explored, many childhood memories left unconscious and unexamined:

> The psychoanalytic treatment of a case of narcissistic personality disorder has progressed to the point of its intrinsically determined termination (has brought about the cure of the disorder) when it has been able to establish one sector within the realm of the self through which an uninterrupted flow of the narcissistic strivings can proceed toward creative expression — however limited the social impact of the achievements of the personality might be and however insignificant the individual's creative activity might appear to others. Such a sector always includes a central pattern of exhibitionism and grandiose ambitions, a set of firmly internalized ideas of perfection, and a correlated system of talents and skills, which mediate between exhibitionism, ambitions, and grandiosity, on the one hand, and ideals of perfection, on the other. [Kohut 1977, pp. 53–54]

For Kohut, self is more important than sex. The material that Kohutian analysis tends not to address is the primary stuff of orthodox analysis. A traditional analysis was thought to have reached the most profound level possible when the sexual and aggressive wishes toward the patient's parents had been uncovered, worked through, and understood — when the "bedrock" of penis envy or castration anxiety reached consciousness. In other words, therapeutic work centered on understanding and being able to sublimate one's sexual and aggressive instincts (drives); narcissism and other preoedipal issues were considered within this frame of reference primarily as defensive maneuvers. In the traditional view the child uses the basic drives and the inevitable oedipal conflict to develop the psychic structure of id, ego, and superego. While Kohut does feel that the so-called structural neuroses can be successfully treated using the drive-based theory, he prefers to place the oedipal issues and the drives in the larger context of the development of self. In other words, sexual and aggressive conflicts most often result from deficits in the self.

REJECTION OF DRIVE THEORY

After examining the transferences and the experiences reported by his patients, Kohut (1977) draws his own conclusions about aggression and pleasure:

> And it is on the basis of studying those aspects of my patients' transferences that relate to the question of the significance of human destructiveness — particularly their "resistances" and their "negative transferences" — that I have come to see their destructiveness in a different light, i.e., not as the manifestation of a primary drive that is gradually unveiled by the analytic process, but as a disintegration product which, while it is primitive, is not psychologically primal. [p. 114]

> Joy is experienced as referring to a more encompassing emotion such as, for example, the emotion evoked by success, whereas pleasure, however intense it may be, refers to a delimited experience such as, for example, sensual satisfaction. From the point of view of depth psychology, we can say, moreover, that the experience of joy has a genetic root different from that of the experience of pleasure; that each of these modes of affect has its own developmental line and that joy is not sublimated pleasure. Joy relates to the experiences of the total self whereas pleasure (despite the frequently occurring participation of the total self, which then provides an admixture of joy) relates to experiences of parts and constituents of the self. [p. 45]

Thus the existence of libido and aggression does not necessitate an acceptance of the drive model of the mind. For Kohut pathological pleasure-seeking or aggressive behaviors do not indicate simply a failure to sublimate ever-present innate drives but instead reveal a history of empathic failures on the part of the caregivers that forced the child to take refuge in satisfactions related to only a small aspect of his potential.

Kohut's (1977) reading of the Oedipus complex follows this enlarged picture, and he explains the Oedipus in terms of the match between the child's needs and the responses of the parents. Just as people who have mastered one task look forward to the challenge of a more demanding one, the oedipal period can be positive. A strong pre-oedipal self minimizes the likelihood that there will be an oedipal "crisis":

> Normal parents experience joy and pride concerning the developmental progress of their oedipal children. [p. 233]

> Parents who are not able to establish empathic contact with the developing self of the child will, in other words, tend to see the constituents of the child's oedipal aspirations in isolation – they will tend to see (even though generally only preconsciously) alarming sexuality and alarming hostility in the child instead of larger configurations of assertive affection and assertive competition – with the result that the child's oedipal conflicts will become intensified – just as a mother whose self is poorly consolidated will react to the feces and the anal region and not to the total vigorous proudly assertive anal-phase self of her child. [pp. 234–235]

> Optimal parents – again I should rather say: optimally failing parents – are people who, despite their stimulation by and competition with the rising generation, are also sufficiently in touch with the pulse of life, accept themselves sufficiently as transient participants in the ongoing stream of life, to be able to experience the growth of the next generation with unforced nondefensive joy. [p. 237]

To summarize, Kohut has tried to give the clinician a new frame of reference with which to understand well-established clinical material. He shifts the central factor, which determines pathology or health from the Oedipus complex to the development of a cohesive self – from the oedipal period to a much earlier time in childhood. What Kohut never states explicitly, but seems to imply, is that all oedipal pathology can be understood as a form, however minor, of pathology of the self. Kohut (1977) does say, though, that a child who has failed to develop a relatively cohesive self in early childhood will not be able to experience the Oedipus complex at all; this is based on his clinical impression that the oedipal material that narcissistic patients often present as analysis nears termination is an entirely new development, a "positive result of a consolidation of the self never before achieved [and not] a transference repetition" (p. 228).

KOHUT'S TOPOGRAPHY

Kohut acknowledges the existence of sexual and aggressive urges, but denies that they are fundamental biological instincts. Accordingly, he does not utilize Freud's second topography—the structural or dynamic point of view—in which the psyche is divided into id, ego, and superego, but instead retains the basic subdivisions into the conscious, the preconscious, and unconscious—Freud's first topography. Kohut develops the notion of vertical and horizontal splits in the structure of the mind. Patients whose appropriate narcissistic needs were not met split off their infantile grandiosity, the yearned-after "I am perfect"; this is the *vertical split*. This grandiosity, a hollow substitute for genuine self-esteem, is used as an escape from the primitive feelings of anxiety, the fear of annihilation, that in fact resulted from the continual failures of the mother and father to provide mirroring or to permit the child to idealize them; this is the *horizontal split*. Repressed below this split is the child's primitive neediness. Until adequate therapeutic work is done in these areas, the poorly consolidated self and its archaic needs cannot be addressed. Treatment strives first to provide the patient with adequate mirroring as well as the opportunity to idealize the analyst; in this context, patients can then expose their archaic narcissistic needs. The patient's preconscious, or conscious, experience against which the grandiosity defends is characterized by low self-esteem, emptiness, depression, and hypochondria.

Kohut proposes the existence of a bipolar self (as discussed earlier) that offers several chances for the child to develop a cohesive self. In addition, he so emphasizes the powerful joy of self-expression and creativity that one wonders whether this, for Kohut, may almost attain the organizing quality of a drive or instinct. This model of the mind stands as Kohut's alternative to Freud's id, ego, and superego, which are structured and powered by instinctual forces and the anxious conflicts they generate as the individual in the environment strives for pleasure.

ANXIETY

Kohut suggests a revised view of the nature of anxiety, for in his narrative, too, it is anxiety that motivates defensive positions such as grandiosity. Freudian anxiety, at its roots, occurs when the individual suffers from excessive excitation such that it cannot maintain homeostasis. There are four later forms that this anxiety may take: fear of the loss of the object, fear of the loss of the love of the object, fear of castration, and fear of loss of the superego's love. These anxieties come into being because of one's forbidden wishes (drives). Kohut (1977) proposes that there is an additional form of anxiety that motivates the defensive process in man: the fear of "the loss of self—the fragmentation of and the estrangement from his body and mind in space, the breakup of the sense of his continuity in time" (p. 105). He believes that the fear of psychological death is the basic and constantly present anxiety from which we suffer.

> Two basically different classes of anxiety experiences exist, rather than only one. The first comprises the anxieties experienced by a person whose self is more or less cohesive—they are the fears of specific danger situations (Freud 1926); the emphasis of the experience lies in essence on the specific danger and not on the state of the self. The second comprises the anxieties experienced by a person who is becoming aware that his self is beginning to disintegrate;

whatever the trigger that ushered in or reinforced the progressive dissolution of the self, the emphasis of the experience lies in essence on the precarious state of the self and not on the factors that may have set the process of disintegration into motion. [p. 102]

The nucleus of the patient's anxiety is, in other words, related to the fact that his self is undergoing an ominous change – and the intensity of the drive is not the cause of the central pathology (precariousness of self-cohesion), but its result. The core of disintegration anxiety is the anticipation of the breakup of the self, not the fear of the drive.

For Freud, then, drives are the basic factor that creates anxiety, motivation, and ultimately, psychic structure. For Kohut, early object relations fulfill these functions. Kohut does allow for a period of primary narcissism based on the (then) current research on infants' capacities, but believes that it is the relationship with the caregivers (i.e., the fact that parents treat babies as though they had rudimentary selves) that accounts for the self in fact beginning to develop. And Kohut also sees continuing dependence on objects as a normal part of adult life rather than as an immature regression from an ideal state of independence and autonomy.

EMPATHY AS SCIENCE

Perhaps Kohut's fundamental contribution, though, is his insistence on the subjectivity of the therapist, on the fact that empathy is the only tool we have with which to investigate our patients. This twentieth-century, post-relativity stance contrasts with Freud's belief in rationality and the self-proclaimed objectivity of nineteenth-century science. There was thought to exist, in Kohut's (1977) words, "a clear distinction between observer and observed" (p. 67). Kohut summarizes beautifully the difference between Freud and himself, and between the concerns of nineteenth- and twentieth-century Western civilization with his concepts of Guilty Man and Tragic Man:

> Man's functioning should be seen as aiming in two directions. I identify these by speaking of *Guilty Man* if the aims are directed toward the activity of his drives and of *Tragic Man* if the aims are toward the fulfillment of the self. To amplify briefly: Guilty Man lives within the pleasure principle; he attempts to satisfy his pleasure-seeking drives to lessen the tensions that arise in his erogenous zones. The fact that man, not only because of environmental pressure, but especially as the result of inner conflict, is often unable to achieve his goals in this area, prompted me to designate him Guilty Man when he is seen in this context. The concept of man's psyche as a mental apparatus and the theories clustered around the structural model of the mind constitute the basis for the formulations analysts have employed in order to describe and explain man's striving in this direction. Tragic Man, on the other hand, seeks to express the pattern of his nuclear self; his endeavors lie beyond the pleasure principle. Here, too, the undeniable fact that man's failures over-shadow his successes prompted me to designate this aspect of man negatively, as Tragic Man rather than "self-expressive" or "creative man." The psychology of the self — especially the concept of the self as a bipolar structure . . . — constitutes the theoretical basis for the formulations that can be employed to describe and explain man's striving in this second direction. [pp. 132–133]

CONCLUSION

Kohut's work offers fresh and effective ways of listening to patients with narcissistic disturbances. His theory paved the way for the research of Daniel Stern and the intersubjective approach. However, Kohut does not adequately acknowledge the extent to which his seeming originality in some areas is a rephrasing of previous thinkers such as Balint (1952, 1968) and Winnicott. And while his clinical insights on narcissistic transferences are brilliant—the idea of the self-object has become an indispensable part of the therapeutic lexicon—his metapsychology may be less persuasive both in his notion of mental structure and in his de-emphasis on the contribution the child makes to his own development in the form of needs and fantasies. Many clinicians in fact combine Kohutian clinical understandings with either ego psychological or object relations theoretical stances. Without Kohut, though, we would lack a sophisticated appreciation of the critical role of empathy in development, adulthood, and psychotherapy.

CASE ILLUSTRATION

Kohut teaches that empathy is both a crucial component in the child's upbringing as well as the tool with which the clinician can help to heal deficits of the self. The self, he feels, is the central psychological structure that is built and maintained by adequate healthy interactions with significant objects. In the earliest relationships, the child experiences these objects as being psychologically fused with himself. Thus, Kohut has referred to the objects as selfobjects.[2] The budding self's first requirement is to be provided with sufficient accurate mirroring responses from important selfobjects; without this, there can be no solid foundation for self-esteem. The following case illustrates the devastating consequences of such a critical early failure.

BACKGROUND

Z., a 28-year-old Asian-American woman, sought psychotherapy when she was applying for a job promotion and had

---

2. Kohut himself wrote of the "self-object," but "selfobject," a less confusing version, has entered general usage.

learned that a long-standing medical condition had been discovered by the company during the physical examination; for no apparent reason, this new piece of data was holding up her much hoped-for new job. Z. had developed rheumatic heart disease as a child, which by this time had caused some problems with the mitral valve and her employer's ostensible concern was about how well her heart would tolerate the physical demands—long hours and travel—that the new position would bring. Z.'s response to these medical issues was shaped by the psychological meaning of her childhood illness, as the history will demonstrate. As treatment began, though, Z. gradually revealed that the company's concerns were not limited to this; for Z., although brilliant in a demanding and specialized field, was severely compromised by her poor ability to get along with her co-workers and with the company's customers. Another concern that led this young woman to seek help was that yet another relationship with a man seemed to be coming to an end, this one having lasted almost two years. Although she was not clear why the relationship had deteriorated, her later conflicts about men suggested that she had not been able to tolerate the pressure to be truly intimate. Over the course of treatment, Z. would have several other relationships that ended under similar circumstances. She did have a number of female friends who proved to be loyal, although each was quirky in her own right.

Z. sought help from Dr. H., a female clinical psychologist of about 50. She entered twice weekly treatment that lasted for four years. At the time treatment began, Dr. H. had not yet become interested in Kohut's work. This case illustration thus is a study of how a competent and experienced clinician found herself unable to help a patient without enlarging her theoretical and clinical bag of tricks. Dr. H. described her first approach to this patient as eclectic/psychodynamic but she was essentially traditional in her basic beliefs about technique and psychopathology. A therapeutic impasse developed after only about a year, and Dr. H.'s profound desire to be of help to this flailing woman prompted her to rethink her theoretical and clinical understanding. Kohut's fascinating account of his own struggle may be found in his well known article, "The Two Analyses of Mr. Z." (1979).

Z. grew up in a medium-sized western city with her father, an insurance executive, her mother, an architect who gave up working in order to raise her children, and two brothers, one older, one younger. The mother seemed to be limitlessly adoring of Z., but in fact her lavish praise was poor camouflage for constant failures in empathy and her obsessive and anxious character. Z. viewed her father as a passive man but remembered him being very available and physically affectionate with her until she was about 5. She remained angry at him for his withdrawing from her, the reasons for which, even well into her adulthood, she could not understand. The ethos, promulgated most actively by the mother, was that their family was an ideal one. It was constantly emphasized that they were an example of perfection on display to the rest of their small community. The family dealt quite poorly with stress of any kind and tended to deny anything problematic. As a result, Z.'s garden-variety childhood illnesses were all but ignored by her parents. One sore throat did not improve on its own and Z. developed a high and persistent fever. It was the school nurse who alerted Z.'s mother to the fact that Z. needed medical attention and ought not to have been in school. Z., in fact, was suffering from a strep infection that, untreated, resulted in rheumatic fever and heart problems. The family perceived this to be a threat to their mythic state of perfection, and Z. herself internalized this attitude abut her medical vulnerability. The parents' insensitivity to their daughter's health reflected a pervasive refusal to see anything that would threaten their precarious self-esteem. Z.'s silence about her suffering signified that by age 9, when this incident took place, she had already learned to protect her parents from what they could not tolerate knowing. Superficially, though, this meant that Z. appeared to all purposes to be a precocious and able child who related well to adults; she did receive much praise for this as well as for her exemplary performance in all areas of academics.

Z.'s older brother became a surgeon and the younger became a prominent local politician; both remained in the hometown, living out their mother's dream of seeing her family as big fish in a medium-sized bowl. Z., however, left home to attend college and graduate school in a technical business field at competitive and prestigious institutions; she returned home reluctantly for vacations and did not choose to begin her career in her hometown. It is interesting to speculate about how the issue of separation affected Z. She was able to separate physically without anxiety, and emotional separation also does not seem to have been a particular issue for her. The time for the establishment of mirroring (though mirroring needs persist throughout life) occurs earlier in childhood than Mahler's rapprochement phase. It is possible that Z. was never able to establish relationships close enough for separation to hold any terror for her. Z.'s problems remained in the more primitive arena of establishing a cohesive self and of being able to establish and tolerate healthy self-selfobject relationships.

Z. did, after a long delay, receive the promotion at work, but this did not bring the immediate happiness and satisfaction she had expected. Instead, she was responsible for supervising a rather large staff and would describe herself to Dr. H. as feeling helpless, as though everything was a terrible mess. Her staff made constant demands on her, even as she was expected to spend at least two days each week visiting client companies. Nonetheless, within a few months, she adjusted to the new level of demands on her and reached a precarious stability. Although she was meeting and exceeding the goals that had been outlined by her boss, she was curt with her staff and co-workers. It was Dr. H.'s conjecture that only Z.'s intellectual gifts and genuine brilliance at her work, which the company recognized, stood in the way of her losing this job. But this success at work provoked further unexpected emotional turmoil in the patient. Z. alternated between a superficial enjoyment of her outstanding achievements and a sense that she was aggressively driving herself to be a success; when she felt this driven, she would become enraged and resentful and would then swing back in the other direction, telling everyone to "screw off." Dr. H. felt that Z.'s inability to take a steady pleasure in her work very likely signified that she was acting out her parents' wishes rather than expressing a consistent personal interest or a desire to do well.

INITIAL TREATMENT STRATEGY

Dr. H. found working with Z. to be like trying to focus a camera on a subject in motion—issues that seemed clear would suddenly disappear. After a year or so of treatment Dr. H. wondered why her interpretations were ineffective. Why was Z. still feeling so awful? Typical exchanges would involve long, exhausted, and frantic descriptions by Z. about how overburdened she felt by some work event. Dr. H. would listen with a growing sense of helplessness and mounting pressure to do something to help Z. She would typically try to help Z. get some perspective on the present difficulty by asking if the event brought anything to mind, sometimes asking (when she knew of specific childhood memories) whether there might be a similarity in the circumstances. Z. would respond by complaining of feeling even more overwhelmed by the demand that Dr. H.'s question itself placed upon her. Interpretations were experienced sometimes as attacking criticisms, and Z. would often be unable to contain her irritation at the therapist. Yet despite the rockiness of the sessions, there was something that kept Z. solidly in treatment, for she never missed a session. Dr.

H. later hypothesized that what had kept Z. there was the accurate perception that, despite the seeming ineffectiveness of therapy, Dr. H. genuinely *wished* to help her; Dr. H.'s struggles to understand how best to be of help were probably obvious to the patient.

The therapist's strategy was traditional in that she encouraged the patient to remember the childhood realities or fantasies — the so-called genetic material — that lay at the root of Z.'s pain. The assumption underlying this strategy is that it is conscious knowledge (cognitive and emotional) of repressed memories or feelings that will be therapeutic. Although Dr. H. was also sensitive to the negative transference as well as to the possibility that Z. was engaged in the re-creation of a libidinally charged masochistic relationship, these themes did not seem to explain Z.'s intense discomfort and pressure, constantly expressed, to be free of the disabling sense of emptiness and depressive episodes. Dr. H. also addressed transference material in a traditional way, assuming that Z.'s feelings about her in the present had been transferred from an object in the past and that the appropriate way to intervene was to elicit memories about that past object; this would be the therapist's tactic in response to the patient's irritation. But this, too, was ineffective, only serving to add fuel to the fire; Z. apparently could not tolerate any of these attempts at understanding. Both therapist and patient were increasingly frustrated.

BREAKING THROUGH THE IMPASSE

During the next few months of treatment Z. essentially maneuvered Dr. H. into a new therapeutic stance by coming to therapy sessions in what amounted to states of panic. At work she was going from one crisis to another (although she managed to give minimal indication of this in the office beyond her usual short temper). During this time Z.'s boyfriend had begun to see another woman, and a final breakup soon followed. Despite her dread of this separation, Z. seemed to react to this loss almost in a generic way revealing through this the degree to which her boyfriend had functioned as a selfobject rather than as a fully constituted individual in his own right.

Although Dr. H. was practically certain that Z. played a large part in creating these difficulties (and thus that insight would help prevent her from repeating these destructive patterns), the degree of Z.'s anxiety during the sessions made it impossible for the therapist to do more than psychological first aid. Dr. H. had to spend each hour calming her down. It is interesting to speculate whether one of the purposes of Z.'s mounting difficulties was in fact just this—to force the benign and caring therapist into providing what Z. needed. And indeed, the therapist came to realize that this altered approach was just what the doctor ordered. As Kohut (1977) explains,

> Some of the most persistent resistances encountered in analysis are not interpersonally activated defenses against the danger that some repressed psychological ideation will be made conscious by the analyst's interpretations or reconstructions; they are mobilized in response to the fact that the stage of understanding—the stage of the analyst's empathic echo or merger with the patient—had been skipped over. In some analyses—though by no means in all—the analyst will even have to realize that a patient whose childhood self-object had failed traumatically in this area will require long periods of "only" understanding before the second step—interpretation, the dynamic-genetic explanations given by the analyst—can be usefully and acceptably taken. [p. 88]

And so Dr. H. changed the way she dealt with this patient. Coincidentally, Z.'s demands took place at the time Dr. H. had begun to explore Kohut's contributions. Dr. H. tried to immerse herself in Z.'s psychic reality in order to establish an empathic understanding. Dr. H. became aware of "not wanting to feel what Z. felt because it felt so awful," and she continually experienced urges to help Z. figure out concrete ways to cope better with all the hassles and crises in her life. This pressure, a countertransference evoked by the patient, can be understood as deriving from Dr. H.'s perception of the patient's ego deficits; the pressure was for her to provide those missing functions for the patient. Dr. H., like Z., was feeling the dread of what lurked beneath the day-to-day problems – the chaos and anxiety that characterized Z.'s emotional life. This insight and the heightened self-awareness that followed helped Dr. H. tolerate the discomfort of listening to Z., and she further intensified her efforts to immerse herself in the patient's emotional world. The patient's panic states diminished as Dr. H. experimented with "being with" the patient rather than "doing for" her through "giving" her interpretations.

Through clarification of the transference Dr. H. also began to understand Z.'s chaos and negativity as an expression of a wish to be healthy. It became clear that Z.'s mother had always taken credit for all of Z.'s achievements; anything good that Z. accomplished was not attributed to Z. Thus negativity was a way in which Z. could achieve some differentiation from her mother – and some self-definition. In the therapeutic relationship, then, Z. experienced traditional interpretations as pressure to be compliant and good, to agree with the therapist's formulation; but it felt to her that being a compliant patient would only serve to signify that Dr. H. was a good therapist. This was a formidable dilemma for the therapist since working on Z.'s negativity would constitute an insult to a very fragile sense of self. The need for respectful mirroring and very cautious acknowledgment of Z.'s accomplishments in therapy and at work left Dr. H. on a tightrope. She addressed Z.'s transference feelings about her only as it was necessary to do so, and she did not urge Z. to explore childhood sources for them. Dealing with feelings in the present had the additional self-building function of affirming (mirroring) the actual experience of the patient (something previous selfobjects had been unable to do). (It should be noted that focusing on the transference in the here and now is not exclusive to the self-psychological approach.)

After about a year of this new approach, Dr. H. had become more able to "feel *with* Z., to stay with her in the experience and not feel the burden of trying to fix her." Z., also, showed evidence of settling down a bit on a daily basis, experiencing the normal stresses of work as slightly less panic-inducing. As Dr. H. began to feel less concerned that she would not be able to help Z., she became aware that she had previously felt that Z. had control over her. Z., in turn, began to expose *her* fear of being destroyed by other people. She would get enraged if Dr. H. was five minutes late in starting a session saying, "How dare you be late. Don't you realize I had to postpone a meeting to be here?" If she wasn't vituperative, she would start distancing herself.

Z. was becoming incrementally more stable in her feelings about work even though the urge to be the best remained strong. In spite of getting some recognition and respect for her unique creative contributions to the company, though, the feeling that she was working primarily to please other people persisted. But when things in her life seemed to be going well, Z. also had difficulty tolerating it and would become over-stimulated and anxious. This severe difficulty in tolerance of affect represented a condition not unusual in a young child, but Z. had never experienced the affective attunement from parents that would have made this no more than a develop-mental phase. She seemed to be balanced on an edge of some sort, superficially doing well in many ways, but more and more exposing in treatment her tendency toward grandiose rage and subsequent emotional withdrawal.

Z. became interested for the first time since the breakup in one particular man. She had previously described all men as pains in the neck who would use her and had had only two dates in three years. A jogging accident that forced her to leave

Kohut *207*

work for several weeks also took her away from this man. She described herself as being in a cloud lying in her room doing nothing: "See what happens when everything starts going well?" she said to Dr. H. Z.'s response to this injury brought into the limelight her crucial and traumatic experience with illness as a child, when she had contracted rheumatic fever as a complication of the untreated strep infection. Following this incident, Z. withdrew from her previous high level of achievement in school, describing this to Dr. H. as "turning away." She had been a "star" both in sports and in the classroom and felt as though the illness had "slapped me down." Although Z. was unable to comprehend that she might also have wanted to turn herself away from the desired and feared budding romance, this event did bring up the issue of her mother's role in her childhood illness, namely, why mother had been so oblivious to what must have been a very sick child.

Z. began discussing various memories of her mother, which Dr. H. understood in a Kohutian framework. Z. began to recall instances when her mother's empathy was inappropriate and thus harmful. Z. remembered her mother saying, "You are miraculous, you're so much smarter than I am, you can do anything—and look at what my life has come to." It seemed to Z. that her mother really meant, "Your accomplishments will redeem me, and I need them, for without them I am worth nothing." Thus Z. felt she had no choice but to strive for the highest possible level of achievement; what would normally have been a strong survival urge, achievement, had been perverted into belonging to her mother. Appropriate empathy would have communicated authentic admiration for Z. and nonpossessive pride in her achievements. Instead, Z. felt that her mother's continuing psychological stability depended on what she did; that receiving love depended on how she performed rather than on who she was. For Z., whose sense of self was based on what she did, the illness constituted a terrible threat to her almost nonexistent core identity. And her mother's

denial of Z.'s illness, indeed of anything that fell short of perfection, was just one reflection of her pathological use of her
daughter as a selfobject. Another inappropriate aspect to the
mother's remark, as Z. recalled it, was the refusal to allow Z. to
idealize her mother. The younger Z. was, the more crucial a
failing this would have been. Both mirroring and idealizing
functions of the mother as selfobject were deficient enough to
compromise severely Z.'s chances to develop a cohesive self.

The mother's failure to take care of Z. was playing itself out
in the transference. Z. was revealing, between the lines, her
assumption that she was so deeply bad and imperfect that Dr.
H. would also find her burdensome. Z. felt like an insatiable,
greedy baby, and the very knowledge of this need engendered
anxiety and self-loathing. This issue was very difficult to
confront, for to do so would require an interpretation of
exactly the sort that Z. did not easily tolerate. What Z. seemed
to need from Dr. H. were constant reassurances in the form of
signs from the therapist that she was emotionally there, and
that she *wanted* to be there. Dr. H.'s goal was to permit Z. to
experience in the therapeutic relationship what she had not
been able to as a child. Taking care of Z. had ceased to be
overwhelming to Dr. H. (as it had been to the mother) as soon
as she had altered her therapeutic style. Thus when Z. was in
seemingly bottomless distress Dr. H. would make remarks such
as, "What would feel helpful for me to say now?" Z. almost
invariably would indicate that all she needed was for Dr. H. to
listen—but the therapist's wish to be of help had been expressed, understood, and Z. would calm down. Behind Kohut's
"'only' understanding" lies the intention to understand, and
Z.'s upbringing had been characterized by such seemingly
deliberate refusal to understand that her basic trust that caregivers were benign was minimal at best. Dr. H. felt she had no
choice but to allow Z. to use her as the archaic selfobject that
just holds.

Behind Z.'s superficially attractive, competent, and sometimes brilliant professional functioning lay a fragmented sense of self that had emerged in full force in the therapeutic relationship with Dr. H. Unfortunately, as the treatment reached this holding pattern in which some work could be done, Z. received another promotion at her company, this one requiring her to move across the country. Due to a corporate restructuring, for Z. to have turned down this offer would have meant losing her job altogether. Although Dr. H. could not be certain about this, it appeared to her from Z.'s account and spontaneous reactions that the patient had not sought this new job, that she had not engineered this move as an attempt to escape the intimacy and power of the treatment. The move came up too quickly for there to be an extended and appropriate termination process, but Z. did seem to be consolidating the gains she had made. The time pressure seemed to function as a challenge to be overcome, and Z. even achieved some distance as they discussed plans for a referral. Although this summary has not emphasized this, Z. was prone to depressions that were sometimes quite severe. She had always refused a referral for a psychiatric consultation to consider medication, but she suggested to Dr. H. that her next therapist ought to be a physician so as to facilitate the use of medication. This is perhaps evidence of Z.'s most important gain—namely, that the relationship with Dr. H. had demonstrated to her that all caregivers were not as willing to ignore her needs as her parents had been, that there were people out there who truly wanted to help her.

8   DANIEL STERN:
THE INTERSUBJECTIVE REALITY
SHARED BY MOTHERS AND INFANTS

Daniel Stern (born 1934) presents thoughtful challenges to the
assumptions about infancy that have shaped psychoanalytic theories of normal development and psychopathology. A psychiatrist
and psychoanalyst, Stern is now based in Switzerland. His major
theoretical work, published in 1985, is *The Interpersonal World
of the Infant.* Its subtitle, "A View from Psychoanalysis and
Developmental Psychology," gives but a hint of the breadth of the
author's mastery of both of these related but distinct fields.
Stern's outline of development has not entered the standard
lexicon of most psychoanalytic clinicians, yet this work is central
to one of the most important current trends in psychotherapy—
the intersubjective approach. With an intellectual pedigree extending from Winnicott ("there is no such thing as a baby"), by
way of Kohut to infant researchers such as Stern, the primary
articulator of the intersubjective viewpoint is Robert Stolorow.
Stern presents an impressive set of observations and theories that
persuasively delineate the intersubjective reality shared by the
mother and her infant; Stolorow and others demonstrate in
clinical work with adults the application of this view that reality is
socially constructed.

Through his studies of normal infants, the *observed infant*, Stern has put psychoanalytic reconstructions of infancy—the *clinical infant*—to the test. His work demonstrates the strengths and weaknesses of both approaches to understanding infancy. As subjective beings we cannot avoid projecting into clinical work our own narratives, beliefs, memories, and fantasies about childhood; as a result, much of the language used to describe infancy is adultomorphic and pathomorphic. Yet our intuitions, when used properly, generate interesting and useful questions that can be studied in experiments done with infants. In experimental situations, "answers" are obtained from infants by monitoring their bodily responses (such as sucking, looking, averting the eyes, turning the head away, and so on)—experimental techniques devised only in the last twenty years. Stern holds that the results of these experiments can confirm or disconfirm our beliefs and moreover that they have the power to suggest further questions to ask ourselves and to use in the therapeutic listening process. Stern's clinical material is straightforward in outline and complex in detail. He sets out to do no less than answer the unanswerable question. "What is the subjective experience of an infant?"

DOMAINS OF EXPERIENCING

Stern proposes that there are four ways in which infants experience themselves and the world. These modes of experiencing develop at about the same chronological ages that other clinicians have noted as signifying changes in the developing infant, but Stern rejects the concept of the "stage" that has a beginning and an end. Rather, he holds that throughout life we continue to experience self and world in all of these modalities. This has implications for the diagnostic process, as any modality of functioning is vulnerable throughout the life cycle. Stern does feel, though, that there exist special vulnerabilites during the time when each modality begins to develop. Stern offers a developmental line of interpersonal relatedness, an account of how the infant comes to be specifically human in affects and capacity for empathy, whereas Mahler constructed a progression of psychological birth from a state of symbiosis to separation and individuation. In a discussion of whether to include intersubjective relatedness among the so-called autonomous ego functions, Stern (1985) asks,

> Are we dealing with a primary psychobiological need? The answer to these questions are actually momentous for clinical theory. The more one conceives of intersubjective relatedness as a basic psychological need, the closer one refashions clinical theory toward the configurations suggested by Self Psychologists and some existential psychologists. From the perspective of infancy research the question is still open. [p. 136]

How each clinician answers this question will depend on his most basic beliefs about the nature of human existence and will determine the methods and goals of psychotherapy he practices.

EMERGENT SELF AND RELATEDNESS

Stern (1985) sees the period from birth until about 2 months not as a time of normal autism or of primary narcissism but as one of active development:

> Infants busily embark on the task of relating diverse experiences. Their social capacities are operating with vigorous goal directedness to participate in social interactions. These interactions produce affects, perceptions, sensorimotor events, memories, and other cognitions. Some integration between diverse happenings is made innately. For instance, if infants can feel a shape by touching an object, they will know what the object should look like without ever having seen it before. Other integrations are not so automatic but are quickly

learned. Connectedness forms rapidly, and infants experience the emergence of organization. A *sense of an emergent self* is in the process of coming into being. The experience is that of the emergence of networks becoming integrated, and we can refer to its domain as the *domain of emergent relatedness*. Still, the integrative networks that are forming are not yet embraced by a single organizing subjective perspective. [p. 28]

Stern stresses that while parents and psychoanalysts have attended mostly to the physical aspects of the care of the newborn, in fact activities such as feeding, rocking, soothing, and bathing entail a great deal of social interaction. Although all experience is ultimately based in the body, physical sensation alone is insufficient to create a psyche. Infants possess inborn psychological talents that are used to perceive and organize the myriad of sensations. Stern (1985) outlines some of these rather amazing early abilities. *Amodal perception* (alluded to in the citation above) is the capacity "to take information received in one sensory modality and somehow translate it into another sensory modality" (p. 51). Research suggests that shape, intensity level, motion, number and rhythm are perceived amodally. There are also *physiognomic categorical affects* – anger, joy, sadness, fear, disgust, surprise, and interest – that seem to be innately recognizable to infants of many cultures. Each affect carries a particular level of intensity or urgency of the feeling level (*activation*) and a particular degree of pleasure or unpleasure (*hedonic tone*). Beyond these, Stern identifies what he names *vitality affects* – "elusive qualities . . . captured by dynamic, kinetic terms, such as 'surging,' 'fading away,' 'fleeting,' 'explosive,' 'crescendo,' 'decrescendo,' 'bursting,' 'drawn out,' and so on" (p. 54). Infants are seen as encountering vitality affects in such "events" as music, warm light, and types of movement by people or things. The infant organizes experience by engaging in activities that Stern dubs *constructionistic efforts* – assimilation, association, accommodation, and the identification of invariants (elements common to different experiences).

Stern attempts to connect deviations from average capacities in these functions to disorders first apparent in young children such as autism and pervasive developmental disorder. Babies who have difficulty with amodal perception may go on to develop learning disorders, for learning does require the capacity to process the visual, for instance, into the auditory or tactile modes. The issue of the match between the mother and the infant is also crucial, for poorly matched temperaments may result in social problems. Listing Stern's conclusions, though, gives little sense of the depth and texture of his work. What is of central importance here is the fact that he has constructed a kind of anatomy of relatedness, an enumeration of the very mechanisms by which the infant develops a relationship with reality. In a sense, what Stern describes as the emergent self might well be considered to be a version of what Hartmann termed the primary autonomous ego functions. Stern's language (certainly more emotionally evocative than Hartmann's) does seem to capture something of the substrate of adult existence, that which we do indeed experience but usually in a distant way, preconsciously or even unconsciously. Although there is no possibility of absolute confirmation, Stern's conception of early infancy as dominated by these perceptions appeals to one's common sense.

CORE SELF AND RELATEDNESS

At the age of 2 to 3 months a change comes about in the way infants are able to relate; they have begun to develop what Stern (1985) terms the *sense of a core self*.

> When engaged in social interaction, they appear to be more wholly integrated. It is as if their actions, plans, affects, perceptions, and cognitions can now all be brought into play and focused, for a while,

on an interpersonal situation. They are not simply more social, or more regulated, or more attentive, or smarter. They seem to approach interpersonal relatedness with an organizing perspective that makes it feel as if there is now an integrated sense of themselves as distinct and coherent bodies, with control over their own actions, ownership of their own affectivity, a sense of continuity, and a sense of other people as distinct and separate interactants. [p. 69]

Note that it is practically impossible to avoid observing and describing these changes in the language of adult affects, despite Stern's stated wish to understand the infant's subjectivity. As Lacan describes in his work on the mirror stage, this is an example of the inevitable process in which identity is shaped by a necessarily alienating language.

In the construction of the core self, the infant's repertory expands to include four major types of experiences (1) *self-agency* — authorship of one's actions and nonauthorship of what others do, volition, control of actions, and knowledge of the consequences of actions; (2) *self-coherence* — feeling oneself to be a physical whole with boundaries and a locus of action while in action and while still; (3) *self-affectivity* — experiencing patterned inner qualities of feeling (affects) that belong with other experiences of self; and (4) *self-history* — having the sense of enduring, of "going on being," in short, having memory. To develop these *self-invariants* of agency, coherence, affectivity, and history, the infant recalls and compares the minor changes as well as the constant elements in often repeated experiences. In other words, infants are able to identify aspects of self and other that do not change as they compare repetitious events; Stern (1985) calls these "islands of consistency." The ability to register episodes in memory, to recall them, and to generalize from several similar episodes is the process through which the infant establishes the self-invariants. The generalized episode (Representation of Interactions that have been Generalized, or RIG) exists in the preverbal infant as an aggregate, an "averaged experience made prototypic," or an expectation of "the likely course of events, based on average experiences" (pp. 96–97). Thus, the more experiences of a particular affective flavor the infant has, the more difficult it is to change the aggregate and thus the expectation; this will mean, however, that failures to meet expectations will be that much more significant in their momentary differences. In this emphasis on the highly affective character of these early months, Stern's material could be seen as lending support to Kernberg's theory of self-affect-other units as the building blocks of mental structure.

So far Stern has looked at how the infant defines a core self by identifying attributes of self experience (*self versus other*); he further seeks to describe the *self with other* and identifies various experiences that take place between infants and their caregivers, namely games and other interactions, that are crucial to forging the capacity to relate to others. By regulating affect, arousal, or physical closeness, caregivers create self-experiences for the infant that could not take place without the other. As Stern (1985) puts it, "There is no such thing as half a hug or half a kiss" (p. 102). The self-regulating other (that is, the one who regulates what the infant experiences) can alter the level of arousal (e.g., by eliciting a larger smile or increasing the intensity of the game), can create a sense of security or attachment (e.g., through cuddling or gazing), can determine which affect the infant will experience (by demonstrating an affect when an unsure infant "checks" back to the parent). "Both infant and caregiver also regulate the infant's attention, curiosity, and cognitive engagement with the world. The caregiver's mediation greatly influences the infant's sense of wonder and avidity for exploration" (pp. 103–104).

Experiences of being with self-regulating others are registered as episodes of memory in the infant, who then generates RIGs— the composite of all similar episodes that becomes the standard against which future episodes in this category of experience are measured. Stern terms this activated memory the *evoked com-*

panion. And mothers themselves have evoked companions that are based on RIGs of their own mothers, and these can act as powerful intergenerational determinants of their responses to their own infants. Transitional phenomena, Stern (1985) suggests, may also have their roots in this process, as infants have been seen to remain entranced by objects their mothers have used with them in play:

> Both while and immediately after the mother imbues the toy with the actions, motions, vitality affects, and other invariant attributes of persons, the infant's interest in the toy is heightened. . . . It has become, for the moment, a self-regulating person-thing, because like a self-regulating other it can dramatically alter experience of self. [p. 122]

In sum, then, the *sense of a core self* and the *domain of core-relatedness* evolve between the ages of 2 and 6 months. They represent a way of experiencing self and other as coherent whole units possessing the capacity to act, wish, feel, create, and recall memories, and engage in relationships with others. The functioning of the core self usually takes place without conscious awareness, yet is obviously an integral part of all adult experience. Problems in the maternal–infant relationship in regard to core-relatedness will predispose the child to difficulties in his future capacity to manage excitement, external and internal stimulation, and anxiety. Overstimulation as well as understimulation ranging from mild to severe can result when either parent or baby cannot adapt to the other.

REPUDIATION OF THE DUAL UNITY OF
MOTHER AND INFANT

In contrast to Mahler and to most generally accepted views of the young infant, Stern (1985) emphasizes the baby's ability to differentiate self and other. Klein's belief in the neonate's vast fund of knowledge, which included by implication some capacity to perceive separateness, did not inspire widespread support in the field. Stern strongly contests the notion that infants at this age believe themselves to be merged (undifferentiated in mental representation) with their mothers, arguing instead that

> the infant's first order of business, in creating an interpersonal world, is to form the sense of a core self and core others. The evidence also supports the notion that this task is largely accomplished during the period between two and seven months. Further, it suggests that the capacity to have merger- or fusion-like experiences as described in psychoanalysis is secondary to and dependent on an already existing sense of self and other. The newly suggested timetable pushes the emergence of the self earlier in time dramatically and reverses the sequencing of developmental tasks. First comes the formation of self and other, and only then is the sense of merger-like experiences possible. [p. 72]

Stern's new timetable challenges the standard psychoanalytic understanding of severe personality disorders. With the development of a core self placed in the first year of life, Stern would seem to suggest that borderline phenomena and pathological narcissism represent difficulties not with the establishment of initial identity but in a later phase. What Stern does not seem to offer, though, is an account of how this would take place. Would "the wish for merger and the fear of engulfment" (p. 105) result from the inability of the infant to achieve a subsequent normal developmental milestone? Or does Stern believe that failures to differentiate self and other do not represent normal development gone awry but rather entirely pathological entities? Is there an alternate narrative that illuminates as parsimoniously the functioning of particular borderline personalities and dysfunctional families? Stern may well be correct in his radical questioning of clinical wisdom and intuitive common sense; just because the baby *was* one with the mother *in utero* does not mean that this fact in any way must necessarily form the basis for the baby's psyche. And he points out that human beings much prefer to hear a story about our psychological roots that speaks of togetherness than that we originate in solitude.

Stern (1985) distinguishes these important experiences of togetherness from fusion, merger, and loss of interpersonal boundaries. Here and throughout, he argues that the preverbal infant's experiences are based in reality rather than fantasy:

> In the position taken here, these important social experiences are neither primary nor secondary mergers. They are simply the actual experience of being with someone (a self-regulatory other) such that self-feelings are importantly changed. During the actual event, the core sense of self is not breached: the other is still perceived as a separate core other. The change in self-experience belongs to the core self alone. The changed core self also becomes related (but not fused) with the core other. The self experience is indeed dependent on the presence and action of the other, but it still belongs entirely to the self. There is no distortion. The infant has accurately represented reality. [p. 105]

SUBJECTIVE SELF AND INTERSUBJECTIVE RELATEDNESS

Between the ages of 7 and 9 months, there unfolds another sense of self.

> This happens when [infants] "discover" that there are other minds out there as well as their own. Self and other are no longer only core entities of physical presence, action, affect, and continuity. They now include subjective mental states—feelings, motives, intentions—that lie behind the physical happenings in the domain of core-relatedness. The new organizing subjective perspective defines a qualitatively different self and other who can "hold in mind" unseen but inferable

mental states, such as intentions or affects, that guide overt behavior. This new *sense of a subjective self* opens up the possibility for intersubjectivity between infant and parent and operates in a new domain — the *domain of intersubjective relatedness* — which is a quantum leap beyond the domain of core relatedness. [p. 27]

Stern (1985) continues his argument for his view of separation when he points out that the subjective self depends on the operation of the core self; without a continuing sense of physical identity and separateness the discovery of "separate minds" (p. 124) would hold little significance for the baby. Note that this age range is typically when stranger anxiety is seen. Stern speaks of the baby's new capacity for *psychic intimacy*, the "desire to know and be known" (p. 126), but there also exists the opposite desire.

The achievement of intersubjectivity signifies that the infant has become aware not only of the results of interactions with parents (e.g., the feeding, the cuddling, etc.) but also of the process by which the parent came to take the action. In other words, the infant is increasingly aware of the empathic process, of the fact that his or her need or feeling state has been understood by the parent. The possibility of sharing psychic intimacy now supplements the bodily closeness of the domain of the core self. This potential to share subjective experience requires that parents begin the process of defining for their infant "what part of the private world of inner experience is shareable and what part falls outside the pale of commonly recognized human experience. At one end is psychic human membership, at the other psychic isolation" (p. 126). From all the affects that the infant manifests, the parents select by their emphases and reinforcements which are acceptable. These selections are made largely unconsciously and they tell the baby which feelings and which degrees or intensities of feelings are okay. It is necessary that parents have the capacity for empathy in order to be able to achieve adequate attunement with the child; significant psychopathology — "neurotic-like signs and symptoms; characterological malformation; and self pathology" (p. 223)—can be the result when appropriate human emotional responses are not acknowledged.

The preverbal infant is capable of sharing intersubjective states in three ways: through sharing joint attention (evidenced by the ability to point and to understand where to focus when mother points at something), sharing intentions (having the expectation that the parent will comprehend and then wish to satisfy the infant's expressed need, such as gesturing toward a bottle), and, most importantly, the sharing of affective states. Stern (1985) develops a concept he calls *affect attunement* to specify the process by which parents transcend simple (or slightly modified) imitation of the infant's sounds and expressions in moment-to-moment interactions. He describes how the mothers he has studied construct their verbal and nonverbal responses so as to match or parallel the contours of the infants' experience. One of his examples:

> A nine-month-old girl becomes very excited about a toy and reaches for it. As she grabs it, she lets out an exuberant "aaah!" and looks at her mother. Her mother looks back, scrunches up her shoulders, and performs a terrific shimmy with her upper body, like a go-go dancer. The shimmy lasts only about as long as her daughter's "aaah!" but is equally exalted, joyful, and intense. [p. 140]

Affect attunement is related to the concepts of other theorists such as *mirroring, echoing, deferred imitation* and *empathy*, but Stern feels it is a simpler and more accurate description of the process.

VERBAL SELF AND VERBAL RELATIONS

The last expansion of the self's capacities begins at about 15 to 18 months when the infant "is able to create shareable meanings about the self and the world." The development of the *sense of a verbal self* and the *domain of verbal relatedness* depends on "a new set of capacities: to objectify the self, to be self-reflective, to comprehend and produce language" (p. 28). While the advantages of being able to use language are rather obvious, the disadvantages are less so. Language, a code of shared symbols, permits increasingly complicated and efficient communication, with vastly increased potential to share subjective experience. In terms of the development of future pathology, though, language has also opened the door to distortions of reality insofar as the toddler has "transcended immediate experience":

> For the first time, the infant can now entertain and maintain a formed wish of how reality ought to be, contrary to fact. Furthermore, this wish can rely on memories and can exist in mental representation buffered in large part from the momentary press of psychophysiological needs. It can carry on an existence like a structure. This is the stuff of dynamic conflict. [p. 167]

On the positive side, infants can use words as transitional phenomena to aid in the process of mastering anxiety, and language allows the construction of a narrative about the infant's own life. Children of this age are also capable of using play in symbolic ways and, Stern believes, their capacity for empathy expands. This would make sense, as language would enrich the perceptive capacities that characterized the subjective self.

The increasing dependence on language, though, causes a rift in the infant's world, and this is the basis for Lacan's radical critique of the institution of the ego (see the later discussion of Lacan's mirror stage). Since emergent, core, and subjective senses and relatedness cannot adequately be translated into complex adult language much less into a child's rudimentary vocabulary, much of this rich experiential material begins to go unheeded. Stern describes the tendency for parents to grant primacy to verbal expressions, and not to pay equal attention to accompanying nonverbal communications. He believes that this encourages children to deny to themselves the existence of the (sometimes contrary) other senses of self.

One of the consequences of this inevitable division into the accountable and the deniable is that what is deniable to others becomes more and more deniable to oneself. The path into the unconscious (both topographic and potentially dynamic) is being well laid by language. Prior to language, all of one's behaviors have equal status as far as "ownership" is concerned. With the advent of language, however, some behaviors come to have a privileged status with regard to one having to own them. "To the extent that events in the domain of verbal relatedness are held to be what has really happened, experiences in the other domains suffer an alienation" (Stern 1985, p. 163). The many messages in many channels are being fragmented by language into a hierarchy of accountability. Stern hypothesizes that the seriousness often observed in children at this age results from their sense of losing access to a great part of their experiencing of the world and not to a lost sense of their own omnipotence or of the omnipotence of the mother.

The dominance of verbal relatedness can facilitate the development of a false self, as some self-experiences are acknowledged and rewarded; what is left out of verbal experience, what is left unsaid or unthought is critical. Stern identifies four "domains of self-experience"—the social, the private, the disavowed, and the "not me"—which represent the continuum from social comfort to the projection of aspects of the self. Language, as a system of symbols, also gives the child the power to engage to a much greater degree in the distortion of reality. Central to how the child will cope with the verbal domain is how well he has previously learned to modulate anxiety and manage stimulation.

STERN'S CONTRIBUTIONS IN CONTEXT

Stern's view of other theorists such as Mahler, Winnicott, Klein, Kernberg, and Kohut is that they base their theories on an incorrect assumption that early infancy carries a normal stage in which the infant believes himself to be fused with mother. Stern is of the opinion that they have attributed to the infant fantasies, wishes, and fears possible only in older children and adults. While he is in harmony with the self psychologists concerning the centrality of the concept of the self and subjectivity to any psychodynamic theory, his work does not fit in the self psychological mold without some friction. Although Stern does not speak extensively about adult psychopathology, in his detailed study of the capacities of the infant there would seem to be an appreciation of the contribution of the child to future problems. To be sure, empathic failures, mediated perhaps through unsatisfactory RIGs in the parents, will cause difficulties for the child (for Kohut, this was *the* source of pathology); but Stern sees that problems will also occur if the child's integrative and perceptive functions were compromised or not firmly "hard-wired." Another way in which Stern sounds slightly different from Kohut is in his stress on the positive aspect of autonomy. He is in agreement with Kohut, however, that the need for selfobjects is lifelong. Stern (1985) tries to fashion a unifying perspective:

> The notion of becoming maturely independent of others and the notion of continually building and rebuilding a more extensive working set of "self-others" as a maturational goal are just opposite ends of the same spectrum. [p. 244]

Concerning another important question, though, it would not seem possible to reconcile opposing points of view. Stern (1985) finds no evidence that classical psychoanalytic theory's Eros and Thanatos exist in the observed infant. He concludes from his extensive observations that the Freudian concepts of innate drives and the theory of psychosexual zones that are sequentially cathected have not been of great use.

> While there is no question that we need a concept of motivation, it clearly will have to be reconceptualized in terms of many discrete,

but interrelated, motivational systems such as attachment, competence-mastery, curiosity and others. It is of no help to imagine that all of these are derivatives of a single unitary motivational system. What is now most needed is to understand how these motivational systems emerge and interrelate and which ones have higher or lower hierarchical standing during what conditions at what ages. The pursuit of such questions will be hampered if these motivational systems are assumed a priori to be derivatives of one or two basic, less definable instincts rather than more definable separate phenomena. [p. 238]

Stern also questions the notion that the pleasure principle precedes the reality principle in chronology. He suggests that in light of what recent research has demonstrated—the infant is born with more abilities that even Hartmann could have imagined—it makes more sense to conceive of a "simultaneous dialectic between pleasure principle and reality principle, an id and an ego, all operating from the beginning of life" (p. 239). And never the twain shall meet!

IMPLICATIONS FOR TREATMENT

The value of this working theory [of the development of domains and of self-experience] remains to be proved and even its status as a hypothesis remains to be explored. Is it to be taken as a scientific hypothesis that can be evaluated by its confirming or invalidating current propositions and by spawning studies that lead elsewhere, or is it to be taken as a clinical metaphor to be used in practice, in which case the therapeutic efficacy of the metaphor can be determined? It is my hope that it will prove to be both. [Stern 1985, p. 275]

The value of any psychodynamic theory to a clinician is in its ability to generate new ways of listening to patients. Stern indeed does that, offering specific guidelines about listening stances. Classical interpretive postures will relate to the patient's verbal self (and the oedipal period is certainly characterized by its verbal quality) while so-called empathic responses will speak to the earlier states. More specifically, empathic interventions may be geared to the core self, for instance if the therapist directs attention to the patient's bodily sensations. Intersubjective states may also be addressed in the empathic mode. All therapists have worked with patients (sometimes termed *alexithymic*) who do not have easy access to their affects, and Stern's work provides another way of listening to this material. Stern (1985) states that "the affective component of [a] key experience usually resides primarily in one domain of relatedness. . . . The clinical question then becomes, what sense of the self carries the effect?" (p. 268). One may then direct interventions to the domain in question, speaking in the terms in which the particular issue at hand would have been experienced by that sense of self. The problem with all this, though, is that clinicians, too, live primarily in the verbal domain, with perhaps little conscious access to other modes of experiencing. But good clinicians undoubtedly utilize information they glean via their intersubjective and core selves, and heightened awareness that these modes of perception exist can only help sharpen clinical acumen.

The suggestions Stern makes on applying his developmental theory to clinical work with adults are largely untested. Mahler's work, in contrast, has provided both a useful sequence in which genetic (historical) reconstructions may be located as well as an effective frame of reference from which to understand the patient's current object relations, including transference material. The intersubjective school does rely on some of Stern's core assumptions that intersubjective relatedness is a basic psychological need, and the following case illustration demonstrates the application of the view that reality is intersubjectively determined. But it is not yet clear that Stern's domains furnish quite as useful a metaphor for work with adults as Mahler's. For the clinical assessment of children and families, however, Stern's ideas are of enormous importance.

CASE ILLUSTRATION

The following case material is included as an example of the intersubjective approach to adult treatment. This is becoming one of the most influential revisions of classical theory and technique in psychoanalytic psychotherapy and psychoanalysis. The core of the matter rests in the understanding of the transference. Originally, Freud used the term *transference* to indicate literally that the affect or idea was directed toward a parent or other important object in the patient's life and that it had been transferred onto the neutral, anonymous, blank-screen analyst. This material will illustrate how the clinician here does not automatically assume that the transference (now used in the wider sense of referring to the patient's reactions to the therapist) represents a distortion of the clinician or a projection of the patient's material. Instead, the analyst carefully considers the patient's reaction, keeping in mind the possibility that the patient may be observing something that analyst has actually done, and that, most importantly, the truth of the matter lies in the emotional dynamic created by the encounter of two subjectivities. Indeed, as will become clear, if the analyst had treated the transference material in the traditional manner, this likely would have played into the sadomasochistic enactment the patient was attempting to create. An important caveat applies to this case — and indeed to all adults in psychoanalytically oriented treatment — and it is articulated by Mark Grunes (1984): when we treat adults, "we are dealing with complex condensations, not only of child and adult, but of pathologically inflamed and updated forms of childhood developmental need. For these reasons alone, the therapeutic object relationship, though similar, is radically different from the parent-child relation" (p. 131).

The patient, N.-P., a single man, was 30 at the beginning of a successful four-times-a-week analysis. He was the youngest of his family's three children, all boys. His father, M. was a career military officer who came from a wealthy family. His mother was a timid and recessive person who was a "good" military wife, supporting her husband in all his moves and tyrannical demands. She defended her husband to the children, never acknowledging his excesses, except indirectly in that she made excuses for his behavior. There is an unusual pre-history to this case, which is, in some ways, more relevant than the patient's actual childhood history. The analyst, Dr. K., had seen N.-P.'s father in episodic once weekly psychotherapy for depression some ten years previously. Thus Dr. K. had some knowledge of the conditions under which N.-P. had grown up. (N.-P. was aware of his father's treatment and was referred to Dr. K. by his father.)

M., the father, was a profoundly narcissistic man, prone to outbursts of violent rage. His choice of career in the military (in which he followed in his father's and grandfather's footsteps) did not serve as an adequate container for his aggression, and he showed himself unable to accept any interpretation that implied even a mild question about his judgment or capacities. Nonetheless, in psychotherapy Dr. K. was able to help M. ameliorate his outbursts of anger to a certain extent. However, he remained by any measure, a difficult man to live with and to please. M.'s need to idealize Dr. K. was intense, as were his demands for Dr. K.'s approval.

M.'s demands on the children took a specific form. First, he wanted them to go into the military and to demonstrate enthusiasm and loyalty toward the military life and ethos. In addition, he was unable to tolerate in his children any signs of helplessness, neediness, or dependency. And this did not refer only to the sort of emotional needs these words might evoke, but also to any demonstration of lack of knowledge. A seemingly innocuous question one son asked concerning his studies at a prestigious military academy brought on beratement, disdain, and rage from his father. The father would tell his children that they could be anything they wanted to be, giving the appearance of believing in their abilities and potential, but he became enraged at the slightest sign that what they wanted for themselves differed in any way from his goals for them. "You can do anything you want" was spoken; left unspoken was the threat, "but it had better be what I want you to do."

The first two sons did not go into the military, but they were ferociously rebellious and aggressive, following their father in personality style if not in career. N.-P., on the other hand, was a shy and sensitive young man who yearned for the life of the mind rather than a life of action and aggression. His ambition was to become an art historian and to teach art appreciation in the education department of a museum. He was 19 when he first saw Dr. K. Like his mother, and unlike his brothers, N.-P. was soft and yielding to his father's rage; he loved his father and desperately wanted his approval. Yet, it seemed impossible for him to obtain this because his desire to enter the museum field and his abhorrence of the military were so strong.

At the time he initially sought help from Dr. K., N.-P. was suffering from a persistent depression. He was in conflict about his relationships with women. A series of relationships had followed a similar pattern: N.-P. would develop an attraction to a young woman, begin an involvement, discover that he did not like her as much as he had expected to—usually because he had realized that she was weird in some way—and then find himself unable to break up with her due to a reluctance to hurt the woman. He experienced guilt about this predicament and saw no way out. The pattern of coping that he had developed within the family, timidly pacifying others so as to avoid conflict and his resulting anxiety, did not work in the world of romantic relationships. The most pressing problem, though, seemed to be his inability to decide upon a career goal. What he wanted to do was something his father deeply disdained;

yet, because he so craved his father's approval, he was stuck.
Dr. K. recommended psychoanalysis to this troubled adolescent, and N.-P. in fact came in for three episodes of four-times-
a-week on-the-couch treatment, each episode lasting only
about three months. Each ending would be precipitated by
mounting pressure from the father that N.-P. had had enough
treatment. These contacts ended up, despite the frequency,
being mainly supportive rather than insight-oriented, although
Dr. K. remained firm in his conviction that psychoanalysis
proper was the treatment of choice for this patient, who had
the intellect, psychological mindedness, and persistence to
benefit from that modality. N.-P. completed the last brief bout
of treatment at age 22 and did not contact Dr. K. again until his
thirtieth birthday; at that time, he requested psychoanalysis.

An obvious concern in this situation is raised by the question of treating two members of the same family. First, it was
clear to Dr. K. at the time he agreed to see N.-P. that M. would
not be returning to treatment with him. He also knew that M.
regarded him as the savior of the entire family and that
accepting this role would be unlikely to harm M. Finally, with
regard to offering psychoanalysis to N.-P., Dr. K. is a sophisticated and gifted clinician, and his judgment that he would be
able to handle any transference manifestations resulting from
this complicated situation was reasonable and accurate. It
should also be noted that Dr. K. is a individual of unusual
openness and warmth. Enactments, though, are the stuff of
psychodynamic treatment, and the prehistory of this case
simply meant that Dr. K. knew in advance what the subject
matter of the first enactment would probably be. Nonetheless,
the circumstances under which N.-P. began treatment were
certainly out of the ordinary.

To give a snapshot of N.-P. at age 30, he had finished college
with some difficulty, having dropped out once to work at a
menial job in the Midwest for a time. Although still passion-

ately interested in the museum field, he was working at an engineering consulting company. His intellectual abilities were apparently sufficient that he was considered to have above average ability in this field; he indeed commanded a more than respectable salary. N.-P. had taken some graduate courses in art history, but he experienced both the sense that he wanted to do this well and simultaneously that he couldn't do this well. To complete the picture, he was involved in a relationship of several years' duration with a woman he had met when he had moved north. She had followed him back to his home city in the South but had moved back home in response to N.-P.'s inability to make a commitment to marriage. The relationship, though, continued on a long-distance basis with regular flying trips on weekends. It was Dr. K.'s impression, too, that this woman did not possess the borderline features he had suspected in the girlfriends of N.-P.'s adolescence. Thus the analysis proper began.

The episode on which we will focus took place about four months into the analysis. Understandably, the transference emerged quickly, as it had been building for years first based on N.-P.'s knowledge of his father's relationship with Dr. K. and then emerging from N.-P.'s own episodic treatment as a late adolescent and young adult. The analysis got off to a good start. Within the first few weeks, N.-P. revealed with a mixture of embarrassment and then relief that he had not told Dr. K. what was really bothering him in the other analyses (that is, the other brief episodes of therapy); he went on to reveal sexual fantasies that were troubling to him. In this matter and in other areas Dr. K. felt that N.-P. was free associating (as much as a beginning analysand can achieve this) in the sessions in a way he had not done before.

N.-P. tended to speak in a vague and quiet way, seemingly a continuation of his pattern of the minimizing and avoidance with which he related to his family. A strange and subtle phenomenon gradually impressed itself on Dr. K., who puzzled

about it for a few weeks before being able to develop a
hypothesis. Dr. K. noticed that N.-P. would react to interpretations with enthusiasm, interest, and apparent thoughtfulness,
seeming truly to pick up on and utilize Dr. K.'s interventions.
But Dr. K. felt uneasy, as though somehow N.-P.'s integration
of the interpretations was illusory. Dr. K. then began to perceive the pattern. That is, N.-P.'s enthusiasm for the insight
seemed to dissipate after a few days, to be replaced by uncomfortable silences and then a litany of vague dissatisfaction,
gradually mounting in intensity. N.-P. would be disgruntled
about the analysis. Was it accomplishing anything? Would it
help him? He would at these moments speak of how hard it was
to resist pressure from his father to end the treatment. To Dr.
K., N.-P. seemed unsettled and irritable, and the repeating
cycle of the enthusiasm for and then inability to use interpretations bespoke a transference issue. Dr. K. wondered whether
it was related to some dissatisfaction with the analyst, and he
pointed out his observations and hypothesis to the patient.

In the interchange that took place during the following
sessions, it became clear that N.-P. regarded Dr. K.'s interpretations as clues to where he was supposed to go, in the analysis
as in life. He would follow along, but somehow started to feel as
though he wasn't getting anywhere. This would usher in the
despondent feelings. He had a firm conviction that Dr. K.
knew, infallibly, what N.-P. needed to do. (Although N.-P. did
not become aware of this negative transference material until
much later into the treatment, there was also a sense that Dr. K.
was willfully withholding his knowledge from the patient.
However, at this early point, the analyst's omniscience was
experienced as benign.) N.-P.'s response certainly suggested
that he was experiencing Dr. K. to be like his father in his
imagined certainty and knowledge. A clinician thinking along
these lines, namely the classical view that transferences represent distortions of the actuality of the therapist, might well
have offered an interpretation at this point: "I think you feel

that I, like your father, know where you're supposed to be going, and that I'm giving you directions." Dr. K., however, took a different view, an intersubjective one that presumed that the truth of the matter lay in the relationship that had developed between them.

Dr. K. closely examined how he viewed N.-P. in the sessions and how he felt about what N.-P. had said. He came to realize that he experienced N.-P. as very needy of his help and that he, Dr. K., did indeed have a subtle but pervasive sense that he knew what N.-P. needed to accomplish; this sense went beyond the ordinary and benign image of one's patient as changed that every therapist needs to have in order to engender the appropriate hope for improvement. But Dr. K. also examined his own feelings very closely and suspected that this impulse to give direction under the guise of interpretations did not emanate from himself alone. In other words, Dr. K. discovered that a transference enactment was taking place in which the patient was evoking his response. It was through the tone and manner of his interpretations — via the music rather than the lyrics[1] — that Dr. K. realized he was indeed behaving like a version of N.-P.'s father, paternalistic and pushing in attitude. While the father was dogmatic in his certainty, though, Dr. K. turned out to be benign, as he was able not only to hear N.-P. say "no" to him but even, as in this vignette, invite the patient to disagree. While Dr. K. did not fly into vituperative rages as did M., he shared with M. a certain tendency toward being controlling. It was this quality in Dr. K. that had made him, for a brief time, an unconsciously willing partner in N.-P.'s enactment. And it took what Stolorow and his colleagues (1987) refer to as "decenter-[ing] from [one's] own reactions" (p. 56) for the enactment to show itself in bold relief. Thus the following exchange took place:

---

1. I thank Newell Fischer, M.D., for this analogy.

Dr. K.:   You have the sense that I've been giving you clues and that I always know what's going on with you and where you need to be going. You know, at first I didn't think I was, but I see now that in a certain way I do. I think I have a picture of where I think you should be going. Even though I try to just focus on understanding, I think that picture has come across in what I say. You hear me subtly giving directions and you seize on what I say because you want so much to feel better. But then because it's mine and not yours, you give up on it.

N.-P.:   I'll tell you one thing you're really wrong about. You keep saying it's my father, that everything is due to my father. But you're wrong, it's my mother.

And as N.-P., with new areas of his thoughts and feelings accessible, began to speak about his shadowy and recessive mother, Dr. K. realized that the treatment had deepened. The change-inducing elements of this interpretation are multiple and include Dr. K.'s willingness to examine his own contribution to the process (countertransference), his assumption that he was not the sole possessor of the truth, and the view that the truth lay in a mutual examination of the jointly experienced but differently perceived interaction.

Stern describes the infantile prototypes of this two-person reality which is at the core of the intersubjective perspective as applied in adult treatment. The above case vignette is particularly apt because of the great likelihood that any other approach would have risked further collusion with the enactment. In other words, if Dr. K. had used the interpretation suggested earlier as an example of the classical strategy ("I think you feel that I, like your father, know where you're supposed to be going, and that I'm giving you directions.") the very nature of this, that the analyst *knows* but does not participate in the process, would have replicated for the patient the sense of his father's distanced judgments.

Note that in this process material, the analyst does not reveal his countertransference experience with the attitude that this reifies the patient's subjective experience. This would be counter to the intersubjective approach, as it would do no more than substitute the analyst for the patient as the arbiter of an objective reality. Rather, Dr. K. uses his experience to stimulate a joint inquiry into the patient's experience and into the ways in which the relationship is a carrier of important intrapsychic data—that is, into the intersubjective field.

As the treatment went on Dr. K. learned about the role of the mother in the complicated family process, and he realized that N.-P. had been right in feeling that he had not understood well enough how significant the mother was to N.-P.'s experience of growing up. N.-P. constantly saw his mother hurt by his father and dreaded each new instance of this. Although the mother would never have considered herself to be abused, she would cry after each burst of rage from M. N.-P. was angry at father for this, and felt deep guilt for not being able to protect mother. Yet, he also felt betrayed by his mother's failure to protect *him* from his father. Thus stuck, he developed the timid, hesitant vagueness that Dr. K. observed. But it was his very helplessness that evoked in the analyst the desire to help and guide N.-P. The central issue in the enactment was the patient pushing Dr. K. to make everything the patient's fault, and this because M., his father, could not tolerate anything wrong with himself (M.) and thus became enraged at the slightest sign of weakness in his children or his wife (who, Dr. K. had concluded, were essentially treated like selfobjects). N.-P. needed to protect his analyst and himself from the dire consequences that would result from the analyst feeling incompetent. Unlike the father, though, Dr. K. was willing and able to identify and tolerate his own imperfections.

The analysis progressed over four years to a successful conclusion. The dynamic described in this vignette was one of the central ones of the treatment and was repeated many times and at deeper and deeper levels of significance. The patient terminated in order to move across the country to marry his very patient girlfriend. He had completed his course work in graduate school and was working steadily on his dissertation. At times N.-P.'s conflict reemerged, and he experienced mild recurrences of the work inhibition due to a sense of obligation rather than pleasure in his new field of work. Each time this took place, N.-P. was increasingly able to engage in self-analysis, which served to dissipate his anxiety; thus, Dr. K. felt confident that the termination was not premature.

The intersubjective perspective that informed Dr. K.'s work acknowledges that communication is comprised not only of verbal elements but also of elements of the earlier domains that Daniel Stern detailed. Enactments occur in which states of mind appear to be magically transmitted. But there is not ESP taking place. Perhaps it would be appropriate to coin a new term—EVP, extra-verbal perception—to point to the myriad ways in which people receive nonverbal communications. These mechanisms are not unrelated to the Kleinian concept of projective identification, yet in important ways they do differ. In the intersubjective view, there is no presumption either that the infant, or patient, had distorted reality or that affects had been projected *into* the therapist. In the words of Stolorow and colleagues (1987):

> A fundamental assumption that has guided our work is that the only reality relevant and accessible to psychoanalytic inquiry (that is, to empathy and introspection) is *subjective reality*—that is, that of the patient, that of the analyst, and the psychological field created by the interplay between the two. . . . *Attributions of objective reality* . . . are *concretizations of subjective truth.* Analysts' invoking the concept of objective reality, along with its corollary concept of distortion, obscures the subjective reality encoded in the patient's productions, which is precisely what psychoanalytic investigation should seek to illuminate. [pp. 4–5]

As Kohut owed a debt (largely unacknowledged) to predecessors such as Balint and Winnicott, so also do Stern and Stolorow owe a debt (openly acknowledged) to Kohut. Their focus on empathy as the primary tool of psychoanalytic work is the standard fare of self psychology, but their fresh consideration of previous analytic concepts of truth and reality adds a new perspective to the therapist's bag of tricks. And it is the work of Stern and other infant researchers that offer tantalizing clues to the earliest forms of human experience and communication.)

9 FRÈRE JACQUES: LEARNING TO PLAY WITH LACAN

While it is helpful to have a working knowledge of Freud's ideas and of the history of psychoanalytic thinking in order to appreciate the contributions of the dramatis personae of this book, it is nonetheless possible to learn a great deal from any one of them without extensive prior knowledge. This cannot be said about the work of Jacques Lacan (1901–1981), the radical French psychoanalyst. Lacan's influence, which is perhaps more profound the further one moves outside the boundaries of psychoanalytic and psychotherapeutic practice, bespeaks his immersion in the intellectual traditions of philosophy, linguistics, anthropology, and literature. Let us not forget that Freud was in a similar way a Renaissance man, often drawing examples from literature or art. I would not discourage a beginner in this field from reading Freud, even though Freud can be easier to understand after one has a sense of how his theories changed over his lifetime. In the case of Lacan, however, it is almost essential to read the commentaries before reading the real thing. In contemplating the difficulty of understanding Lacan, I am reminded of what I was once taught about the use of the image of the strawberry in Hieronymus Bosch's painting, *The Garden of Earthly Delights*. The strawberry is delicious, a true experience of temptation and pleasure, but the pleasure is an evanescent one, for the flavor does not remain on the palate after the morsel is swallowed. The work of Lacan is as jarring and moral in its message as that of Bosch, and yet it seems to vanish from the mind in the very process of learning, I suspect because the ideas are so unfamiliar that we do not yet know quite how to assimilate them. This chapter, then, outlines the major Lacanian contributions and places them in the context of the preceding material in this book; the scope of Lacan's thought, though, vastly exceeds what will be included here.

It is important to appreciate the cultural context in which Lacan lived and wrote, for the place of intellectual discourse in France is quite different from most other places in which analytic thought has become a significant force. Perhaps the most vivid way of illustrating this is to point out that one of the most popular television shows in France in the 1980s was "Apostrophe," a Sunday evening program, their "60 Minutes," as it were; prominent intellectuals, writers, academics, and artists participated in a roundtable discussion of recent works. Another show, "Le Divan," consisted of an interviewer positioned behind an oversized couch on which the interviewee reclined. Also, what Mitchell (1985) has termed the "preposterous difficulty of Lacan's style" (p. 4) is not wholly unrelated to the fact that Paris is the fashion capital of the world; the French are more likely to appreciate a difficult style as expressive of the complexities of the theorist and the theory. Lacan is said to have pointed out with characteristic accuracy and arrogance that "It is an empirical fact . . . that after ten years time, what I have written becomes clear to everyone" (Turkle 1981, pp. 239–240).

One source of the difficulty of reading Lacan's texts is that he himself intended them to be difficult. Also, the reception of his work was not unaffected by his personal qualities. Even Stuart Schneiderman (1983), one of Lacan's analysands and admirers, writes, "Accusations of imbecility and the like flowed from Lacan as naturally as water flows downstream" (p. 19). And Lacan's influence was so great that there developed a polarization of French psychoanalysts—one was either with him or against him. In fact, analytic institutes had split because of his very presence. The International Psychoanalytic Association, led by Heinz Hartmann, condemned Lacan's practices, withdrew his authority to be a training analyst, and refused to allow him to present his ideas under their auspices; Rudolf Loewenstein, who had been Lacan's analyst, participated in these deliberations. This is only the proverbial tip of the iceberg, a mere taste of the controversy that seemed to emanate from Lacan. So, what was all the fuss about? Are Lacan's ideas truly dangerous?

To address the knottiness of Lacan's metapsychological naughtiness (Lacan's work is riddled with wordplays more elegant than these), we will begin in the middle with his best known clinical heresy—his failure to respect the sanctity of the 45- to 50-minute analytic hour. His treatment "hours" were of unpredictable length, often as short as five minutes. What can be the rationale for this seemingly wild technique? To begin with, Lacan saw himself first and foremost as a reader of Freud and as one who picked up where Freud had never quite been able to get due to the chronological accident that structural linguistics had not yet been developed. Lacan does his best to persuade us that Freud really did have embedded in his writings, on the tip of his tongue, as it were, the philosophy that Lacan later articulated. As Lacan said, in 1980, "C'est à vous d'être lacanien, si vous voulez. Moi, je suis freudien." ("It's for you to be a Lacanian, if you wish. I, myself, am a Freudian.") (Schneiderman 1983, p. 91, my translation). And the Freud to which Lacan returned was not the Freud later co-opted by the American ego psychologists, but rather the earlier Freud whose work focused on discovering meanings rather than delineating mechanisms of the processes of the mind (Turkle 1981). From *The Interpretation of Dreams* (1900), in which Freud declared dreams to be structured like language, Lacan took language as the stuff of psychoanalytic meaning. And Freud's (1923) pronouncement, "Wo Es war, soll Ich werden," usually translated "Where Id was, there Ego shall be," Lacan reinterpreted to read "Where It was, there ought I to become" (Schneiderman 1983, p. 169).[1] In 1953 (the year in which he resigned from the Société Psychoanalytique de Paris over the issue of training nonmedical candidates), as described by Jonathan Scott Lee (1990), Lacan elaborated that "the ego or *moi* is fundamentally an illusory identity, inherently weak, alienating and alienated, and a clear hindrance to the curative aims of psychoanalysis" (p. 32). Again, the pl/knot thickens – what is all of this about? The answer lies in the mirror.

THE MIRROR STAGE

In 1936 Lacan attempted to deliver a paper on what he termed the mirror stage, only to be interrupted by Ernest Jones after ten minutes. He finally in 1949 delivered in its entirety his paper entitled, "The Mirror Stage as Formative of the Function of the I as Revealed in Psychoanalytic Experience," in which he describes how the child assumes "the armour of an alienating identity" (Lacan 1977, p. 4). Between the ages of 6 and 18 months (note that this is Lacan's first and last "developmental" contribution to the field) the child has the experience of recognizing himself in the mirror. Now this is to be understood not only literally, that there is an actual mirror image, but also figuratively in that the child sees his reflection in the responses of his parents. The key point Lacan insists on is that at the time this occurs the child exists in a state of physical and mental dis-unity and uncoordination. Thus, what Winnicott and Kohut welcomed as a positive and organizing effect of this reflection for Lacan represents the institutionalization of a false sense of unity for the baby.

---

1. For a fascinating discussion of the problems of the translation of Freud's work, see Bettelheim (1983).

There develops an irreparable and inevitable gap (*béance*) between the experience, however fragmented, of the bodily self and the falsely whole mirror image, the self objectified – seen through the eyes of the Other. In Lacan's words,

> We have only to understand the mirror stage *as an identification*, in the full sense that analysis gives to the term: namely, the transformation that takes place in the subject when he assumes an image – whose predestination to this phase-effect is sufficiently indicated by the use, in analytic theory, of the ancient term *imago*. [p. 2]

In other words, this recognition of the self in the mirror is, in Lacan's view, a *méconnaissance*, a misrecognition.

Although Lacan does not put it in these terms, this concept seems not wholly unrelated to Winnicott's true self and false self. This brings to mind, too, Daniel Stern's description of the baby's early modes of experiencing that are overtaken by the power of the verbal domain. When Lacan (1977) refers to the "*specific prematurity of birth* in man" (p. 4), that the human infant is indeed born incompetent to cope, it foreshadows Mahler's later concept of psychological birth (she does not include a reference to Lacan in her 1975 book, *The Psychological Birth of the Human Infant*). Lacan, though, repudiates what Jacqueline Rose (1985) calls the "very ideology of oneness and completion" so central to object relations theory and self psychology. He simultaneously, in Lee's (1990) words, rejects ego psychology's "quasi-scientific, alienating objectifications that psychoanalysis ought to be helping subjects in the modern world escape" (p. 83). Although Lacan uses the term *intersubjective* in his descriptions of the therapeutic relationship, this must not be taken to be identical to Stolorow's usage. Stolorow, and Stern for that matter, presume the existence of independent centers of subjective experience in infant and mother; Lacan, on the other hand, understands the mirror phenomenon to create a fundamentally divided and decentered self (Turkle 1981) in which the very experiencing of subjective phenomena becomes inextricably intertwined with how one is experienced by an Other. A certain, if perhaps grudging, admiration is due to Lacan; it took originality to find a way, with this one paper, to alienate analysts (that is, those who would actually read the paper) from all theoretical positions, contemporary and yet to come.

LANGUAGE

From the consequences of the mirror stage emerges perhaps the central feature of Lacan's thinking, that is, the significance of language and speech. (Lacan felt that both ego psychology and object relations underestimated this element in theory and in clinical practice.) It cannot be emphasized strongly enough that the infant is born into an already-existing system of language and symbols—signifiers—and that this language, no matter how much it helps a child to communicate, is at its origin an alienating force in the psyche. And it will be the goal of psychoanalysis, paradoxically through the vehicle of language, to expose this gap between the assumed language and the experiencing of the subject. The term *subject*, then, can be partially understood to refer to this pre–mirror-stage true self (Lacan does not use this terminology) that is excluded from the *moi* (ego) formed by identifications. It must be recognized that Lacan had no privileged position regarding knowledge of what an infant actually experienced; his assertion that there is an experience of bodily incompetence or disunity may seem logical or persuasive but is no more than an assumption, and one based on work with adults rather than extensive infant observation. Like seasoned child observers, though, Lacan sees the age of 18 months to be a developmental turning point and dates the ending of the mirror stage to this time, at which the child figures out that the parents "are not entirely responsive to inarticulate demands" (Schneiderman 1980a, pp. 4–5). Mahler has identified this moment as the beginning of the rapprochement crisis when the toddler has learned that the world is not his oyster.

Another question has to do with how free from the social/ linguistic system the preverbal child actually may be. Schneiderman (1980b) suggests, "The fact that a child cannot speak does not mean he exists outside the net of language; on the contrary, to the extent that he cannot speak, I would assert that he is more thoroughly captured in that net" (p. 14). Here it is important to distinguish between language and speech. In the words of Ferdinand de Saussure, the Swiss linguist who first outlined the principles of structuralism, "language is not a function of the speaker, it is a product that is passively assimilated by the individual. It never requires premeditation. . . . Speaking, on the contrary, is an individual act. It is willful and intellectual" (Lee 1990, p. 36).

Although Lacan, it is reported, compared language to "a parasite, the form of cancer with which human beings are afflicted" (Miller 1977), there would seem to be an advantage for a child in learning to speak, progress over the passive embeddedness in the system of language. Recognizing his profound skepticism about the benefits of the individual's adaptation to society, one can discern at this point at least a partial answer to the question of whether Lacan's ideas are dangerous; in fact Lacan's ideology played a part in the 1968 uprisings in Paris (Turkle 1981).

In a sense one can imagine language as a sort of cyberspace, comprised only of individual workstations, yet having an existence somehow greater than the sum of its parts. We as individuals use language in speech acts, yet the language also shapes our very subjectivity. Our sense of ourselves as being centered, as agents and the source of our own thoughts, is an illusion, for we are inhabited by society through the language that we learned. In Lacan's view, the only one who escapes this fate is the psychotic who refuses to use speech in a conventional way (Turkle 1981). Psychotic language precisely does not partake of the common usage of the signifier. This term *signifier* comes from the field of structural linguistics and is to be distinguished from the paired idea of the *signified*, the idea to which the signifier refers. Language is understood to be a system of signifiers that are essentially floating. They have no real or fixed meaning, no signifieds attached to them in an absolute way, but rather they derive their sense from their relation to the entire system of signifiers. A speech act is also an inherently social event. Schneiderman (1980b) notes, "As Lacan has said, speech is dialogue" (p. 13), similar to Winnicott's (1960a) "There is no such thing as an infant." Lacan (1951) here applies this to the therapeutic process: "What happens in an analysis is that the subject is, strictly speaking, constituted through a discourse, to which the mere presence of the psychoanalyst brings, before any intervention, the dimension of dialogue" (p. 62).

R.S.I.: REAL, SYMBOLIC, IMAGINARY

THE IMAGINARY

Lacan and his followers rely for their conception of psychic structure not on the traditional categories of id, ego, and superego, but rather on another classification of mental experience — the "orders" or "registers" of the Real, the Symbolic, and the Imaginary (R.S.I.).[2] Although not entirely unrelated to the Freudian protocol, it creates more confusion than clarification to try to make any consistent correspondence between the two ways of thinking. Lacan's orders are difficult to understand and explain, in part at least because they try to capture precisely what cannot be put into words. Lacan believes that all three orders remain potent and interdependent forces in mental life throughout the

---

2. Note that the French pronunciation of the letters R-S-I is 'hérésie' — heresy.

life span, although they are attained in a developmental progression. (Note the similarity to the way in which Stern conceives of his various domains.)

The Imaginary has its roots in the images, the *imagos*, of the mirror stage. The misrecognition — *méconnaissance* — of the mirror stage is related to both narcissism and aggression. In seeing a reflection of unity and wholeness in the mirror, as opposed to a more accurate representation of the infant's actual state of mental and physical uncoordination, the baby is like Narcissus, looking in the pond and seeing only his own beauty, what he wants to see. But accomplishing this requires the expulsion of what he does not want to see, that which is dangerous or disorganizing. (Note the similarity to the projective tendencies Klein ascribes to the infant.) As Madan Sarup (1992) describes,

> Wherever a false identification is to be found — within the subject, or between one subject and another or between subject and thing — there the Imaginary holds sway. The Imaginary performs the function of *méconnaissance* (misrecognition) and is to be distinguished from knowledge (*connaissance*). [pp. 101–102]

To give an example from clinical practice, consider a bright young man who had just received his doctorate in anthropology. This psychotherapy patient was unsure of how others would respond to his sometimes original formulations; despite his ability to think beyond existing theory in his field, he seemed at times to be profoundly unable to acknowledge his own creativity of thought. Early in the treatment (before this dynamic had fully emerged) after some weeks when a particular subject had been on the patient's mind intellectually and in his mind in the process of working through related issues for himself, the therapist commented that perhaps the patient would write something on this topic at some point in his career. This intervention (which might be described as a suggestion, possibly deriving from a countertransference pressure) became a nodal point of the treatment. The patient described how, from that point on, he had a solid sense of the therapist's belief in his abilities and potential, a sense of hope, and a sense of his own worth as thinker. This can be understood to be a manifestation of the Imaginary in the sense that this patient's sense of unity, competence, and organization resulted from seeing himself "mirrored" in his therapist's eyes as he hoped to find himself. Later in the treatment, the patient was able to examine his self-doubt more fully and came to realize the significance of that early intervention. Perhaps the Imaginary can be understood to bear some relation to the idea of the unconscious fantasy, that silent but constant mental partner to consciousness, which flickers like the lights on the tape deck even when the volume is turned off.

The Imaginary register is thus this falsely organizing domain in which infants and later adults believe themselves to have found images of their own wholeness. There seems to be an assumption in this that the infant does indeed see a beautiful and positive reflection in the mirror, just as when Mahler wrote of object constancy she was referring to good-object constancy. But there exists bad-object constancy as well, that of a baby who has formed a steady intrapsychic representation of a frustrating mother. One question about the Imaginary and the mirror stage concerns the fate of the child who sees a reflection more negative, more dis-unified, less pleasing than he is; this would constitute a form of trauma, of experience beyond description, and would represent the intrusion of the Real, Lacan's last order. It is in this sense, of an experience that cannot be encoded into the Symbolic, the language, that the Real is defined as "the impossible." Although Lacan's effort was to be more metaphorical than developmental in his descriptions of the orders, it seems as though the mirror stage, the domain of the Imaginary, is seen if not as a developmental need at least as a maturational inevitability under normal circumstances. And despite his scorn for the object relations school's idealization of "wholeness," the Imaginary, the false but perhaps developmentally necessary sense of wholeness, is dependent on the quality of the mirroring functions available to the infant.

THE SYMBOLIC

For Lacan, the ego, *le moi*, which is the carrier of neurosis – and not the seat of mental health – is formed by the imaginary alienating identifications that persist beyond the mirror stage. And this phenomenon, the inevitable failure to assume fully the Symbolic order, is central to the Lacanian view of psychopathology and clinical technique. Schneiderman (1980a) writes:

> In psychoanalytic work, the symbolic manifests itself in the form of the family romance or the mythic structure of the Oedipus complex. This discourse is the conjuncture into which the subject was born, and it determines the success or failure of his maturation or development. When there is a failure of psychosexual or psychosocial maturation, relating it to a moment in a developmental process is secondary to analyzing the specific signifiers that the patient uses to talk about it. [p. 6]

Simply put, the Symbolic order is characterized by the common lexicon and grammar which permits the understanding of behavior and speech among members of society (Lee 1990). If the Imaginary is understood to represent dyadic and narcissistic experiences of object relations, then the Symbolic involves a progression to the triadic and the truly social interaction that is mediated by use of the language. The assumption of language is at once a victory, for with it the child can communicate more effectively, and a defeat, for the child must take one further step away from subjectivity (even though subjective experiencing had been infiltrated by language). The Imaginary is relinquished as the child comes to accept the use of language as an intruder in the relationship with the mother.

It is not quite right to say that Imaginary is to Symbolic as preoedipal is to oedipal, although it is not quite wrong either. As Mahler saw that it is the father who can rescue the toddler from a too intense or destructive symbiosis or rapprochement experience, so also does Lacan reinvent the role of the father. In Rose's (1985) words, "The father is a function and refers to a law, the place outside the imaginary dyad and against which it breaks" (p. 39). Lacan emphasizes that the Oedipus complex is dependent not on the presence or absence of the actual father, but rather on his presence as the representative of the post-Imaginary experiencing:

> To speak of the Name of the Father is by no means the same thing as invoking paternal deficiency (which is often done). We know today that an Oedipus complex can be constituted perfectly well even if the father is not there, while originally it was the excessive presence of the father which was held responsible for all dramas. But it is not in an environmental perspective that the answer to these questions can be found. So as to make the link between the Name of the Father, in so far as he can at times be missing, and the father whose effective presence is not always necessary for him not to be missing, I will introduce the expression *paternal metaphor*. [Rose 1985, p. 39]

This is a persuasive explanation for both the success of many single mothers raising sons as well as the development of transsexual wishes in little boys from seemingly intact families. In general, Lacanian theory can be said to remedy what was seen as an overdependence on the mother–infant dyad by Klein and her followers; although perhaps Freud had not paid adequate attention to the early influence of the mother (this would no doubt be practically impossible to capture in a self-analysis), Lacan nonetheless returns to the Freudian emphasis on the central role of the father (Rose 1985).

To return to the issue of the Symbolic order, there is a further fragmentation of the individual. In addition to the alienation from subjective bodily experience that took place in the process of the identifications of the Imaginary order, the imaginary *moi* (ego, me) is further alienated by the subject (*je*, I) as it comes to be defined in the Symbolic register, that is, in relation to the Others who use the language. As Lee (1990) notes, "The *moi* is basically a product of pre-oedipal relations with imaginary others, while the subject is fundamentally a product of oedipal relations articulated in a symbolic system" (p. 65).

THE REAL

There is no way to address the third order, the Real, without the risk of being provocatively enigmatic. The term itself invokes the feel of *1984*'s Ministry of Truth, for "the Real" is not equivalent to "reality." Perhaps the least impenetrable analysis of the Real is provided by Alan Sheridan, the translator of Lacan's (1977) *Écrits*. The Real "describe[s] that which is lacking in the symbolic order, the ineliminable residue of all articulation, the foreclosed element, which may be approached, but never grasped: the umbilical cord of the symbolic" (p. x). Here is a selection of even more elusive circlings around this concept:

- "The very idea of the real entails the exclusion of any meaning. Only insofar as the real is emptied of all meaning can we apprehend it a little" (Lacan 1977; cited in Julien 1994, p. 103).
- "The Real is that which is outside the Imaginary and the Symbolic. The Real is that which is excluded, the impossible to bear" (Sarup 1992, p. 104).
- "The Lacanian concept of the Real harks back to the Freudian id; it is associated with the sudden, the disconcerting and the unpredictable" (Sarup 1992, p. 104).
- "The Real comes close to meaning 'the ineffable' or 'the

impossible' in Lacan's thought. It serves to remind human subjects that their Symbolic and Imaginary constructions take place in a world which exceeds them" (Sarup 1992, p. 105).

- "The real is the scene of the trauma; the subject is constituted in an encounter with a traumatic situation" (Schneiderman 1980a, p. 6).
- "Lacan identifies the real as 'that which prevents one from saying the *whole* truth about it'" (Lee 1990, p. 136).
- "The real is that which is 'prohibited' (*interdit*), but also that which 'is said between the words, between the lines'" (Lee 1990, p. 171).
- "As human beings we are fully part of the real even as we stand outside of it ('ex-ist') by inhabiting the orders of the symbolic and the imaginary" (Lee 1990, p. 186).
- "The dead . . . are real, and not merely because death creates holes in the real. The gods and the dead are real because the only encounter we have with the real is based on the canceling of our perceptual conscious, of our sense of being alive: the real is real whether we experience it or not and regardless of how we experience it. The real is most real when we are not there; and when we are there, the real does not adapt itself to our being there. The concept of the real implies the annihiliation of the subject. When the Greeks named the wind or the sea after a god, they recognized that it is only through the structure of the symbolic order that things become real, not through perception or consciousness, not through the agency of a subject" (Schneiderman 1983, pp. 76–77).

And the list could go on. How, then, to make any sense of this tantalizing yet evanescent concept? The Real would seem to be an integral part of human existence yet not a part of ordinary conscious perception, an aspect of experience not captured in Imaginary or Symbolic terms; it is related to the unconscious, to the ongoing sense of existing and to time itself. The Real breaks through the Symbolic and Imaginary when external events (trauma, and the unconscious as represented by what was thought to be impossible) coincide and intervene. Christopher Bollas has coined the evocative phrase, "the unthought known." Perhaps there is some truth to be found in the way we describe as "unreal" happenings either traumatic or too good to be true, for these represent those unconscious wishes or fears we had thought to be impossible. Although it cannot be captured by language—the Symbolic—the Real is closer to the Symbolic than to the Imaginary, and perhaps could be thought of as being inconsistent with the Imaginary, that is, with the ego (*moi*). The Symbolic can name the Real and can mediate ruptures in it, as, for instance, in the rituals associated with mourning (Lee 1990). The concept of the Real begins to approach another central aspect of Lacan's thinking that will shape his clinical technique, and that is the relationship of the living to the dead and to our own inevitable deaths—to temporality.

NEEDS, DEMANDS, DESIRES

Lacan also expands upon Freud's thinking on the subject of needs, wishes, and object relations. Lacan distinguishes three categories: needs, demands, and desire. Freud defined a drive as possessing four components—an object, a source, pressure, and aim. Lacan's "need," although requiring the intervention of another, aims for "a transformation in the organic state of the animal or person who needs" (Lee 1990, p. 75). In Freud, all desires are ultimately based in the psychobiological substrate of the drives and aim toward a reduction of tension. Lacan goes on to specify the ways in which satisfaction cannot be defined by this aim. Lacan (1958a): "Demand in itself bears on something other than the satisfaction which it calls for. It is demand for a presence or an absence" (p. 80). The aim of a demand, then, is to effect a change in the Other to whom one directs the demand (Lee 1990). (Kohut, too, suggests this when he points out that even infants do not require just food but rather empathically modulated food-giving.) Michèle Montrelay, a member of the Lacanian school, situates demand as distinct from need in the early hallucinatory process: "To permit the hallucinated breast to exist for the child is to open for him a place other than the one which concerns the satisfaction of need" (Montrelay 1977, p. 84). Freud originally identified libido, as distinct from a purely biological need, from the phenomenon of thumb-sucking.

The third category, desire, refers to something that goes largely unarticulated, and that is the wish for recognition, the striving to be reckoned with as a being. Demand, which begins as the putting into words of the experienced bodily needs, and desire are atttempt to repair the *béance*, the gap created by the alienation of the mirror. As Lee (1990) puts it,

> No matter what the child or adult demands, it is always merely an object that might satisfy need. Were he to demand recognition explicitly, this demand would require an explicit recognition of the subject's essential want-of-being, something that simply cannot be put into words at all. In the desperate and vain attempt to articulate desire, the desiring subject continually moves from one demand to another, from one signifier to another. [p. 59]

A note about translation is of interest on this subject. What has been translated from the German *Wunscherfüllung* to English as "wish-fulfillment" entered the French language as "realization of desire" (Schneiderman 1980a, p. 3).

DRIVES AND AFFECTS

Behind needs, demands, and desires lie the drives, but Lacan (1977) retools Freud's concept of drives to fit in with his linguistic approach.

[The drive] is that which proceeds from demand when the subject disappears in it. It is obvious enough that demand also disappears, with the single exception that the cut [e.g. the fading or eclipse of the subject] remains, for this cut remains present in that which distinguishes the drive from the organic function it inhabits: namely its grammatical artifice, so manifest in the reversions of its articulation to both source and object – Freud is unfailingly illuminating on this matter. [p. 314]

In other words, the drives as we conceive of and experience them are shaped by the language that inhabits us. The body zones that were theorized to be the seat of the drives are themselves organized by the language that infiltrates the subject's self-experience. As Lee (1990) points out, Lacan relates the drives to the Symbolic order: "What is taken by many commentators on Freud as little more than a biological instinct becomes in Lacan the effect of a signifying chain inscribed on the subject's very body" (pp. 148–149).

Although Lacan stresses the role of language, his revised thinking about drives bears something in common with Kernberg's in that they both focus on the acquired rather than on the innate characteristics of drives as motivation. Kernberg postulates that affects are central to the process, while Lacan in his theory of affects insists on the supremacy of language over the body. In an interview on French television, Lacan (1987) pointed out "the need to approach them [affects] via the body, a body which is, as I say, affected only by structure" (p. 26). By structure Lacan means language, and he is thus arguing that it is language that leads to affects; note that this is the opposite of Kernberg's belief that it is units of affective experience that create mental structure. But, to reconsider Kernberg's hypothesis in a Lacanian light, it is not unreasonable to assume that even the Kernbergian infant must partake of the background language system in the very process of organizing the positively valenced and negatively valenced object-affect-self units of experience. (Ironically, Lacan's position on affects and language foreshadows the work of the cognitive therapist Aaron Beck.)

FADING AND THE *OBJET A*; OR, WHAT DID LACAN SAY TO DESCARTES?

Lacan refers above to a "cut," explained as the fading of the subject; this and the notion that there is a fundamental lack of satisfaction even when demands are "satisfied" are concepts foreign to orthodox theory (although Lacan claimed this fading accompanied the splitting of the ego described by Freud) (Mitchell and Rose 1985). To understand the concept of fading we reconsider the mirror stage and the falsely unified subject that results from identifications. In the face of manifestations of the authentic self, that is to say in confrontations with the Real as expressed in dreams, slips, traumata, the subject is said to shrink away. Indeed in contrast to Descartes' "I think, therefore I am," one might say here, "I shrink, therefore I am." In one interpretation of "*Wo es war* . . ." ("Where id was . . .") Lacan (1977) seems to suggest that in fading there lies hope: "'I' can come into being and disappear from what I say" (p. 300).

Fading of the subject occurs in relation to desire as well and is related to the impossibility of satisfaction, for desire is intimately bound up with loss. If the baby had not "lost" the breast, if it were not absent, then there would be no need for a hallucination. Although the baby's hunger for food can be met, although the demand for responsiveness can be satisfied, there yet remains that core of the loss of the object that originally spurred desire. It is, thus, desire that fundamentally cannot be satisfied. As Safouan (1975) phrased the question, "What is there to want when want persists as pure want?" (p. 133). And it is in the face of this want that the linguistically constructed subject fades and is eclipsed by the desire that transcends it. The object that occasions desire

Lacan terms the *objet petit a. Objet* means "object"; *petit a*, "little a," refers to the word *autre*, "other," as distinct from *Autre*, "Other," referring to a linguistically constructed and perceived real person. The *objet petit a* is real in the sense that fantasies are real and represents, in Lee's (1990) words, "a substitute to take the place of the lost, all-satisfying object" (p. 144).

The *objet petit a*, this "point of lack" where "the subject has to recognize himself" (Lee 1990, p. 144) leads to yet another major area of Lacan's thinking, the subject of the phallus. And this leads us back, again, to the mirror stage where the baby is influenced, shaped, by the fact of his mother's unsatisfied desire. Her *objet petit a*, the unattainable object of desire for the mother, is the phallus. The baby must disappoint the mother in this regard, and so one identification will be with the mother's perception of the baby as lacking. And when the baby sees the mother, she is found wanting. The baby cannot fulfill the mother's desire any more than the mother and the father could not do for their mothers. This first phallic conflict concerns the wish to *be* the phallus; later struggles are about *having* the phallus.

THE PHALLUS

To begin to unpack this controversial proposal it is important to understand that "phallus" is not equivalent to "penis." And it is not only the mother but the father, too, who desires a phallus; since phallus does not equal penis, neither man nor woman possesses it. As Lacan (1958a) explains,

> In Freudian doctrine, the phallus is not a fantasy, if what is understood by that is an imaginary effect. Nor is it as such an object (part, internal, good, bad, etc. . . .) in so far as this term tends to accentuate the reality involved in a relationship. It is even less the organ, penis or clitoris, which it symbolises. And it is not incidental that

Freud took his reference for it from the simulacrum which it represented for the Ancients.

For the phallus is a signifier, a signifier whose function in the intrasubjective economy of analysis might lift the veil from that which it served in the mysteries. For it is to this signified that it is given to designate as a whole the effect of there being a signified, inasmuch as it conditions any such effect by its presence as a signifier. [pp. 79–80]

Of course, there is no need of a signifier to be a father, any more than to be dead, but without a signifier, no one would ever know anything about either state of being. [Lacan 1977, p. 199]

What the phallus signifies is the father as the third term that ruptures the mother–infant dyad, the Symbolic that interrupts the Imaginary. It is the law, the Name of the Father that the child must come to accept, and that the father must come to personify. In fact, Lacan believes that a father's inability to represent the law results in psychopathology in the child (for an extreme example, see Safouan [1975]). The phallus, insofar as it is the instrument of transition from the Imaginary to the Symbolic, comes to stand for the irreparably divided nature of the human self. Lacan's story about the phallus is as much about separation as it is about oedipal wishes or fear of castration. The child must accept the father's phallic power, and relinquish the dyadic relationship with the mother, if he wishes to have a place in the family and society. Sarup (1992) clarifies how Lacan integrates the Oedipus complex into his theory of language and the self:

In connection with the Oedipus complex Lacan often uses the term "paternal metaphor." This refers to the prohibition of the father. The father stands for a place and a function which is not reducible to the presence or absence of the real father as such. In other words, an oedipus complex can be constituted perfectly well even if the father is not there. Lacan argues that in order to escape the all-powerful, imaginary relationship with the mother, and to enable the constitution of the subject, it is essential to have acquired what he calls the "name-of-the-father." The father introduces the principle of law, particularly the law of the language system. . . . When this law breaks down, or if it has never been acquired, then the subject may suffer from psychosis. [p. 122]

But the phallus is not entirely disconnected from the actual penis. For the mother is seen not to possess one. But—to link this to the centrality of the language system—there is nothing natural about perceiving this as a deficit. To experience something as being missing means that one already has a conceptual schema, that is to say a linguistically acquired sense of categories, such that an absence could be experienced as a lack. As Turkle (1981) puts it, "The penis can take its role in psychic development only when it is transformed into a symbol, the phallus, which is a signifier, a carrier of information about the set of meanings *socially* conferred upon the penis" (p. 75). Note, too, that in Lacan's oedipal story, there is no natural heterosexual maturational urge in the child that creates the oedipal crisis. Rather, the Oedipus is seen as a necessary breaking up of the mother–infant dyad, without which the child would not be a social being. For Lacan, "social" means triadic. Thus, the Oedipus begins to occur with the achievement of the Symbolic, with the acquisition of language; in this sense, Lacan's developmental timetable is probably closer to Klein's than to Freud's. It is therefore language itself, the interrupter of the Imaginary, that represents the beginning of triadic oedipal relations and the paternal presence and law, the Name of the Father.

THE OEDIPUS COMPLEX

Freud and Lacan have different views on the Oedipus story, as though each was describing a different refracted element of a light shone through a prism. For Freud, this is primarily a tale of a biologically induced developmental crisis. Both girls and boys are faced with the "fact" of castration, for girls, or the fear of it, for boys. As Lee (1990) succinctly describes it,

> The Lacanian notion of castration itself is virtually divorced . . . from any biological framework by his insistence that the phallus is a signifier (and not the penis). Where the Freudian drama of castration involves the child's coming to grips over time with the implications of his or her biological gender, the Lacanian drama is made up of a lifelong sequence of variations revolving around the basic language-created split, which structures the human being as a subject. The only developmental fact of significance for Lacan is the fact that language is acquired, the fact that children do grow up in a world richly structured by various symbolic (and castrating) systems. [p. 174]

Lacan believed that the castration complex was not a result of biological development but rather an artifact of the perceptions of self and others that the preexisting language shaped. Moreover, it is the assumption itself of this language that is the central castrating force in life, the force that permanently and inevitably decenters and divides the self.

The differences between Freud and Lacan go beyond this, although Lacan might have protested that he was simply clarifying or refining Freud's writings. For Freud, the acquisition of knowledge plays a central role in development; toddlers engage in sexual researches and discover the "fact" of their mother's castration. For Lacan, what the child also learns is something about knowledge itself, that is that the father already knows this information; the child discovers the fact of his or her own ignorance (Clavreul 1980). This adds to the traumatic potential of the oedipal crisis, for the child has also had to give up the Imaginary idea of being the central focus of his parents' life. And finally, the child's narcissistic needs for bodily integrity (for the boy) and for affection from the parents (for both genders) must outweigh the wish to possess the romantically loved parent of the opposite sex.

VIVE LA DIFFÉRENCE!

It is certainly not incorrect to say that Lacan's theory is phallocentric. Indeed, his effort is to reassert the importance of the father, the paternal metaphor, and undo the influence of the object relations school. But, nonetheless, many feminists have embraced Lacanian theory. How can this paradox be explained? By returning once again to a focus on language and the mirror stage, it follows logically that if the importance of the phallus is as signifier and not as biological organ, then the concept of gender, too, must be marked by language. Anatomical difference comes to stand for gender difference, but there is no natural reason for the phallus to confer privilege. It is indeed an unstable source of male identity, for it disappears under the scrutiny of its linguistic basis. As Rose (1985) explains,

> When Lacan is reproached with phallocentrism at the level of his theory, what is most often missed is that the subject's entry into the symbolic order is equally an exposure of the value of the phallus itself. The subject has to recognise that there is desire, or lack in the place of the Other, that there is no ultimate certainty or truth, and that the status of the phallus is a fraud (this, for Lacan, is the meaning of castration). The phallus can only take up its place by indicating the precariousness of any identity assumed by the subject on the basis of its token. [p. 40]

Thus, in Lacan's view sexual identity itself is an artifact of the language rather than being rooted in biology and primitive, nontraumatic identifications leading to primary gender identity (Stoller 1976). For Lacan, all identifications create a divide in the self. Lacan did not try to argue that biology had no effect whatsoever on destiny but that the effect of language was powerful and pervasive, influencing and organizing development.

One of Lacan's more controversial assertions was "Woman does not exist." Another: "There is no sexual relation." And: "[I]f there was no sexual difference how could I say there was no sexual relation?" (Rose 1985, p. 56). Lacan was not denying that women as actual biological beings exist. This is instead an emphasis on the fact that language consists of signifiers and that there is no absolute category of "woman," except in men's fantasies, and men need this category in order that they may "confirm" their identity as men. If the phallus is a fraud, so, too, is woman. But man needs woman to be his *objet petit a*, that which will compensate him for his loss, the phallus that he is not, the self he lost through language. It is this narcissism at the base of man's sexual desire that leads Lacan to the conclusion that there is no sexual relation (Lee 1990). (This relationship that Lacan sees as less than fully acknowledging of the woman as a total human being bears close resemblance to what Kohut would later describe as a selfobject need.) The *objet petit a*, that is to say the motivator of fantasy, has different substrates in men and women; while man needs woman to represent or "be" the phallus (hence the fetishistic attraction to the various parts of a woman's body), for woman, man appears to "have" the phallus she lacks. But it is really a case of smoke and mirrors, as Lacan (1977) points out: "The fact that the phallus is a signifier means that it is in the place of the Other that the subject has access to it" (p. 288). (By "the place of the Other" Lacan refers to the fact that language is indeed learned from others, but language was and is just as "Other" for those others, too.)

DEATH

The Oedipus story is not only about desire, though; it is a tale of death and murder, actual and imagined, unintentional and desired. And death is a central organizer of Lacan's ethos. To begin, the acquisition of identity and language in the mirror stage and beyond represents a partial death of the individual. The full acceptance of the Symbolic register, the father's law, gives one access to rituals that both permit mourning and also preserve a place for the dead in thoughts. And oedipal wishes are for the death of the parent of the same sex. But if one wishes to take the place of that parent, then the wish for one's own death cannot be far removed. Lacan also shifts the emphasis of the oedipal story from the theme of patricide to that of theft: stealing the desired parent, to be sure, but mainly stealing life itself from one's parents and from the dead. Schneiderman (1983) writes: "Lacan did not teach people how to get along with other people, interpersonally, but rather how to negotiate and to enter into commerce with the dead" (p. 63). This is not as crazy as it at first may sound when we recall that language itself is inherited from the dead, and that the identifications that divide and shape us are predicated on a partial death/castration of the self. Remember, too, that desire itself does not occur without an experience of loss in the sense of an unmet need. Thus the dead with whom we converse live on in our own minds. For Lacan, dealing with the dead and with the fact of our own death is the central human responsibility. It was around this that he constructed his own version of psychoanalysis. This inquiry into Lacan's metapsychology began with the clinical question about his "wild" five-minute hours. The answer can now perhaps be gleaned, that this was Lacan's way of making certain the issue of death would enter into the consulting room.

CLINICAL IMPLICATIONS

THE ANALYTIC STANCE

Like Freud, Lacan saw cure as an accidental by-product of psychoanalysis rather than its goal. But unlike Freud, he devel-

oped a different view of the role of the analyst regarding neutrality. The Freud who treated Dora had not yet entirely learned that
telling a patient some "truth" about herself would not in itself be
therapeutic. Recall Freud's insistence with Dora that he was right
and that she needed to admit the correctness of his interpretations. Freud certainly knew of the relevance of transference
before he worked with Dora (Davis 1990), but it was not until
later in his career that he truly learned the lesson Dora had
taught him and granted primacy to transference and resistance
and to the neutrality of the analyst—although it must be acknowledged that Freud's neutrality and anonymity were, at best, dis-
tantly related to even liberal current practices.

Lacan (1979) returns to Freud's early stance in a partial and
paradoxical way. For he believes simultaneously that the analyst
does not possess privileged knowledge about the patient and that
it is the job of the analyst to make certain that the patient learns
particular lessons about life:

> [Analytic] experience itself extends between this consistently de-
> based image of the father and an image our practice enables us more
> and more to take into account and to judge when it occurs in the
> analyst himself: although it is veiled and almost denied by analytic
> theory, the analyst nevertheless assumes almost surreptitiously, in
> the symbolic relationship with the subject, this position of the figure
> dimmed in the course of history, that of the master—the moral
> master, the master who initiates the one still in ignorance into the
> dimension of fundamental human relationships and who opens for
> him what one might call the way to moral consciousness, even to
> wisdom, in assuming the human condition. [pp. 407–408]

"The human condition" refers, above all, to the omnipresence
of death. So even while it is the analyst's role to guide the patient
into the full realization of mortality, the analyst must also demonstrate to the patient that the Other does not have the answer
the patient seeks. Analytic abstinence hence does not refer in
Lacan only to nongratification of libidinal or aggressive wishes

but also to the very process of interpretation. It is the patient who must do the analyzing, who must come to be the one who knows. As one might imagine, a Lacanian analysis is not for the faint-hearted, and yet this is not entirely alien to aspects of standard therapeutic practice; for experienced clinicians recognize that an insight achieved by the patient is likely to have far more value than anything that is told to him.

TECHNIQUE

Lacan believes that speech is inherently social, that speech is dialogue. To which speech does the analyst respond? Lacan develops the terms *Full Speech* and *Empty Speech* to describe the verbal material of the patient. The gift and opportunity of free association rapidly becomes a burden in the face of the frustrating silence of the analyst. The patient is gradually faced with the false identifications that have structured his *moi*, his ego. He comes to realize that there does exist a gap in his being, the *béance*, that his self is fundamentally divided and uncertain.

> Shall we ask where . . . the subject's frustration comes from? Does it come from the silence of the analyst? A reply to the subject's empty speech, even—or especially—an approving one, often shows by its effects that it is more frustrating than silence. Is it not rather a matter of a frustration inherent in the very discourse of the subject? Does the subject not become engaged in an ever-growing dispossession of that being of his, concerning which—by dint of sincere portraits which leave its idea no less incoherent, of rectifications that do not succeed in freeing its essence, of stays and defences that do not prevent his statue from tottering, of narcissistic embraces that become like a puff of air in animating it—he ends up by recognizing that this being has never been anything more than his construct in the imaginary and that this construct disappoints all his certainties? For in this labor which he undertakes to reconstruct *for another*, he rediscovers the fundamental alienation that made him construct it *like another*, and which has always destined it to be taken from him *by another*.

The ego, whose strength our theorists now define by its capacity to bear frustration, is frustration in its essence. [Lacan 1953, pp. 41–42]

Full speech is that which is cognizant of the temporality of the human condition; it is that which acknowledges divided identity and of the deficits inherent in the very existence of the ego (it is not without cause that the psychoanalytic establishment excluded Lacan). It is the analyst's role to confer recognition on the achievement of Full Speech and to structure the treatment in such a way as to encourage the development of Full Speech rather that the Empty Speech of unstructured so-called free associations. Talking too much, it is clear, can function as a resistance (Schneiderman 1983).

The session of unpredictable length was one of Lacan's tools in this endeavor. He referred to it as a form of punctuation, pointing out that it is the commas and periods that give sense to our speech. Lacan thus would terminate a session that seemed to him was filled with Empty Speech. He would also use the ending of a session to punctuate or to mark the achievement of insight, or Full Speech. Procrastination, the refusal to face the issue of temporality, and its symptom, intellectualization, were to be short-circuited by the termination of "empty" sessions. Obviously, the potential for countertransference intrusion into this process is immense. How does the analyst know when speech is empty or full? The role of the analyst changes from analyzing to judging (but Lacan is clear that he does envision the therapist to be the moral master). It is crucial for the analyst to know his own desire so as not to mistake his projections for the patient's symbolic world. Lacan strenuously objected to the analyst interpreting the significance of nonverbal material, seeing this not only as an invitation to the introduction of the analyst's countertransference but also as a dangerous departure from the focus on speech as the carrier of psychopathology. This is not to say that the nonverbal plays no role in Lacanian work. The analyst is instructed, to the contrary, to pay attention to aspects of the patient's history "that are not part of his lived experience" (Schneiderman 1983, p. 150). The danger is that the analyst will "search for a reality lying behind or beyond the analysand's speech" (Lee 1990, p. 41).

Lacan, like Freud, did have a solid sense that analyst and patient were made of the same psychological material, an emphasis that was perhaps missing from much medicalized analytic writing in the middle of the century. Thus he wrote with supreme irony: "What nobility of soul we display when we reveal that we ourselves are made of the same clay as those we mould!" (1958b, p. 226).

TIME

Like Freud, who only reluctantly wrote a few papers on technique, Lacan did not particularly prescribe his methods for all analysts, and his use of this method was not universally successful.[3] It is interesting and more than a little ironic to realize that even in the 1930s Lacan was experimenting with this time-limited treatment, in a sense utilizing a form of what would later be called short-term anxiety-provoking psychotherapy. Unlike later models of short-term treatment, however, and unlike his behavior regarding the length of individual sessions, Lacan did not designate an ending point of treatment. Rather, it was the patient who, ideally, was supposed to make this decision at the point when he realized that there was no more to be gained from the process. In this sense, the patient has stolen life from the analyst and casts him off as a no-longer-needed witness to his speech. But termination for Lacan took on not only a clinical but

---

3. See Schneiderman (1983) for a testimonial of Lacan's skill as a clinician and Turkle (1992) for Didier Anzieu's description of how negative an effect Lacan's style could have.

also an ethical and existentialist dimension. Schneiderman (1983), one of his patients, describes the effect of the retelling and analyzing one's own life story:

> There is a point at which you have to answer for what you have or have not done, for what you have or have not been. And no amount of astute analysis can obviate that responsibility, which is ethical and thus beyond analysis.
>
> At the least this makes clear why people like to do analysis and why the termination of analysis is never anticipated with any great joy. It is more fun, more secure, to analyze than to be in the position of the dead, to be judged in a situation where a heart of gold and all the analytic acuity in the world mean nothing. [p. 71]

At best, then, Lacanian analysis results in a realization of the profound state of discomfort that is the human condition—that we are decentered by the assumption of language, that we must account for our time from birth in the context of the inevitable limit of death, that we must relate to the dead in the form of their symbolic representation in our minds and in the Real. For Lacan, the greatest risk was that treatment would bolster a patient's false (Imaginary) sense of unity and self-completion (Rose 1985). This philosophy has implications for Lacan's management of the transference.

TRANSFERENCE AND COUNTERTRANSFERENCE

Transference is the centerpiece of treatment, and the "wild" short hours represent but one way of manipulating it. The goal for Lacan was to block both the traditional transference in which the patient expected to receive knowledge from the analyst and the Winnicottian transference in which dyadic needs were fulfilled. The goal was not for the patient to identify with the analyst in any simple or comfortable way, for this would only be a repetition of the mirror phenomenon, the taking on of an alien self-image. The analyst, instead, was to confer recognition on Full Speech, and the patient was to assume this analytic function for himself. Lacan felt that the analyst must avoid meddling (Schneiderman 1983)[4] in the patient's life (although his manipulation of session lengths would certainly seem to be inconsistent with this).

Lacan's view was that transference and countertransference were intimately related; as speech is dialogue, so transference is constituted within a relationship, although it also reflects repetitive ways of being "[T]he transference is nothing real in the subject other than the appearance, in a moment of stagnation of the analytic dialectic, of the permanent modes according to which it constitutes its objects" (Lacan 1951, p. 71). Thus transference love or hate is not entirely new but also not entirely a repetition. Lacan has a harsh understanding of the patient's acting out as representing an aspect of the transference that the analyst has been unable to attend to. Freud learned his lesson about transference at Dora's hands, and it is in a discussion of the Dora case that Lacan (1951) writes,

> I believe, however, that transference always has this same meaning of indicating the moments where the analyst goes astray, and equally takes his or her bearings, this same value of calling us back to the order of our role—that of a positive non-acting with a view to the ortho-dramatisation of the subjectivity of the patient. [p. 72]

CASE ILLUSTRATION

This vignette will describe but a few interpretive strands in a complex, multifaceted clinical encounter. The clinician's understanding of this patient's inability to be successful in work and in love is informed by a Lacanian perspective.

---

4. Compare this to Winnicott's concept of nonimpingement.

G., a Polish-American Catholic man of 34, consulted Dr. V., a psychiatrist in his late 30s, after discovering that his wife of five years had been having an affair. This knowledge was particularly distressing to G. because the lover was taller than he and hence, in G.'s mind, more masculine. G. recognized that he had given his wife substantial reason to feel unhappy in the marriage, and he thus sought help for himself. The single nonconflictual subject in the marriage was their son, a 3-year-old, adored by both G. and his wife. Child-rearing seemed to be largely occurring in a smooth fashion with both parents in agreement about limit-setting and other thorny areas—a remarkable achievement for a man with a deeply comprised childhood of his own.

BACKGROUND INFORMATION

G. was born to immigrant parents. The mother was a housewife while the father worked in a factory. By the time G. was born, the father had already suffered several minor occupational accidents and lived in constant if low-grade pain; he was probably moderately depressed. In any case, the father was a physical presence in childhood but G.'s life was directed and textured by his doting mother. The relationship with her could be characterized as symbiotic, with the mother doing her best to solve every problem and fix everything that went wrong for her son. As a result, G. lived a life of excessive gratification in which he never learned to solve his own problems or adequately to tolerate frustration.

As he described himself to Dr. V., G. was aware that his early years had affected him in a less than healthy way. G. had been somewhat small as a boy, timid and frightened, especially of the dark. When this brooding anxiety prevented him from sleeping, an appeal to his mother would invariably result in an invitation to sleep in his parents' bed. This ritual of fear and escape from it was an almost daily occurrence. The father was present but seemed to play no part in it save for his tacit approval of his wife's handling of G.'s fear. In Lacanian terms, what the father failed to do was to offer G. the possibility of the third term, the Name of the Father, the Symbolic register, as a way of escaping from this symbiotic cycle of dependence on and excessive gratification from his mother. In other words, well into his preadolescence, the gratifications of the Imaginary dominated G.'s mental life; in his view, everything could be made all right by this almost magically responsive mother who was ill-preparing her son for the world. But the pressures of maturation intruded into the Imaginary. It was G. who made the pressured decision to leave the safety of the parental bed, this at age 13 when he began to develop anxiety almost to the point of panic each night in their bed. G. did not make the conscious connection that seemed apparent to Dr. V. between this anxiety and the pubertal redawning of sexual desires.

G. had some friends in school, but his early adolescence was filled with a pervasive fear of being found out by his friends to be less than he ought to be, to be found out to be a fool; the memory around which this fear crystalized was of slightly wetting his pants once after laughing uncontrollably at a friend's joke. In fact, G. had suffered from enuresis until his early teens. G. developed a compensatory machismo attitude which by and large fooled his peers. But there was a sense of unreality about his existence both at school and at home, as though life were a game whose rules he could make up. G. had trouble with authority figures in a variety of situations, for he had not accepted the legitimacy of authority—and certainly had not internalized an ideal of authority or morality in his own mind. In his marriage, too, he made up the rules, for he had periodic one-night affairs. There was a way in which G. had married a woman and fathered a child without accepting that he had become husband and father. Interestingly, at the time he presented for treatment, his son was at the age when he would increasingly need G. to behave like a father, to be available as an alternative to the dyadic maternal relationship. G. displayed his inability, literally, to integrate the Name of the Father: he spoke on and off for years about renaming his shop his father's original Polish name (which his father had Americanized) but never took any actual steps to accomplish this. G. worked as an artisan but never made an adequate income; he once attempted to invest in a business and then got cold feet and backed out, in the process losing thousands of dollars of his wife's money. All this forced his wife to work full time, although she would have preferred to stay at home with their son.

The Real intruded in G.'s young adulthood on two notable occasions. First, when G. was in college on his way to a vaguely conceived career as a potter, he took an art history course and cheated on a quiz in order to get a passing grade. This was discovered by the professor who gave him a failing mark. Although he ended up passing the course, he described to Dr. V. getting from this for the first time in his life a sense that somebody out there was serious and that this was more than a game. This professor, in Lacan-speak, functioned as the paternal metaphor, as the Law, as G.'s own father had not done. The second and highly traumatic event was the sudden death of G.'s father from yet another industrial accident. G., in fact, witnessed at the hospital the unsuccessful attempts to resuscitate the dying man. This occurred about five years before treatment and G. had still not really begun the work of mourning; this is, in a sense, not surprising, for the difficulty of mourning a shadow is considerable. G. had continued, emotionally, to be his mother's welcomed "little shadow," and this certainly was one factor leading to difficulties in his marriage. However, this brief summary in its attempt to follow one theme may make G. seem more impaired than he actually was. G., after all, had completed school with some success, had a certain artistic talent, and did in fact move to his own apartment, support himself (albeit minimally), date a number of women, and marry. Despite the undertow of inferiority, G. had also managed to maintain over many years a few close friendships with male peers.

TREATMENT

And so G. presented himself to Dr. V., whose impression was that this patient had a certain intelligence, some areas of psychological strength, and the capacity for empathy; G. was attempting to take responsibility for his actions and their effect on his marriage by seeking help for himself where a man with borderline personality organization would be blaming everything on somebody else and would be able to see both positives and negatives in himself and others, as G. immediately demonstrated he was able to do. These strengths outbalanced Dr. V.'s concerns about G.'s poor ability to tolerate frustration, and so he agreed to accept G. into psychoanalysis, the treatment G. had requested. G.'s anxiety about exposing his weakness and vulnerability characterized the opening phase of treatment. His passive attitude toward Dr. V. was notable, extending even to what he felt free to say and feel in the office. Dr. V.'s interpretations were taken as welcomed directives; for instance, a comment that G. sounded angry was heard as an invitation to be angry whether G.'s feeling had been going in that direction or not. Dr. V. understood this attitude to be based on G.'s expectation that "mother will always take care of me and make everything turn out all right." Treatment thus began with G. assuming that the form of Dr. V.'s help would take place in this Imaginary register in which a toddler can believe that mother's kiss will cure a boo-boo.

In the transference, G. continued his struggle to avoid the Symbolic. Dr. V.'s impression was that G. took refuge in a brother transference, focusing on the realistic similarity in ages between the two of them. To understand this developmentally, G.'s mirror stage in which he consistently found an ideal self in the reflection provided by his mother had never been interrupted by the paternal metaphor. Thus G. continued to seek in Dr. V. the same sort of mirror image (not unrelated to what Kohutians would term a twinship transference). Seeing his analyst as a father figure would also have risked a terrifying repetition of finding the seemingly secure Dr. V. to be underneath as degraded and humiliated as his actual father had been. G.'s father, although he had a penis, certainly did not behave as though he had the Phallus, and G.'s fear was of becoming as castrated himself as he experienced his father to be. Having had only a weakened father with whom to identify, G.'s masculine identity was not deeply anchored in his psyche; thus passivity also carried the unconscious threat of homosexual attraction. Both the macho and the passive behavior that G. displayed resulted from his identification with the Imaginary father who was seen, alternately, as greatly aggrandized and then as castrated. (When the child achieves the Symbolic order, the castration at the hand of the language, there has been an acceptance, a working through, such that actual castration becomes less of a preoccupation. Obviously, this had not taken place for G.) Nor was it a solution to see Dr. V. (or the father) as a maternal figure, for a feminine identification, too, would undermine G.'s masculinity. But Dr. V. did feel pressure in the relationship to supply the kind of magical solution that mother had. G.'s difficulty could be understood as a resistance to accepting the Symbolic; he did not want to know that wishes had to be put into words, that it was not possible to solve everything while remaining in the realm of the Imaginary. All patients have fantasies of how psychotherapy or psychoanalysis will cure them and this was G.'s. Thus Dr. V.'s refusal to furnish easy support and facile solutions combined an empathic stance with Lacanian provocation. As Schneiderman (1980b) puts it,

> Analysis is a dialectical process in which the analysand analyzes. He analyzes not the Self but the Other, insofar as the Analyst in the transference is supposed to occupy its place. Because of the nature of the transference, the Analysand will form an idea of what the analyst wants to hear and will speak accordingly. . . .
>
> [The analyst's] role is to bring the analysand to recognize that this Other that had been supposed to have the answer is defined as lacking something, as defective at precisely the place where the answer should have been forthcoming. [pp. 13–14]

Interpretations were difficult for G. to accept, representing as they did the absence of what he was seeking. In effect, interpretations were crucial encounters with the inevitable *objet petit a* for this patient whose mother had done her best to evade these moments.

G.'s "magical cure" fantasy is not wholly unrelated to his inability to have mourned his father, in that they both reflect a resistance to the developmental task of trying to cope with the Real via the Symbolic. They also represent a refusal to deal with the passage of time, for Lacan perhaps the crucial measure of mental health. G. was almost phobic about committing to anything—his work, his marriage—and this procrastination bespeaks his denial of the human condition of mortality. In the analysis this was expressed in G.'s frequent telling of amusing anecdotes under the guise of free association. Where Lacan might have drawn attention to this Empty Speech by the abrupt termination of the session, Dr. V.'s technique instead was to point out to G. what he was doing and wonder whether he was trying to "keep things light and airy, . . . no fuss, no bother, no conflict." G. was able to admit that it made things easier for him as well. Further exploration revealed profound fears that Dr. V. would try to take advantage of G., would try to put something over on him, or leave him. Resistance to Full Speech, to meaningful participation in the analysis, represented G.'s fear of trusting and engaging in a real relationship with Dr. V. It was G.'s conscious expectation that he would pay Dr. V. a fee and in return the doctor would perform a treatment that he would tolerate passively but with cooperation. The wish behind this was that the analyst would bestow on him a "painless miracle cure that require[d] nothing more of him than patience," as Dr. V. phrased it. But beneath this pleasant fantasy of an Imaginary cure, lay a disturbing unconscious fearful fantasy in which Dr. V. becomes an unscrupulous and tyrannical child abuser who castrates him—the stranger to whom he must not speak, as his mother had warned him in his childhood.

CONCLUSIONS

As this brief vignette demonstrates, it is not necessary to throw out the baby with the bathwater when it comes to Lacan. An appreciation of Lacan's ideas does not obligate the clinician to replicate his clinical practices. The developmental hypothesis of the mirror stage and the metapsychological registers of Imaginary, Symbolic, and Real provide yet another hermeneutic strategy with which we can decipher our patients' stories. These concepts can enrich our ability to listen to language and speech in the consulting room as we evaluate not only if the patient has achieved Full Speech with us but also whether his life possesses an equivalent capacity to struggle to acknowledge the Real.

Lacan's take on the concept of analytic nongratification of wishes deepens our understanding of what we already are doing, for instance, when we refuse to answer patients' questions. By showing ourselves not to satisfy at the moment when satisfaction is demanded, we open the door for our patients to explore what leads them to want in the first place; in doing this we encourage patients to look inward toward their own thoughts, to examine their expectations, to assume Full Speech. If this seems to risk disturbing our patients, it is because the human condition is disturbing as well. But there is no greater gift we can offer our patients than the power to understand their own thoughts and to face their mortality to the best of their ability.

REFERENCES

Aichhorn, A. (1925). *Wayward Youth.* New York: Viking, 1945.

Akhtar, S. (1994a). Discussion of L. LaFarge's "Transferences of Deception." Meeting of the American Psychoanalytic Association, New York City, December.

—— (1994b). Lecture. Philadelphia Psychotherapy Training Program of the Philadelphia Psychoanalytic Institute and Society, Spring.

Baker, H., and Baker, M. (1987). Heinz Kohut's self psychology: an overview. *American Journal of Psychiatry* 144(1):1–9.

Balint, M. (1952). *Primary Love and Psychoanalytic Technique.* New York: Liveright.

—— (1968). *The Basic Fault.* London: Tavistock.

Benedek, T. (1938). Attention to reality in early infancy. *Psychoanalytic Quarterly* 7:200–214.

Bergman, A., and Ellman, S. (1985). Margaret S. Mahler: symbiosis and separation-individuation. In *Beyond Freud: A Study of Modern Psychoanalytic Theorists,* ed. J. Reppen. Hillsdale, NJ: Analytic Press.

Bettelheim, B. (1983). *Freud and Man's Soul.* New York: Knopf.

Casement, P. (1990). The meeting of needs in psychoanalysis. *Psychoanalytic Inquiry* 10:325–346.

Clavreul, J. (1980). The perverse couple. In *Returning to Freud: Clinical Psychoanalysis in the School of Lacan,* ed. S. Schneiderman, pp. 215–233. New Haven, Yale University Press, 1980.

Davis, D. (1990). Freud's unwritten case. *Psychoanalytic Psychology* 7(2):185–209.

Eissler, K. (1958). Notes on problems of technique in the psychoanalytic treatment of adolescents. *Psychoanalytic Study of the Child* 13:223–254. New York: International Universities Press.

Erikson, E. (1950). *Childhood and Society*. New York: Norton.

—— (1961). Reality and actuality: an address. In *In Dora's Case*, ed. C. Bernheimer and C. Kahane, pp. 444–455. New York: Columbia University Press.

Freud, A. (1966). *The Ego and the Mechanisms of Defense*, revised edition. New York: International Universities Press.

Freud, S. (1895). Project for a scientific psychology. *Standard Edition* 1:238–387.

—— (1900). The interpretation of dreams. *Standard Edition* 4/5.

—— (1901). The psychopathology of everyday life. *Standard Edition* 6.

—— (1905a). Fragment of an analysis of a case of hysteria. *Standard Edition* 7:3–122.

—— (1905b). Three essays on the theory of sexuality. *Standard Edition* 7:125–243.

—— (1905c). Jokes and their relation to the unconscious. *Standard Edition* 8.

—— (1912). Recommendations to physicians practicing psycho-analysis. *Standard Edition* 12:109–120.

—— (1913). On beginning the treatment (further recommendations on the technique of psycho-analysis). *Standard Edition* 12:121–144.

—— (1914). Remembering, repeating, and working through (further recommendations on the technique of psycho-analysis-II). *Standard Edition* 12:145–156.

—— (1915). Instincts and their vicissitudes. *Standard Edition* 14:109–130.

—— (1917). Mourning and melancholia. *Standard Edition* 14:237–258.

—— (1923). The ego and the id. *Standard Edition* 19:3–66.

—— (1926). Inhibitions, symptoms, and anxiety. *Standard Edition* 20:75–174.

—— (1930). Civilization and its discontents. *Standard Edition* 21:51–145.

—— (1933). The dissection of the psychical personality. *Standard Edition* 22:57–80.

Freud, S., and Breuer, J. (1893). Studies on hysteria. *Standard Edition* 2.

Gay, P. (1988). *Freud: A Life for Our Time*. New York: Norton.

Gilligan, C. (1982). *In a Different Voice.* Cambridge, MA: Harvard University Press.

Greenberg, J., and Mitchell, S. (1983). *Object Relations and Psychoanalytic Theory.* Cambridge, MA: Harvard University Press.

Grunes, M. (1984). The therapeutic object relationship. *Psychoanalytic Review* 71(1):123–143.

Guntrip, H. (1975). My experience of analysis with Fairbairn and Winnicott (How complete a result does psychoanalytic therapy achieve?). *International Review of Psycho-Analysis* 2:145–156.

Hartmann, H. (1948). Comments on the theory of the instinctual drives. In *Essays on Ego Psychology*, pp. 69–89. New York: International Universities Press, 1964.

——(1950). Comments on the psychoanalytic theory of the ego. In *Essays on Ego Psychology*, pp. 113–141. New York: International Universities Press, 1964.

——(1951). Technical implications of ego psychology. In *Essays on Ego Psychology*, pp. 142–154. New York: International Universities Press, 1964.

——(1958). *Ego Psychology and the Problem of Adaptation*, trans. D. Rapaport. New York: International Universities Press.

——(1959). Psychoanalysis as a scientific theory. In *Essays on Ego Psychology*, pp. 318–350. New York: International Universities Press.

——(1964). *Essays on Ego Psychology.* New York: International Universities Press.

Julien, P. (1994). *Jacques Lacan's Return to Freud: The Real, the Symbolic, and the Imaginary*, trans. D. Simiu. New York: New York University Press.

Kernberg, O. (1975). *Borderline Conditions and Pathological Narcissism.* New York: Jason Aronson.

——(1976). *Object Relations Theory and Clinical Psychoanalysis.* New York: Jason Aronson.

——(1980). *Internal World and External Reality: Object Relations Theory Applied.* New York: Jason Aronson.

——(1984). *Severe Personality Disorders.* New Haven: Yale University Press.

—— (1992). *Aggression in Personality Disorders and Perversions*. New Haven: Yale University Press.

Klein, M. (1926). The psychological principles of infant analysis. In *The Selected Melanie Klein*, ed. J. Mitchell, pp. 58–68. New York: Free Press, 1986.

—— (1928). Early stages of the Oedipus conflict. In *The Selected Melanie Klein*, ed. J. Mitchell, pp. 69–83. New York: Free Press, 1986.

—— (1929). Infantile anxieties reflected in a work of art and the creative impulse. In *The Selected Melanie Klein*, ed. J. Mitchell, pp. 84–94. New York: Free Press, 1986.

—— (1930). The importance of symbol formation in the development of the ego. In *The Selected Melanie Klein*, ed. J. Mitchell, pp. 95–111. New York: Free Press, 1986.

—— (1936a). The psychotherapy of the psychoses. In *Object Relations and Psychoanalytic Theory*, ed. C. Greenberg and S. Mitchell. Cambridge, MA: Harvard University Press.

—— (1936b). A contribution to the psychogenesis of manic-depressive states. In *The Selected Melanie Klein*, ed. J. Mitchell, pp. 116–145. New York: Free Press, 1986.

—— (1946). Notes on some schizoid mechanisms. In *The Selected Melanie Klein*, ed. J. Mitchell, pp. 176–200. New York: Free Press, 1986.

—— (1952). The origins of transference. In *The Selected Melanie Klein*, ed. J. Mitchell, pp. 201–210. New York: Free Press, 1986.

—— (1955). The psycho-analytic play technique: its history and significance. In *The Selected Melanie Klein*, ed. J. Mitchell, pp. 35–43. New York: Free Press, 1986.

—— (1956). A study of envy and gratitude. In *The Selected Melanie Klein*, ed. J. Mitchell, pp. 211–229. New York: Free Press, 1986.

—— (1959). Our adult world and its roots in infancy. In *Object Relations and Psychoanalytic Theory*, J. Greenberg and S. Mitchell. Cambridge, MA: Harvard University Press, 1983.

Kohut, H. (1971). *The Analysis of the Self*. New York: International Universities Press.

—— (1977). *The Restoration of the Self*. New York: International Universities Press.

—— (1979). The two analyses of Mr. Z. *International Journal of Psycho-Analysis* 60:3–27.

Kris, E. (1934). The psychology of caricature. In *Psychoanalytic Explorations in Art*, pp. 173–188. New York: International Universities Press.

Lacan, J. (1936). The mirror stage as formative of the function of the I as revealed in psychoanalytic experience. In *Ecrits: A Selection*, trans. A. Sheridan, pp. 1–7. New York: Norton, 1977.

—— (1951). Intervention on transference. In *Feminine Sexuality: Jacques Lacan and the Ecole Freudienne*, ed. J. Mitchell and J. Rose, trans. J. Rose, pp. 61–73. New York: Norton, 1985.

—— (1953). Function and field of speech and language. In *Ecrits: A Selection*, trans. A. Sheridan, pp. 30–113. London: Tavistock.

—— (1958a). The meaning of the phallus. In *Feminine Sexuality: Jacques Lacan and the Ecole Freudienne*, ed. J. Mitchell and J. Rose, trans. J. Rose, pp. 74–85. New York: Norton.

—— (1958b). The direction of the treatment and the principles of its power. In *Ecrits: A Selection*, trans. A. Sheridan, pp. 226–280. New York: Norton, 1977.

—— (1977). *Ecrits: A Selection*, trans. A. Sheridan. New York: Norton, 1936.

—— (1979). The neurotic's individual myth. *Psychoanalytic Quarterly* 48:405–425.

—— (1987). Television. *October* 40:7–50.

Laplanche, L., and Pontalis, J.-B. (1973). *The Language of Psycho-Analysis*, trans. D. Nicholson-Smith. New York: Norton.

Lee, J. S. (1990). *Jacques Lacan*. Amherst, MA: University of Massachusetts Press.

Little, M. (1990). *Psychotic Anxieties and Containment: A Personal Record of an Analysis with Winnicott*. Northvale, NJ: Jason Aronson.

Mahler, M. (1968). *On Human Symbiosis and the Vicissitudes of Individuation: Infantile Psychosis*. New York: International Universities Press.

Mahler, M., Pine, F., and Bergman, A. (1975). *The Psychological Birth of the Human Infant: Symbiosis and Individuation*. New York: Basic Books.

Miller, J.-A. (1977). Teachings of the case presentation. In *Returning to*

    Freud: Clinical Psychoanalysis in the School of Lacan, ed. S. Schneiderman, pp. 42–52. New Haven: Yale University Press, 1980.

Mitchell, J. (1985). Introduction-I. In *Feminine Sexuality: Jacques Lacan and the Ecole Freudienne*, ed. J. Mitchell and J. Rose, trans. J. Rose, pp. 1–26. New York: Norton.

—— (1986). *The Selected Melanie Klein.* New York: Free Press.

Mitchell, J., and Rose, J. (1985). *Feminine Sexuality: Jacques Lacan and the Ecole Freudienne*, trans. J. Rose. New York: Norton.

Montrelay, M. (1977). The story of Louise. In *Returning to Freud: Clinical Psychoanalysis in the School of Lacan*, pp. 75–93. New Haven: Yale University Press, 1980.

Moore, B., and Fine, B. (1990). *Psychoanalytic Terms and Concepts.* New Haven and London: American Psychoanalytic Association and Yale University Press.

Parens, H. (1991). Separation-individuation theory and psychosexual theory. In *Beyond the Symbiotic Orbit: Advances in Separation-Individuation Theory—Essays in Honor of Selma Kramer, M.D.*, ed. S. Akhtar and H. Parens. Hillsdale, NJ: Analytic Press.

—— (1994). Lecture: Personality development course. Philadelphia: Psychoanalytic Institute, Fall.

Pulver, S. (1970). Narcissism: the term and the concept. *Journal of the American Psychoanalytic Association* 18:319–340.

Rapaport, D. (1958). A historical survey of psychoanalytic ego psychology. In *The Collected Papers of David Rapaport*, ed. M. Gill, pp. 745–757. New York: Basic Books, 1967.

—— (1967). *The Collected Papers of David Rapaport*, ed. M. Gill. New York: Basic Books.

Rose, J. (1985). Introduction-II. In *Feminine Sexuality: Jacques Lacan and the Ecole Freudienne*, ed. J. Mitchell and J. Rose, trans. J. Rose, pp. 27–57. New York: Norton.

Rothstein, A. (1995). A perspective on analysts' evaluating, diagnosing, and prognosticating. Lecture: Philadelphia Psychoanalytic Society, September.

Safouan, M. (1973). Contribution to the psychoanalysis of transsexualism. In *Returning to Freud: Clinical Psychoanalysis in the School of*

Lacan, ed. S. Schneiderman, pp. 1–8. New Haven: Yale University Press, 1980.

—— (1975). Feminine sexuality in psychoanalytic doctrine. In *Feminine Sexuality: Jacques Lacan and the Ecole Freudienne*, ed. J. Mitchell and J. Rose, trans. J. Rose, pp. 123–136. New York: Norton, 1985.

Salyard, A. (1994). On not knowing what you know: object-coercive doubting and Freud's announcement of the seduction theory. *Psychoanalytic Review* 81(4):659–676.

Sarup, M. (1992). *Jacques Lacan*. Toronto: University of Toronto Press.

Schneiderman, S. (1980a). Lacan's early contributions to psychoanalysis. In *Returning to Freud: Clinical Psychoanalysis in the School of Lacan*, pp. 195–212. New Haven: Yale University Press.

—— (1980b). The other Lacan. In *Returning to Freud: Clinical Psychoanalysis in the School of Lacan*, pp. 9–16. New Haven: Yale University Press.

—— (1983). *Jacques Lacan: The Death of an Intellectual Hero*. Cambridge, MA: Harvard University Press.

Segal, H. (1981). *Melanie Klein*. Middlesex, England: Penguin.

Sheridan, A. (1977). Translator's note. In J. Lacan, *Ecrits: A Selection*, pp. vii–xii. New York: Norton.

Spitz, R. (1945). Hospitalism: an inquiry into the genesis of psychiatric conditions in early childhood. *Psychoanalytic Study of the Child* 1:53–74. New York: International Universities Press.

Stern, D. (1985). *The Interpersonal World of the Infant: A View from Psychoanalysis and Developmental Psychology*. New York: Basic Books.

Stoller, R. J. (1976). Primary femininity. *Journal of the American Psychoanalytic Association* 24(5) supplement–Female Psychology: 59–78.

Stolorow, R. D., Brandchaft, B., and Atwood, G. E. (1987). *Psychoanalytic Treatment: An Intersubjective Approach*. Hillsdale, NJ: Analytic Press.

Turkle, S. (1981). *Psychoanalytic Politics: Freud's French Revolution*. Cambridge, MA: MIT Press.

—— (1992). *Psychoanalytic Politics: Jacques Lacan and Freud's French Revolution*, 2nd ed. New York: Guilford.

Winnicott, D. W. (1950s). Ideas and definitions. In *Psychoanalytic Explorations*, ed. C. Winnicott, R. Shepherd, and M. Davis, pp. 43–44. Cambridge, MA: Harvard University Press, 1989.

—— (1951). Transitional objects and transitional phenomena. In *Playing and Reality*, pp. 1–30. Middlesex, England: Penguin, 1971.

—— (1958). The capacity to be alone. In *The Maturational Processes and the Facilitating Environment*, pp. 29–36. New York: International Universities Press, 1965.

—— (1960a). The theory of the parent–infant relationship. In *The Maturational Processes and the Facilitating Environment*, pp. 37–57. New York: International Universities Press, 1965.

—— (1960b). Ego distortion in terms of true and false self. In *The Maturational Processes and the Facilitating Environment*, pp. 140–152. New York: International Universities Press, 1965.

—— (1961). Psycho-neurosis of childhood. In *Psycho-Analytic Explorations*, ed. C. Winnicott, R. Shepherd, and M. Davis, pp. 64–72. Cambridge, MA: Harvard University Press, 1989.

—— (1962). The aims of psycho-analytical treatment. In *The Maturational Processes and the Facilitating Environment*, pp. 166–170. New York: International Universities Press, 1965.

—— (1963). Dependence in infant-care, and in the psycho-analytic setting. In *The Maturational Processes and the Facilitating Environment*, pp. 249–259. New York: International Universities Press, 1965.

—— (1964). The importance of the setting in meeting regressions in psycho-analysis. In *Psycho-Analytic Explorations*, ed. C. Winnicott, R. Shepherd, and M. Davis, pp. 96–102. Cambridge, MA: Harvard University Press, 1989.

—— (1965). *The Maturational Processes and the Facilitating Environment*. New York: International Universities Press.

—— (1971). *Playing and Reality*. Middlesex, England: Penguin.

—— (1989). *Psycho-Analytic Explorations*, ed. C. Winnicott, R. Shepherd, and M. Davis. Cambridge, MA: Harvard University Press.

Wolman, T. (1995). Separation-individuation viewed through a Lacanian lens. Unpublished paper.

Young-Bruehl, E. (1992). Lecture: Freud course. Haverford College, Haverford, PA.

CREDITS

The author gratefully acknowledges permission to reprint material from the following sources:

From *Feminine Sexuality* by Jacques Lacan, edited by Juliet Mitchell and Jacqueline Rose, translated by Jacqueline Rose, translation copyright © 1982 by Jacqueline Rose. Copyright © 1966, 1968, 1975 by Editions du Seuil. Copyright © 1975 by Le Graphe. Reprinted by permission of W. W. Norton & Company, Inc., Macmillan Press Ltd., and Editions du Seuil.

From *Ecrits: A Selection* by Jacques Lacan, translated by Alan Sheridan. Copyright © 1966 by Editions du Seuil. English translation copyright © 1977 by Tavistock/Routledge Publications. Reprinted by permission of W. W. Norton & Company, Inc. and Tavistock/Routledge Publications.

From *New Introductory Lectures on Psycho-Analysis* by Sigmund Freud, translated by James Strachey, translation copyright © 1965, 1964 by James Strachey. Reprinted by permission of W. W. Norton & Company, Inc., Sigmund Freud Copyrights, the Institute of Psycho-Analysis, and the Hogarth Press.

From *The Ego and the Id* by Sigmund Freud, translated by James Strachey, translation copyright © 1960 by James Strachey, renewed 1988 by Alix Strachey. Reprinted by permission of W. W. Norton & Company, Inc., Sigmund Freud Copyrights, the Institute of Psycho-Analysis, and the Hogarth Press.

From *Psychiatry as a Revolution* by Hector Manus and by permission of International ... . Copyright © ... by International ... published.

From *Ego Psychology* and the *Problem of Adaptation* by Heinz Hartmann, International Universities Press, Inc., New York. Copyright © 1958 by International Universities Press.

From *The Discovery and* the *Self* by Alice Kahler, by permission of International Universities Press. Copyright © 1977 by International Universities Press.

From *The Fifty-Minute Hour* ... by ... Used by permission of International Universities Press, ... copyright © 1980 by International Universities Press.

From *The Ethnography of Law* ... and the *Emergence of ...* ... by L. E. A. ... by permission of International Universities Press. Copyright © ... by International Law ...

From *The Interpretation of Dreams* by ... by ... by K. Scott & Co. Used by permission of ... and publishers.

... has been made in ... to the sources of copyrighted materials ... for the selections used in this volume ... and to obtain permission to reprint copyrighted passages. The author will be pleased to acknowledge in future editions to correct any inadvertent error or omission that may be pointed out.

INDEX